Investor Relations

Also by Anne Guimard

LA COMMUNICATION FINANCIÈRE: Théorie et Pratique

Investor Relations

Principles and International Best Practices in Financial Communications

2nd Edition

Anne Guimard

© Anne Guimard 2013
Softcover reprint of the hardcover 2nd edition 2013 ISBN 978-1-137-33739-9

All rights reserved. No reproduction, copy or transmission of this publication may be made without written permission.

No portion of this publication may be reproduced, copied or transmitted save with written permission or in accordance with the provisions of the Copyright, Designs and Patents Act 1988, or under the terms of any licence permitting limited copying issued by the Copyright Licensing Agency, Saffron House, 6–10 Kirby Street, London EC1N 8TS.

Any person who does any unauthorized act in relation to this publication may be liable to criminal prosecution and civil claims for damages.

The author has asserted her right to be identified as the author of this work in accordance with the Copyright, Designs and Patents Act 1988.

First published 2013 by
PALGRAVE MACMILLAN

Palgrave Macmillan in the UK is an imprint of Macmillan Publishers Limited, registered in England, company number 785998, of Houndmills, Basingstoke, Hampshire RG21 6XS.

Palgrave Macmillan in the US is a division of St Martin's Press LLC,
175 Fifth Avenue, New York, NY 10010.

Palgrave Macmillan is the global academic imprint of the above companies and has companies and representatives throughout the world.

Palgrave® and Macmillan® are registered trademarks in the United States, the United Kingdom, Europe and other countries.

ISBN 978-1-349-46380-0   ISBN 978-1-137-34234-8 (eBook)
DOI 10.1057/9781137342348

This book is printed on paper suitable for recycling and made from fully managed and sustained forest sources. Logging, pulping and manufacturing processes are expected to conform to the environmental regulations of the country of origin.

A catalogue record for this book is available from the British Library.

A catalog record for this book is available from the Library of Congress.

Contents

List of Illustrations	xi
Introduction	xii

1 Competing for Capital   1
  1.1 Why Go Public?   2
  1.2 The Four Phases of Investor Relations in an IPO   6
  1.3 Investor Relations for Private Companies   18
  1.4 Private Equity Investor Relations   20
  1.5 Debt Investor Relations   20

2 Seven Keys to Successful Investor Relations   24
  2.1 Clearly Defined Goals   24
  2.2 Importance of Senior Management Commitment   25
  2.3 The Efficient Investor Relations Organization   25
    2.3.1 A Flexible and Scalable Investor Relations Organization   29
    2.3.2 Position in the Organization   30
    2.3.3 Responsibilities of the Investor Relations Department   32
      2.3.3.1 Coordinating financial and strategic communications   32
      2.3.3.2 Building internal awareness of investor relations   33
      2.3.3.3 Being the company's spokesperson in the financial markets   34
      2.3.3.4 Keeping management aware of the market's perception   38
    2.3.4 Investor Relations: Profiles and Job Descriptions   39
      2.3.4.1 Profiles   40
      2.3.4.2 Job descriptions   41
      2.3.4.3 Investor relations as a career   46
    2.3.5 External Investor Relations Service Providers and Advisors   50
      2.3.5.1 Scope of assignments   51
      2.3.5.2 Identification and selection process   52
      2.3.5.3 Efficiency and performance assessment   54

	2.3.6	Investor Relations Tools	55
		2.3.6.1 Contact database	55
		2.3.6.2 Monitoring tools	56
	2.3.7	Investor Relations Budgets	59
2.4	Quality of Information and Reporting Systems		61
2.5	Understanding and Complying with Legal Requirements		62
	2.5.1	Price-Sensitive Information	63
		2.5.1.1 Main characteristics of price-sensitive or privileged information	63
		2.5.1.2 Insiders	65
		2.5.1.3 Disclosure of price-sensitive information	66
	2.5.2	Periodic Disclosure	69
		2.5.2.1 Financial accounting information	69
		2.5.2.2 Annual general meetings	70
		2.5.2.3 Financial transactions	71
2.6	Anticipating Changes in Investor Relations		74
	2.6.1	Endogenous Factors	74
		2.6.1.1 Time elapsed since listing	74
		2.6.1.2 Size and breakdown of share capital	74
		2.6.1.3 Size, renown, and recognition	75
		2.6.1.4 Image and reputation	75
		2.6.1.5 Sectors and countries in which the company does business	75
		2.6.1.6 Internal organization	76
		2.6.1.7 Expansion policy and strategic priorities	76
		2.6.1.8 Financial structure and strategy funding	76
		2.6.1.9 Research and development	76
		2.6.1.10 Shareholder returns	77
		2.6.1.11 Maintaining a positive image even if you delist your shares	77
	2.6.2	Exogenous Factors	79
		2.6.2.1 The competitive environment	79
		2.6.2.2 Macroeconomic and geopolitical environment	79
		2.6.2.3 Technology changes	79
		2.6.2.4 Regulatory changes	80
	2.6.3	The Adoption of New Reporting Standards and Tools: XBRL, IFRS	80
		2.6.3.1 XBRL	80
		2.6.3.2 Ensuring Smooth Migration to International Financial Reporting Standards (IFRS)	80
		2.6.3.2.1 Challenges and opportunities for investor relations	81

		2.6.3.2.2 The European experience	82
		2.6.3.2.3 The investor relations roadmap for IFRS	84
		2.6.3.2.4 The IFRS toolkit	84
2.7	Investor Relations and Cross-Border Listings		85
2.8	The Convergence of Investor Relations and Corporate Communications		88
	2.8.1 Convergence Is Here to Stay		88
	2.8.2 Integrated Communications as a Value Driver		88
	2.8.3 Ensuring Consistency across Communications		89
3	**Implementing Best Practices in Investor Relations**		**92**
3.1	Identifying Shareholders		92
	3.1.1 Legal Means		93
		3.1.1.1 Notification of threshold crossing	93
		3.1.1.2 Identification by a central securities depositary	94
		3.1.1.3 Analysis of voting results	94
	3.1.2 Technical Means		95
		3.1.2.1 Free shareholder identification techniques	95
		3.1.2.2 Fee-based identification tools	95
		3.1.2.3 Financial intermediaries	96
3.2	Attracting and Retaining Shareholders		97
	3.2.1 Intelligent Targeting		98
		3.2.1.1 Meeting with hedge funds	102
		3.2.1.2 Activist shareholders or the limitation of institutional targeting	102
	3.2.2 The "Seed, Harvest and Lock" Approach to Investor Relations		103
3.3	Understanding Market Expectations		103
	3.3.1 Form		104
	3.3.2 Content		105
3.4	Developing the Financial Calendar		107
	3.4.1 Who Prepares the Financial Calendar?		107
	3.4.2 Financial Calendar Content		112
	3.4.3 Publication of the Financial Calendar		112
	3.4.4 Quiet Periods		113
	3.4.5 Black-Out Periods		114
3.5	Crafting Compelling Messages		115
	3.5.1 Writing Clearly		117
	3.5.2 Financial and Strategic Messages		117
		3.5.2.1 The business environment	117

		3.5.2.2 Organization	118
		3.5.2.3 Human resources	119
		3.5.2.4 Commercial, technological, and financial performance	119
		3.5.2.5 Business model	120
		3.5.2.6 Strategy	121
		3.5.2.7 Risk and uncertainties	122
	3.5.3	Outlook	123
		3.5.3.1 Forecasts, objectives, outlook, and guidance	124
		3.5.3.2 Selecting guidance indicators	125
		3.5.3.3 Choice of time horizon	126
		3.5.3.4 Changing the way you provide outlook and guidance	127
		3.5.3.5 Stopping earnings guidance	130
		3.5.3.6 Profit warnings and pre-announcements	131
	3.5.4	Shareholder value creation	132
	3.5.5	Mergers and Acquisitions	134
	3.5.6	Corporate Governance and Internal Control	135
	3.5.7	Corporate Social Responsibility and Sustainable Development	136
		3.5.7.1 From sustainable development to environmental, social, governance (ESG)	136
		3.5.7.2 Integrated reporting: the future of financial reporting?	138
	3.5.8	Investor Relations for Employee Shareholders	140
	3.5.9	Bridging the Language Divide	141
3.6	Selecting and Implementing Investor Relations Tools		143
	3.6.1	Press and News Releases	144
	3.6.2	Visuals, Presentations, and Slideshows	146
		3.6.2.1 Form	146
		3.6.2.2 Content	146
	3.6.3	Online Investor Relations	147
		3.6.3.1 Basic principles for website construction	148
		3.6.3.2 Site content	149
	3.6.4	Blogs and Social Media	151
	3.6.5	The Annual Report	153
		3.6.5.1 The purpose of the annual report	154
		3.6.5.2 Structure of the annual report	154
		3.6.5.3 Distribution of annual reports	155
	3.6.6	Shareholder Letter	157

	3.6.7	Financial Advertising	157
	3.6.8	Press Kits	158
	3.6.9	Public Meetings	158
	3.6.10	Solving the "Who Meets Who" Problem	159
	3.6.11	Successful Investor Relations Meetings Tactics	160
	3.6.12	One-to-One Meetings	161
	3.6.13	Roadshows	163
		3.6.13.1 Roadshow format	163
		3.6.13.2 To go solo or to use an investment bank	163
		3.6.13.3 Roadshow participants	164
		3.6.13.4 Ten rules for successful roadshows	165
		3.6.13.5 International roadshow checklist	167
	3.6.14	"Reverse Roadshow"	167
	3.6.15	Conferences	168
	3.6.16	Analyst and Investor Days	168
		3.6.16.1 Objectives	168
		3.6.16.2 Planning	169
		3.6.16.3 Location	170
		3.6.16.4 Content	170
		3.6.16.5 Feedback and debriefing	170
	3.6.17	Conference Calls	170
		3.6.17.1 Making the best use of technology	171
		3.6.17.2 Script and presentation	172
	3.6.18	Open Days	174
	3.6.19	The Annual General Meeting (AGM)	174
	3.6.20	Factbooks	177
	3.6.21	Written Disclosure Policy	177
	3.6.22	The Shareholder Guide	178
	3.6.23	Corporate Social Responsibility Report	178
	3.6.24	Fact Sheets	179
	3.6.25	Deploying Technological Innovation in Investor Relations	179
3.7	Enhancing Shareholder Loyalty and Retention		180
	3.7.1	Extracting Value from the Shareholder Base	180
	3.7.2	Combining Financial and Corporate Communications Strategies	181
3.8	Dealing with Crisis Communication in Investor Relations		181
	3.8.1	Anticipating, Just in Case…	183
	3.8.2	Joining Press Relations and Investor Relations Forces	183
4	**Measuring the Value of Investor Relations**		**188**
4.1	Quantitative Factors		189

4.1.1	Stock-Market Criteria	189
4.1.2	Equity Research on the Company	189
4.1.3	The Shareholder Base	190
4.1.4	Financial Criteria	191
4.1.5	The Investor Relations Program	191
4.2	Qualitative Factors	192
4.2.1	Perception Studies	192
4.2.1.1	Areas of focus	193
4.2.1.2	Methodology	193
4.2.2	Awards	194
4.2.3	Investor Relations Organizational Structure	194
4.2.4	Assessment by Senior Management	195
5	**Conclusion**	**198**
6	**Resources**	**199**
6.1	The CEO Investor Relations Checklist	199
6.2	Daily Stock Trading Datasheet	200
6.3	Sample Investor Relations Resume	201
6.4	Earnings Presentation Evaluation Form	204
6.5	Analyst & Investor Day Checklist and Timeline	205
6.6	Analyst & Investor Day Evaluation Form	206
6.7	Investor Relations Contact Form	208
6.8	Request for Roadshow Proposal	209
6.9	Earnings Announcement Timeline	211
6.10	Corporate Fact Sheet	212
6.11	Examples of ESG Performance Metrics	213
6.12	Basic Site Map Template for an Investor Relations Website	214
Index		215

List of Illustrations

Figures

1.1	Players and Objectives in Issuing Securities	3
1.2	The Stock Price Drivers	7
1.3	The Four Phases of Investor Relations in an IPO	8
1.4	Preparation of the IPO (Phase 1)	8
1.5	The IPO (Phase 2)	12
1.6	Beginning of the Aftermarket (Phase 3)	16
1.7	Stabilization (Phase 4)	18
2.1	The Investor Relations Relationship Framework	26
2.2	Company Management in the Role of the Supplier to the Capital Market	26
2.3	Company Management in the Role of a Client of the Capital Markets	27
2.4	Capital Markets in the Role of Suppliers to Company Management	27
2.5	Capital Markets in the Role of Clients of Company Management	27
2.6	Investor Relations Organizational Chart	39

Tables

2.1	The Target Audiences of Investor Relations	35
2.2	Costs and Benefits of Migrating to IFRS	81
2.3	Communication Plan for IFRS Conversion	83
3.1	The Benefits of a Diversified Shareholder Base	98
3.2	Comparative Advantages of Shareholder Types	99
3.3	Roadshow Matrix	104
3.4	Sample Financial Calendar for Fiscal Year Ending December 31st	108
3.5	Investor Relations Messages by Theme	116
3.6	Risks and Uncertainties	124
3.7	Example of Analyst Day Agenda	171

Introduction

All things being equal, the quality of Investor Relations (IR) is a key competitive differentiator that can result in higher valuation.

This is not only my firm belief, it has also been my experience after more than 25 years of practice in Investor Relations, both in-house and as an external advisor to public as well as private companies around the globe, of all sizes and sectors.

Traditionally, the key principle of Investor Relations is to help promote the securities issued by publicly traded companies—shares, bonds, or hybrid products—in compliance with regulations, with a particular emphasis on providing everyone with equal access to information. All players in financial markets should, therefore, have enough information to assess the fair value of these securities.

The world of Investor Relations and of financial communications is constantly changing, because of technology, regulation, and globalization. The information content is expanding much beyond the presentation of financial statements. Non-financial factors like patents, commercial successes, market shares, and management's reputation now carry as much weight in determining the value of a company as the quality of its financial performance. Lawmakers are increasingly requiring companies to detail their management compensation, corporate governance, and sustainable development policies. Accounting standards are also likely to evolve further, maybe even converge.

In this context, Investor Relations is not only a multi-faceted discipline, but also a major corporate responsibility in generating trust. As such, Investor Relations is a strategic lever for corporate development because of its influence on the cost of capital—share prices and credit ratings—and on reputation. This is why I am convinced that Investor Relations deserves "a seat at the table" and needs to be fully integrated with the company's communications framework and strategy.

There can be no question that Investor Relations are increasingly complex and target a wider and more demanding audience. Ever greater professionalism is thus required in an environment where the stakes and risks are real and growing.

With this book, my goal is to share with you a wealth of both strategic and tactical advice on how to understand and implement Investor Relations, wherever you are located, whether private or public. Because rules and regulations, a key aspect of the practice of Investor Relations,

Introduction   xiii

can differ from one country to another and evolve over time, I have given particular attention to international best practices. These can be easily implemented to comply with the most frequently adopted regulatory requirements, as well as to appeal to the global investment community.

Even if, originally, Investor Relations exclusively referred to a finance function within companies whose equity was traded on a stock exchange, they can, and should, actually be actively implemented by other categories of companies that are competing for capital, regardless of their size, their sector, or their financial track record. While this book is chiefly devoted to potentially or already publicly traded companies, most of the recommendations it contains will, therefore, be useful to any organization. Whether you are seeking to raise capital by attracting venture capitalists or private investors without going through the stock market, or whether you belong to a state-owned enterprise or a sovereign entity that is intending to tap the bond markets, you will be taken through the essential steps for understanding, conveying and, ultimately, marketing value.

The book combines the art and science of marketing, financial analysis, and Investor Relations in a single source. It offers expert advice, helpful tips, and successful ideas, including sample documents or templates in the appendix titled "Resources". Because it was written with the goal of offering clear and comprehensive information, the book is intended for the novice and for the sophisticate alike.

Divided into four comprehensive parts, this book clearly describes the entire process, from the decision to design a dedicated Investor Relations strategy to the measure of its return on investment.

Chapter 1 shows that going public means entering a new competitive environment where thousands of other companies are also competing on capital markets. It describes the various objectives for getting listed on a financial market: issuing new shares or bonds to help fund expansion; diversifying the shareholder base; building employee loyalty; extracting more value from the asset portfolio; and enhancing awareness of the company, for instance.

It then moves on to describe the four-step process of Investor Relations in the initial public offering (IPO), from the structuring of the transaction on the primary market to the post-IPO or "after market" life. As such, it puts particular emphasis on the need for Investor Relations to be adequately positioned within the company to ensure optimal performance in capital markets over the long term. It presents the role of the Investor Relations function in a two-dimensional manner that is comparable to customer–supplier relationships.

Chapter 2 analyzes the key factors needed to create successful Investor Relations. It first focuses on the value of senior management commitment to the program, and stresses that being able to rely on robust information systems is an absolute prerequisite. The reader will also learn why it is important to fully understand disclosure requirements and comply with legal obligations. Practical insight is then provided on how to professionally structure and implement a strategic Investor Relations program. It aims to answer questions such as, "Whom should the Investor Relations department report to?" "What are the major responsibilities of Investor Relations?" "How do you budget Investor Relations actions?" "How do you decide between outsourcing Investor Relations and keeping it in-house?".

Chapter 3 explains how to articulate a methodological approach to design a winning Investor Relations strategy with which companies can attract and retain shareholders or fund providers, ranging from effective annual reports to crisis communications management. The Investor Relations strategy will help get coverage from the media and financial analysts. In addition to highlighting the impact of corporate governance and socially responsible investment on corporate reputation, topics discussed include the following: shareholder identification and targeting; gathering of financial and industry information to develop consistent and compelling corporate messaging; financial calendar planning; and implementation of communications tools to be used in outreach programs to investors and key stakeholders.

Chapter 3 also offers many workplace-tested techniques such as how to write financial press releases, organize a roadshow, develop a contact list, and take advantage of innovation in communication technologies.

In Chapter 4, the book offers perspective on Investor Relations measurement. Assessing the value of Investor Relations on the basis of share price improvement is far from being the one and only metric, as many factors come into play; therefore, it is hard to separate the role of Investor Relations in that complex equation. I am suggesting different empirical methods framework to measure the results of an Investor Relations strategy against initial objectives, with a clear focus on steady improvement and value creation. This chapter lists not only the quantitative criteria that include stock-market-related metrics, but also the evolution of the earnings consensus, the shareholder base, for instance. It also considers qualitative parameters, such as awards or perception studies. It describes how to launch cost- and time-effective audits that are meant to provide senior management with useful and unbiased market sentiment.

Since the book was first published in 2008, the world has changed quite dramatically, affecting the way Investor Relations is performed. This second edition is therefore substantially enlarged with many new sections to help international Investor Relations practitioners navigate an ever evolving macroeconomic, financial, regulatory and technology environment where competition for capital is accelerating. The global financial crisis has taught many lessons with direct consequences for IR: growth prospects are more difficult to predict and investors are turning to companies that can provide sustainable returns, albeit more limited. I have therefore added actionable recommendations in the following areas: how to revise a guidance policy, how to discuss risks and uncertainties affecting business performance, how to delist while maintaining a visible presence with the financial community, how to integrate more environmental, social and governance issues in IR, while preserving your company's reputation.

Furthermore, the macroeconomic environment in the US and Europe has deteriorated sharply, bringing country risk back to the foreground and forcing investors to look at other investment opportunities beyond their traditional geographies. As emerging markets are fast gaining momentum as the next investment frontier, this is the opportunity for those companies to raise their profile in the global investment community and attract the capital they need to fund their growth or to achieve a fair valuation. They are already quite often busy implementing best practice in Investor Relations to achieve these goals. New resources have therefore been added that should be useful to many: a basic site map for an IR web site, an international roadshow checklist to take with you before you board the plane, tips on how to translate IR into foreign languages without losing impact, a sample Investor Relations resumé and an indepth analysis on IR as a career. The pros and cons of cross-listings are also described from an IR angle.

Regulations continue to be strengthened here and there, aiming at protecting investors and (re)building the trust in financial markets. In parallel, technological innovation has also accelerated further allowing for faster, broader dissemination of information to a wider, and often younger, audience; this blurs the lines between stakeholder groups thus forcing companies to take a more holistic approach to engagement by breaking down the communication silos. Also discussed are such areas as how to migrate smoothly to International Financial Reporting Standards, how to adopt social media for IR.

This second edition is also designed to reflect the feedback and many most helpful suggestions that readers from all over the world have been kind enough to provide me with. I greatly value their contribution and want to thank them here. I will always welcome criticism and any suggestions to improve future editions, both in form and substance.

In the conclusion, I will be reiterating my firm conviction that, regardless of the future changes in technology or regulation, the quality of Investor Relations, in form and content, will continue to act as a major catalyst in the fair valuation of a company by the capital markets.

1
Competing for Capital

Bringing in new shareholders, getting listed—or going public, as it is also called—or issuing new securities implies competing against hundreds or even thousands of companies all looking for partners to finance their development. These companies are often referred to as "the issuers." They may be from the same sector or come from entirely different economic areas. They may be of comparable size, larger or smaller. And they may be active in their own country or run global operations.

If two issuers have comparable financial results, the quality of their Investor Relations can be a differentiating factor and a real competitive advantage, which will be reflected in their valuation.

This is true both for companies that are considering a stock-market listing and for those that want to work with private investors or venture capitalists. Likewise, if a government decides to privatize a state-owned company, it is important that the entity which is being put up for sale is presented to potential investors in the most attractive and honest way.

As early on as possible, before the planned transaction becomes reality, the management of the companies in question needs to be fully aware of the challenges it will face once the companies become issuers:

- Meeting significant demands and high expectations from new "clients": financial analysts, institutional investors, individual shareholders journalists both domestic and international;
- Striking the balance between the short-term expectations of financial markets and their own long-term objectives;
- Maintaining and increasing investor appetite for their securities.

The goal is to tell an investment story that is convincing and consistent over the long term, while complying with the regulatory framework of the market (or markets where the securities are listed) and with international best practices. At the same time, the highest possible level of quality and consistency in terms of content and style needs to be applied. The rules that must be observed to achieve quality and consistency are as follows:

- Prepare for the transaction rigorously and with professionalism;
- Comply fully with a wide range of legal obligations;
- Aim for excellence in defining the methods and tools used to deliver financial information and communication to capital markets;
- Be clear, concise, and convincing;
- Inspire confidence;
- Devote the necessary time and resources to retaining the attention, and remaining on the radar screens, of journalists, analysts, and investors.

All of this requires a transparent and healthy relationship with both investors and the media. It means objectively separating information that is truly strategic and which needs to remain confidential, insofar as its disclosure could go against the company's legitimate best interests, and that which is required for valuation purposes. Those who consider that living happily means living secretly should think twice before they decide to get listed, and wait until they come to believe that being thrust into the spotlight can in fact help them grow faster than competition. In addition, going public is an extremely strenuous exercise for these companies, one that can slow or even stop growth. In some cases, it may make sense, and be much wiser, to postpone the listing decision.

1.1 Why Go Public?

Companies may turn to capital markets at a given point in time in their history to fund their expansion, build their corporate reputation, or enable existing shareholders to sell their shares at the best possible price.

While this book is not intended as a complete guide to initial public offerings (IPO), it aims at focusing on the mission-critical role of Investor Relations throughout the process and well beyond (see Figure 1.1).

Providing it offers and maintains a consistently clear understanding of its activities and strategies (microeconomic factors) along with updates on the environment in which it is operating (macroeconomic picture) on a regular basis, the company will be able to achieve the following:

- *Raise capital on the financial markets to help fund its development.* Capital can be raised through debt (if the company issues bonds) or equity (if shares are issued). These two types of security can also be combined into hybrid instruments. The company's Investor Relations program will relate to all of the securities issued since they are designed to

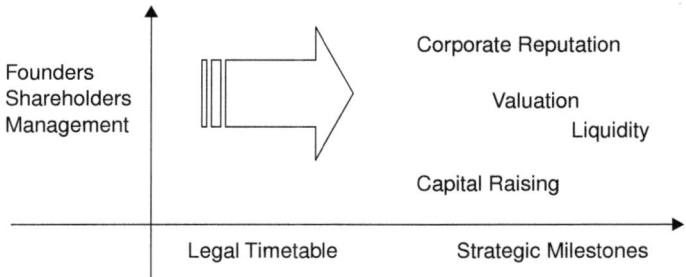

Figure 1.1 Players and Objectives in Issuing Securities

reflect not only its overall image, but also to promote a specific category of securities. Equity can be a less expensive source of funding than bonds, but can be counterproductive if new issues dilute earnings per share. Different factors, such as financing costs and balance sheet structures, can prompt companies to issue other types of securities (bonds or hybrid instruments). The terms of the offering, notably the price, will have an impact on the success of the transaction, but investors are less likely to be interested if they are only a little, or not at all, familiar with the company, its track record, its management team, and its development strategy.

- *Increase valuation.* In general, public companies enjoy a higher valuation than private enterprises. Researchers and market specialists agree that valuation multiples tell whether an Investor Relations policy is successful. In other words, the market prices take into account transparency, clearly presented businesses and strategies, in addition to applying other more strictly financial stock selection and valuation criteria. In practical terms, this means that companies must provide the following:
  ○ More information about their different activities by giving detailed segmental descriptions of their profit streams, strategies, and managers or, in some cases, by organizing site visits. This will help investors evaluate the company's competitive advantages (market share, pricing power between competitors, etc.) and distinguish between growth and mature businesses;
  ○ More open discussion about its financing and accounting practices (for instance, its policy with regard to risk provisions, management compensation).
- *Take advantage of sector valuation discrepancies between geographies.* For instance, listing your shares abroad, because your main competitor is listed there and is relatively better valued or better covered by the analysts' community than your own stock.

- *Provide liquidity.* By going public, including via an international listing, a company creates a market for its share where buyers and sellers are able to trade the share. In general, shares in a public company are much more liquid than stock in a private enterprise. Liquidity is created for the investors, institutions, founders, owners, and venture capital professionals. It can also supply an investor or company owner with an exit, merger, and acquisition strategy, and portfolio diversity. As a consequence, enhanced liquidity will also allow for the diversification of the initial shareholder base.
- *Raise visibility and increase corporate reputation.* The objectives here are manifold. It is worth using the publicity around the listing to make a company's brand known to a wider market, with clients and suppliers becoming shareholders, multiply business opportunities and even attract new business partners: These are likely to feel more confident in dealing with a company whose credibility is boosted by its complying with strict regulations and by the regular publication of audited financial statements. Getting listed is also about enhancing the company's overall image by associating quality products with a proactive policy geared to retail investors. For instance, banks or consumer goods firms may decide to give their shareholders special status as customers (or vice versa!). This brings us well outside the framework of Investor Relations, particularly when it comes to promoting a company's industrial or commercial strategy in a foreign country, even when it is not listed on the local market. It, however, only adds value to the necessity to design and implement a fully integrated communications strategy. It is also worth knowing that some investors actually have a tendency to hold long-term positions in companies that are household names. Public companies are more likely to appear in major newspapers and media than a private enterprise.
- *Attract and retain employees.* Visibility improves as financial information about listed companies is communicated via an increasingly wide range of media on a daily basis. Many medium-sized companies, the share prices of which are given regularly on TV or the radio in the local currency, gain much more publicity this way than they would through costly advertising campaigns with few measurable results. This allows them to attract and retain talented personnel they might otherwise not be able to reach and offer them attractive remuneration. These can take the form of stock-based compensation or be indexed to the evolution of the share price or result in a combination of both. In addition, through dedicated share ownership schemes, employees can become partial owners of the company where they work. Significant employee share holdings is often very well regarded by the investment community. It gives a strong sense of loyalty and commitment to productivity, and can prove a most efficient anti-takeover weapon.

It is clearly in listed companies' interest to target the highest possible valuation in order to achieve the following:

- *Ward off hostile bids and shareholder activism.* Hostile moves are based on the target company's share price, and potential predators tend to be scared off by higher market capitalizations. That said, let us be realistic: Institutional investors are accountable to their own shareholders and may have no choice but to sell their shares if the offer price is attractive.
- *Protect themselves against excessive market reactions to adverse news flows.* For instance, investors can overreact to economic data or major swings in exchange rates. Such sudden changes in the environment need not have a significant impact on a company's share price when the market has the proper level of understanding. If shareholders know that the company purchases as much as it sells in a given currency, then they know that a sharp increase or decrease in that currency may not necessarily impact its earnings in the same proportion. It can take the Investor Relations Officer (IRO) a few hours or days to get this message across, or in significantly less time, if he or she
  - discusses the potential issue during regular descriptions of the company. Making sure that the IRO gets regular and objective feedback from the market and is well aware of the company's perception by the investment community will be helpful in preparing for this eventuality;
  - responds immediately to the spate of phone calls that will inevitably pour in.
- *Be better positioned than competitors.* When building their portfolios, investors can choose from a vast selection of players within the same economic sector or with similar business models, at the national or the international level, relying on a host of ratios and forecasts calculated by financial analysts. Given a choice between two companies with similar valuations, they will in many cases opt for the one that provides the most detailed and readily accessible information. With tens of thousands of companies now listed throughout the world, they have more options than ever before. Better communications are synonymous with a better valuation, and this, in turn, is a significant competitive advantage over other listed companies—even more so, in the case of private ones. For the latter, their past financial performance and future prospects are not in the public domain, which may be a cause for concern to a potential shareholder.
- *Issue securities at any time at an attractive price.* It is important to bear in mind that much time may elapse between issues, possibly several years. Even if the decision to tap the capital market is made several months or weeks ahead of time, the light only turns green a few days

at best before the event. Regular Investor Relations can help lay the groundwork well ahead of time. In Investor Relations, closing a door that was once open can have damaging consequences. As the saying goes, "Markets have a long memory." Likewise, suddenly shifting to a higher gear, for no apparent reason, can also put operators on guard.
- *Reduce their cost of capital.* It is common knowledge that quality Investor Relations are a direct source of value creation, notably because they can be instrumental in driving share prices higher, thus pushing financing costs down. Investor Relations supports the company's financial strategy.
- *Diversify their shareholder base.* That is, achieve a better balance between the different categories of shareholders (institutional and retail investors, core shareholders who own a substantial portion of the share capital, employees and shareholders from the country of origin and from foreign countries—the no-resident shareholders). The goal here is to spread the risk more evenly, as some investors obviously have more investment power than others. Moreover, not all have the same responsiveness, and some manage their funds with a view to the short (in some cases very short!) term while others are truly focused on the long term. Meanwhile, should a crisis occur, foreign investors, most of whom are institutional, may be prompt to sell their holdings very quickly and repatriate the funds to their domestic markets. Some issuers are also keen to develop a shareholder base that reflects the geographic spread of their businesses, using their revenue breakdown as a model.

1.2 The Four Phases of Investor Relations in an IPO

Regardless of the timing of the IPO, the quality of Investor Relations is determined by how rigorously and thoroughly the process of going public is going to be thought out and implemented.

As in many life-changing events, there is a "before" and an "after." This applies to getting listed as well (see Figure 1.2).

The pre-IPO stage, which is by nature much shorter than the post-IPO one, should be designed with a view to simultaneously prepare for the after market. Bearing in mind that a positive image cannot be developed overnight, but can take months or even years to accomplish, the earlier you get started, the better.

Adopting this approach may seem to add complexity to an already strenuous process, but failing to do so is bound to create more trouble and higher costs ahead. Going public is similar in a number of ways to launching a new product, or having a child without thinking ahead about the room the baby is going to require to grow up in, or the school to apply to in order to ensure a place at the right time in the future.

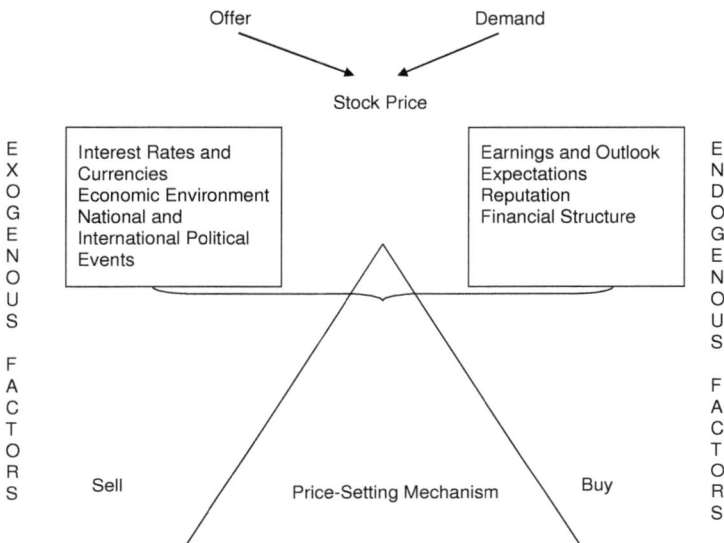

Figure 1.2 The Stock Price Drivers

Like any other major strategy, taking your company public requires careful planning and tactics to ensure success. From a methodology standpoint, the Investor Relations process is divided into four phases, each involving a plan of action as described below (see Figures 1.3–1.6).

As early as two to three years before the IPO, you should begin acting like, and functioning as, a public company, both internally and externally. As you go through the process, keep in mind that running a company and completing an IPO is challenging. Choosing the right advisors at this critical time can make all the difference for the success of your IPO.

During the IPO preparation, the company may want to "practice" Investor Relations well ahead of the actual listing, in order to get its organizational structure in order and validate its going-public strategy. This preparation work involves the following:

- *Take control.* Investment banks have their own agenda. So it is vital that you don't give them exclusive control of the IPO process, and certainly not as far as Investor Relations are concerned.
- *Begin early to bring information systems up to speed* (see Chapter 2, Section 2.4). This means getting comfortable with the rhythm of quarterly and annual reporting requirements, their content, and costs. Reporting and management tools must be able to deliver exhaustive, reliable, and relevant data, within the timeframe imposed by regulations. This phase is all

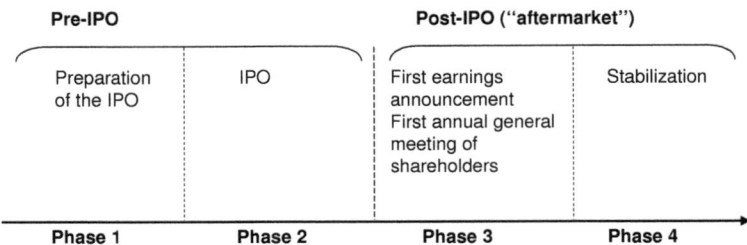

Figure 1.3 The Four Phases of Investor Relations in an IPO

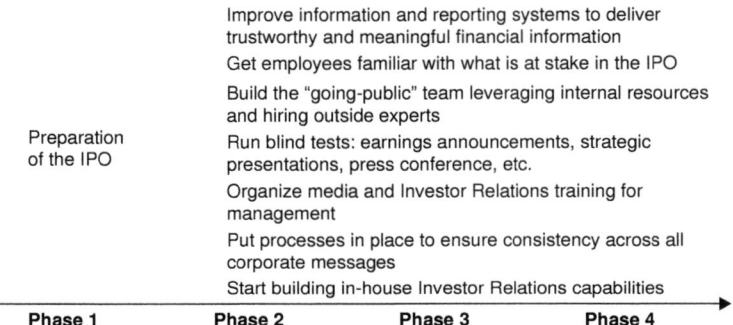

Figure 1.4 Preparation of the IPO (Phase 1)

too often taken lightly, or in some cases ignored altogether by IPO candidates. But the fact is that if information systems are not reliable and set up in time, management is unlikely to establish its credibility over time. This also implies that management has made sure that it has a minimum of two to three years of audited financial statements available before starting the IPO process. All in all, it is highly recommended to make sure that internal processes are robust enough to ensure smooth production of the entire set of data and internal controls that will be required before, during, and after the IPO. A good sanity check is to ask yourself whether your company can meet its quarterly reporting obligations in time and see what needs to be done to achieve this goal before the IPO goes live.

- *Ensure that employees are aware of the benefits as well as of the new obligations arising from the IPO.* It can be an opportunity to turn employees into shareholders, to attract new staff by advertising the company's name, and to strengthen the sense of belonging. However, the IPO also means new obligations for all, especially where privileged or price-sensitive information is concerned. This is why, during phase 1, some companies opt to draft an internal code of conduct or amend an existing one, to make everyone aware of these new obligations.

- *Gather market intelligence.* The goal is twofold: identify the other listed companies with which your company is going to be compared, and analyze both the content and form of their investor relations program and corporate communications. The first step is to build a peer group from a selection of companies. Then, you will examine their reported metrics and which performance indicators they have chosen to give objectives for (or guide the market on) and the time horizon they allow themselves to meet these targets: Do competitors give quarterly, annual, or medium-term guidance? The next step is to look at whether they release their earnings on a quarterly or on a semi-annual basis and to read the research published about these competitors to see whether the market has any appetite for the sector. This exercise is invaluable in shaping your investment case that will be presented to the market at the time of the IPO. The information should not be too difficult to access. If needed, help can be provided by financial intermediaries or investment banks. In parallel, you should also take time to learn the rules of the market(s) where you are going to be listed and the needs of local investors. You will complete this research by reviewing the peer group's Investor Relations actions: disclosure and guidance policies, earnings release dates, conference call times and content, website use; information kits, and the event program, such as participation in broker-sponsored conferences.
- *Build the "going-public" Investor Relations team.* Build the "going-public" Investor Relations team that will manage the messaging and disclosure process. This working group should be comprised of members of the management team, chief executive officer (CEO), chief finance offer (CFO), controller, internal IRO, corporate communications, and general counsel. They will be assisted by the lead investment bank or broker and by a financial communications firm, often combining Investor and Public Relations capabilities.
- *Build a positive public image.* Build a positive public image that will enhance the initial sales effort and maintain the public's interest in the stock in the aftermarket. More specifically, focus your attention on those who will buy the company's stock and on those who influence that buying decision (financial analysts, stockbrokers, the financial press, and industry publications). You may have to hire Investor Relations and Public Relations firms well in advance of the IPO. These firms can assist you in getting your company's "story" out early enough, adding analysts and business press editors to your mailing lists, participating in trade shows and conferences that are attended by analysts, and publicizing key employee appointments.
- *"Practice" Investor Relations and financial communications.* This involves preparing marketing materials, and drafting of earnings press releases,

planning financial presentations, creating a graphic identity, developing a glossary of the technical terms used in the company's business in appropriate languages, holding press conferences to which journalists and analysts are invited, and educating managers about the needs of investors. These tests can take the form of "dry runs," with the company only sharing the results with its advisors as if it were already a public company. The latter strategy is sometimes adopted by large companies that have already issued bonds but no shares and are well-known enough to move straight to this phase. That is particularly true with state-owned companies that are privatization candidates. It is during this process that executives and operations managers familiarize themselves with financial markets, particularly the press and financial analysts, and test how their messages are perceived. Meanwhile, analysts get to know the future issuer and build the valuation models they will use once the company is effectively listed. The process is always instructive, and much appreciated by the target audiences. That said, the legal obligations associated with this type of exercise intensify as the IPO approaches. This is particularly true of information delivered to prospective investors, the content and distribution of which are subject to strict regulations. In addition, the investment case presented by the company must be consistent with the one bankers will use to secure the IPO's success.

- *Set up methods and processes.* Set up methods and processes to ensure that messages are consistent over time and across the various communications channels of the company. During this phase, both external and internal communications are integrated with employee communications, with product and service marketing messages. It may not be necessary to establish a hierarchy between the different areas. The idea is that, relying on the communication experience its marketing department is likely to have, the company should try to deliver a core set of messages to different stakeholders and thus ensure that the company "speaks with one voice." The more integrated and the more consistent the messages, company-wide, the more convincing they will be. This is a real asset when it comes to shaping the company's financial image. It also fosters internal cooperation between marketing, finance, and communications teams.
- *Develop and coordinate the Investor Relations organization and procedures.* These guidelines, which will be used all the way up to top management, must be designed to evolve as the IPO approaches and to expand thereafter. In particular, they will apply to all the other employees who are not authorized spokespeople, giving them direction on where to reroute incoming inquiries.

- *Appoint a limited number of authorized spokespersons.* Appoint a limited number of authorized spokespersons in order to keep messaging consistent over time and across spokespeople: the CEO, the CFO, possibly a chief operating officer (COO) and divisional heads as appropriate, in addition to senior communications representatives. Of these, only one or two, usually the CEO and CFO, should be responsible for direct contact with analysts, investors, and the financial media. Have them properly trained to converse comfortably with analysts, investors, and members of the media while reinforcing the story and preventing accidental disclosures of non-public information. Educate them on stock-market regulations, disclosure rules, and Investor Relations best practices.
- *Establish a dedicated team.* Establish a dedicated team headed by a project coordinator. In most cases, he or she will work with investment banks to identify internal resources and select outside contractors, notably to handle the technical and logistical aspects of investor and media relations if the company does not have in-house resources. This also entails the implementation of process and staff to respond to incoming investor and media inquiries, which will be advertised in the Investor Relations section of the website. The same coordinator will monitor budgets and the timeline, assuring that it is updated regularly. If the IPO is a success, this coordinator may be appointed to run Investor Relations in the "aftermarket."
- *Determine the stock's sector.* Listed companies are divided into sectors internationally, and this classification has an impact on Investor Relations. Equity research firms are often organized along the same lines. Advisors will study which sector the company is likely to be placed in, the compartment in which its competitors are situated, and the respective valuation multiples of each sector. It is important to bear in mind that companies are rarely reclassified into another sector once they are listed, barring significant shifts in their business profile.

In phase 2 (see Figure 1.5), you launch the active preparation of your company's Investor Relations strategy ahead of the IPO. This phase is very strictly regulated. Your objectives will include the following:

- *Crafting key messages.* This is the task of the investment banks that are helping management develop the "investment case," also called the "equity story." This helps determine the stock's future positioning on the market and is critical in more ways than one: It forces managers to explain, in words and numbers, the strategy that will subsequently be presented to the public in company documents. The main goal is to

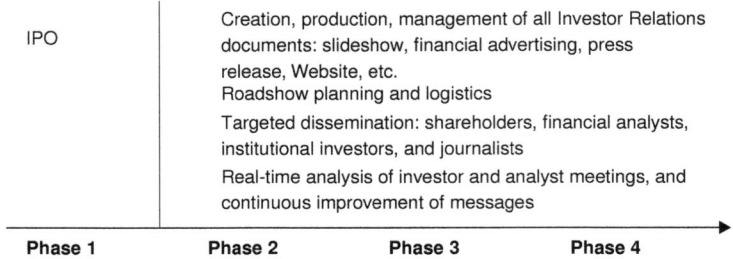

Figure 1.5 The IPO (Phase 2)

come up with an equity story that will appeal to the investors to whom the investment banks will be marketing the shares. Conflicting interests can be a serious issue during this stage: Shareholders will want to see the highest possible valuation while investment banks will want to ensure that the IPO is successful, hence potentially sell it off at an initially lower price. Needless to say, it can also be the other way around. This is going to impact the size of the "free float" (the portion of the share capital that will be actually tradable with the public) and share price once the shares are listed. Therefore, managers must pay special attention to how they define their strategic messages, describe their growth prospects, and set their objectives. This phase would not be complete without real "dress rehearsals" in every language in which information meetings or private meetings will be held. These "dry runs" should include intensive Q&A sessions. You can already start getting ready to respond to some of these most frequently asked questions in these instances: "Does your company have a profitable track record? What makes you confident that you will be able to maintain strong sales and earnings growth in the future? What are your key competitive differentiators?" These rehearsals can also help determine which executives or operating officers will be presenting to the investment community, based on not only their position within the organization, but also on their speech and communication skills in any given language. In most cases, it is useful to bring in a media trainer and speech coach.

- *Defining the guidance policy for strategic objectives and financial targets.* This will be an area of maximum attention, internally and externally, a far-reaching one that will influence a new issuer's disclosure policy, its relationships with analysts and investors, and its public company image long after the IPO is over. Management will be held accountable for the objectives to which they will have committed. While more practical recommendations will be provided in Section 3.5.3. (Chapter 3) of this book on how to provide guidance to the market, it is important that management realizes as early as possible in the IPO process that

they need to be prepared to talk about and quantify their plans for the next one, five, or ten years. They will have to strike a fine balance between being too generic (a usual tendency) and giving long-term divisional targets (a traditional investment bank's recommendation). Factors impacting this choice will including the company's financial visibility, sector dynamics, and peer company behavior.
- *Developing and managing the Investor Relations toolkit.* Companies have a wide range of options, depending on the key audiences, the size of the transaction in question, and the attention they wish to attract. Selection of appropriate tools at the outset enables companies to maintain consistency, visibility, and quality over time. Some of these tools are mandatory. Here is an overview of the most usual ones (see Section 3.6 in Chapter 3):
  - *Slideshows.* These are chiefly used for information meetings with the press, financial analysts, and institutional investors. A convincing presentation will address all potential issues, including the negative ones, with a view to anticipate and optimize investors' questions.
  - *Financial advertising in all types of media, including online media.* In certain countries, this is specially geared to attracting retail investors and can be the subject of proper advertising campaigns for major transactions, such as privatizations.
  - *Press releases.* Every major event during the entire IPO process will be the subject of a dedicated press release: launch, terms and conditions, structure of the offering, filing with and clearance by the market authorities, results, and so on.
  - *Press kits.* These are designed for journalists. In addition to the above-mentioned materials, the press kit should at least include biographies and photos of company management, a reproduction of the company's logo in a digital format and, where appropriate, videos that explain more about the company's history and business.
  - *The corporate website, with a section specially devoted to Investor Relations.* This primary communications tool is just as important as the others and should be designed as early as possible before, and not after, the IPO. You should bear in mind that the Investor Relations section can be subject to specific regulatory requirements. Make sure yours comply.
- *Organizing roadshows with potential investors and managing event logistics.* The schedule, which is often intensive and can involve international travel, should be planned in close cooperation with the investment banks that are going to arrange the meetings with their institutional clients. One, or several, teams representing the company will be sent to meet with prospective investors. This will require significant planning, along with thorough and rigorous training. Also, one of the goals will

be to make sure that executives who are temporarily acting as "traveling salesmen" do not have to worry themselves with "housekeeping" issues. It is a good idea, for instance, to have enough business cards printed beforehand in the languages of the countries to be visited, to inquire about their dietary requirements, or favorite hotels in the cities that will be included in the tour.
- *Disseminating Investor Relations information.* The first step here consists of building the distribution lists, from the company's internal sources or from third-party vendors, prior to pricing. It will allow the company to announce itself the completion of its IPO. The Investor Relations distribution list will contain key sell- and buy-side analyst and investor contacts. An Investor Relations firm can be called in to supply prospective contacts in the investment community, who may eventually be interested in covering or in investing in the company. Depending on the communications strategy elected by the company, these lists can also include business partners, commercial suppliers, in addition to the media and the investment community. Once the IPO supporting documents and materials have been validated, they are to be delivered to these target audiences in target regions (retail investors, financial analysts, institutional investors, and journalists) in at least two languages if English is not the company's official language.
- *Analyzing meetings with analysts and investors in real time to improve the equity story and key messages.* Writing down every single question asked during meetings will help managers prepare their aftermarket presentations, and keep the Q&A bible up to date. Ideally, they should be briefed regularly on how their responses are perceived by investors and analysts, beyond what financial research or media clippings might suggest, which will benefit, whenever possible, from suggestions on where to improve their presentations, and how to appear more confident and convincing. Future issuers should also take advantage of these meetings to learn more about their potential stakeholders, taking every opportunity to inquire about the amounts they manage, their investment policies, and their expectations in terms of Investor Relations. This dialogue opportunity is often overlooked, to the dismay of fund managers. All information gathered from these meetings will be invaluable to the company during the subsequent phases.

Throughout this second phase of the Investor Relations process during an IPO, it is essential that IROs and staff are organized and trained to:

- provide back-up during road shows;
- take on much heavier and more intense workloads. Outside help can be called in (temporary staff, private contractors, or outsourcing) to

respond to the flow of inquiries resulting from the IPO marketing frenzy;
- ensure that the messages delivered are consistent and instructive. In the run-up to the strategically important first day of trading, IROs and staff should have maximum access to all the information they deem necessary. They should be closely involved in:
  ○ developing the investment case to support the IPO price;
  ○ selecting the investors that the underwriting banks will target.

The Investor Relations team will also see to it that:

- the company's Investor Relations comply with best practices starting from day one on the first day into the capital markets. The team will notably guarantee that all analysts and investors, regardless of their relations with the lead underwriters, have equal access to information, and particularly to public meetings;
- the selection of investors targeted by the road show is detailed, justified, and personalized;
- the final results of the IPO are recorded with the utmost precision, going so far as to specify the names of the fund managers within each institution that subscribed to the offering;
- a perception study is conducted with the analysts and investors met during the road show.

Thanks to these measures, the Investor Relations team should have, after the IPO:

- an exact picture of the new breakdown of the share capital, both in terms of shareholder categories and geographic locations;
- an initial earnings consensus of "sell-side" analysts, including their recommendations and target prices.

This information will be used to develop the Investor Relations strategy in phase 3 (see Figure 1.6), independently of the lead banks that handled the IPO. The strategy will not only involve solidifying the new shareholder base, but also developing a marketing plan for promoting the share. Much will need to be done to retain existing shareholders, identify new targets, and steadily attract new investors and analysts.

Phase 3 marks the beginning of the aftermarket period, which starts on the first day of trading in the newly issued stock. The company is now listed and, so to speak, "on its own." Here are a few essentials to get off to a good start and set up the right tools to manage a winning Investor Relations program:

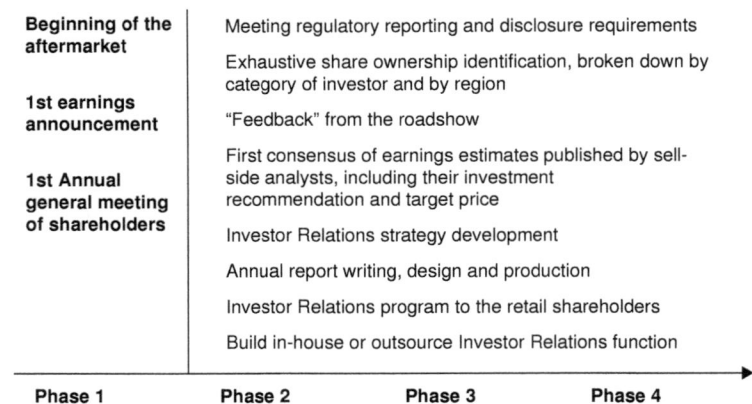

Figure 1.6 Beginning of the Aftermarket (Phase 3)

- *The exact breakdown of the shareholder base, both in terms of categories and geographic location.* The banks that have placed shares with their clients will be required to provide the most accurate information possible. If this information is used to build the company's contact database, an absolute prerequisite for any Investor Relations program, it needs to include all relevant information about the institutional investors that established positions and the number of shares acquired in the IPO. Regrettably, new issuers often find themselves with no more than a list of financial institutions, with no addresses or individual names. The only solution in this case is to enter the information from the business cards collected during the road show into the computer to create a database, far enough ahead of the next press releases to be sent out.
- *Feedback from road shows.* While the subscription rate and trend in the share price in the first few days of trading do give an indication of the IPO's success, it is just as important to find out why certain investors did not subscribe. Did they find the shares too expensive? Did management make a poor impression? Do they find the sector too risky? Rapid debriefing should be conducted as soon as possible once the IPO road show is over.
- *The initial consensus of financial analysts.* In most cases, this will reflect their earnings estimates for the current year and the two following fiscal years, their buy, sell or hold ratings, and their price targets for the months ahead.

The company should, by the end of phase 3, have what it needs to develop and implement the tools to manage its Investor Relations program, such as:

- Understanding of the structure of the company's initial shareholder base;
- The investor and analyst contact data base with which it will maintain the dialogue initiated during the IPO;
- The analysts' earnings consensus;
- Highlights of the Q&A sessions, portions of which can be integrated into the frequently asked questions, "FAQ," page of its website.

In addition, the company will want to put into place:

- Data sheets showing daily movements in the share price and trading volumes (see Table 6.2 in Resources section);
- A financial calendar (see Section 3.4) to assure compliance with legal reporting and disclosure requirements and keep the investment community informed of upcoming financial announcements;
- Internal procedures to ensure the timely disclosure of material information. Investor Relations consultants and law firms will help the company become familiar and comply with the obligation to disclose all price-sensitive information, favorable and unfavorable, as soon as possible.

If it is not yet effectively the case, the newly listed company will need to appoint someone in charge of managing these tools as well as Investor Relations in general. As suggested earlier, this may be the project manager who coordinated the teams that conducted the IPO, or possibly the CFO, if it is a small company. If enough financial analysts are covering the stock, the company may consider hiring an IRO from outside or consider outsourcing at least a part of its Investor Relations program to experts while it establishes its presence on the market during phase 4 (see Figure 1.7).

Phase 4 begins approximately 18 to 24 months after the IPO. In the interim period, the company will have complied with legal obligations and reported revenues and earnings on a regular and quite often quarterly basis. It will have also published its annual report and held the annual general meeting of shareholders.

The messages presented at the time of the IPO will have been reiterated, and the company will have provided updates on its progress toward its stated objectives.

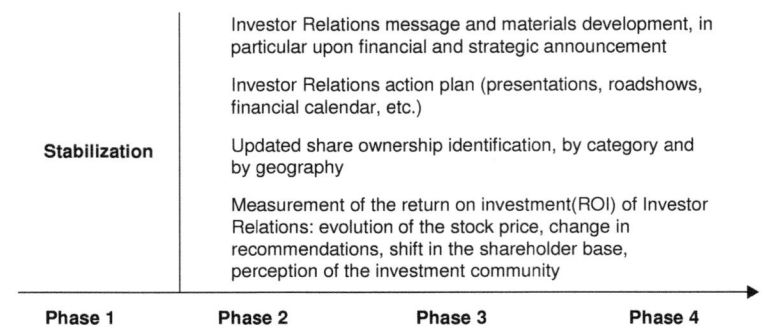

Figure 1.7 Stabilization (Phase 4)

Maintaining or putting the company on the radar screens of analysts and investors long after the IPO spotlights are switched off is going to require tremendous work. Meetings with new analysts and investors will have been held, the share price will have trended higher or lower, and the composition of the free float will probably have changed. In addition, certain deadlines, such as lock-up periods, may have been in place beyond the IPO. They will be known to the market and mentioned in the IPO prospectus. Once large shareholders or groups of institutional investors have potentially taken advantage of these periods to sell their shares within these deadlines, the share price will be able to move more freely.

All of this gives the company enough experience to:

- identify areas in which it can improve the organization of its Investor Relations program;
- add other Investor Relations management tools;
- conduct ongoing analysis of its shareholder base by category and geographic location;
- evaluate the return on investment of its Investor Relations as evidenced by the share price, equity research on the company, stock recommendations, the consensus, and perception studies focusing on its financial image.

1.3 Investor Relations for Private Companies

Prior to obtaining venture capital or considering a public listing at some point in time in their growth strategy, emerging companies or "start-ups" will benefit from implementing minimum corporate governance standards and financial communications procedures. Most of them were described earlier in Section 1.2 and correspond to phase 1 of Investor Relations in an IPO.

If they opt for private equity financing, formal board presentation will be a condition to obtain equity. You will have to know how to:

- present your business and financial track record so far;
- articulate your growth strategy and the business model that goes with it;
- justify your need for capital with realistic result and achievement objectives.

You can learn from Investor Relations specialists and from best-practice-oriented publicly traded companies, by studying the form and content of their financial communications and corporate governance principles.

Furthermore, it is very likely that the CEO will have his or her vision and targets aggressively challenged by potential investors. Adequate training and rehearsing will be a prerequisite.

Once the funds have been cashed in the composition of the board of directors is, in most cases, going to incorporate representatives of the private equity firms that have contributed to the equity-raising process. They will be hardly different from other institutional investors in their information requests and expectations. For instance, this is going to entail:

- keeping them informed of industry and companies issues, in real time;
- scheduling meetings at regular intervals.

This process may seem tedious at first, but it has many advantages for private companies, the foremost among which are:

- getting used to high standards of communications;
- becoming familiar with valuation mechanisms;
- understanding how to build an efficient board of directors.

In other words, the sooner you get organized and ready for this very specific communications exercise, the better.

1.4 Private Equity Investor Relations

The stock market is far from being the only way to raise capital to build or grow businesses. In this respect, private equity firms have always provided companies with alternative financing sources. These firms are raising funds from investors (limited partners or "LPs") who require just as much attention as do portfolio managers investing in a listed company. The rapid expansion of the private equity market is generating heightened competition for capital, thus prompting firms to develop proper Investor Relations programs in-house or outsource to specialized service providers.

Their primary goals are to:

- create visibility in the market, through effective media relations;
- develop the fund's positioning and strategy;
- create marketing materials;
- market the fund to potential LPs;
- prequalify potential investors;
- process all documentation for investor transactions into funds;
- build and manage relationships between fund raisings with current and potential LPs;
- track the fund's performance and benchmark it against competitors;
- hold annual investor meetings;
- produce and distribute investor reporting.

1.5 Debt Investor Relations

Issuers in the state-owned sectors and listed companies alike tap the international capital markets by raising debt. For the latter, credit conditions may, at times, make it even cheaper than equity.

Because debt and equity are closely related, it makes sense for investors to want and for companies to deliver a single, consistent message, encompassing the equity and the debt story. Therefore, there is no reason why equity and fixed-income analysts from the same institution should not be invited to Investor Relations meetings.

The organization of debt Investor Relations varies from one company to another. Either it is incorporated into Investor Relations or, more often than not, it is managed by the central treasury function. Whatever the structure, it is essential that consistency in messages is maintained by both teams, because in today's environment, investors and analysts want to understand the company's capital structure in its entirety and be able to compare return expectations.

Key Principles to Remember

- Getting listed or tapping the capital market is not for the timid. Success calls for advance planning, discipline, professionalism, and management's full-time dedication
- Investor Relations are a core part of companies' operations and necessitates a proactive development of client–supplier relationship with the capital markets
- Between two companies with similar economic and financial performances, investors will prefer the one with the higher quality of Investor Relations.

International Best Practices	
Pre-IPO	Post-IPO ("aftermarket")
• Establish rigorous and professional processes, including robust financial reporting systems • Go for excellence in terms of Investor Relations and proactive communications with capital market players • Build a strong financial image that speaks of quality and consistency, in form as well as in content • Inspire confidence be clear, concise, and convincing.	• Understand and conquer the competition: the *other* listed companies • Comply with strict regulatory constraints • Find the optimum between short-term requirements of the financial markets and the company's longer-term objectives • Maintain and increase the interest generated by IPO • Know how to devote time and resources to remaining on the analysts' and investors' radar screens.

2
Seven Keys to Successful Investor Relations

In order to use Investor Relations effectively as a competitive differentiator on financial markets, a specific mindset needs to be adopted by the company. It is going to be a combination of the following:

- Clearly defined goals;
- Management's commitment;
- Organizational efficiency;
- Quality information systems;
- Understanding of and compliance with legal obligations;
- Ability to anticipate future changes in financial communications

Applying each of the principles listed above, with an integrated vision shared by the entire executive team, is going to be mission critical in achieving best-practice Investor Relations in a measurable way.

2.1 Clearly Defined Goals

Investor Relations is often viewed as a cost, and therefore, something that should be kept to a minimum, or even avoided. In times of recession and economic slowdown, it is often one of the first overheads to be cut from the company's budget. However, it should be managed as an investment that can generate actual returns, providing its objectives are

- realistic;
- aligned with management's expectations;
- tied in to the company's overall strategy;
- measurable qualitatively and quantitatively.

2.2 Importance of Senior Management Commitment

This is, and will remain, the primary determinant of success, the one that will end up differentiating companies from one another. Management can see Investor Relations either as a necessary evil or as a strategic tool for enhancing the company's valuation and their own personal image.

In the first case, Investor Relations is seen as being too expensive and time consuming and yielding unpredictable, possibly even mediocre results. Companies that take this view have a hard time hiring good Investor Relations Officers (IROs) because they have little respect for this activity. They consider it to involve merely tracking the share price and they are unwilling to offer any career advancement prospects beyond Investor Relations. This particular type of management has no desire to be face to face with analysts, investors, or the media. This attitude of ignorance, or in some cases contempt, tends to grow, and become mutual. These executives consider that analysts should come to them, not the other way around. They barely involve themselves in defining the company's financial and strategic communications and delegate this work to ad hoc committees, even though they are legally liable for its content. They are never around when bad news is announced because they cannot handle it with the required humility and objectivity. It is often difficult for companies that behave this way to get back into the good graces of the market, which rarely forgets being cold-shouldered in this fashion.

In the second case, management does not see Investor Relations as a burden but rather as an excellent opportunity to take advantage of the company's presence on capital markets, and an essential tool for meeting the targets set at the time of the initial public offering (IPO), for instance. These managers recognize that it is a part of corporate responsibility and a real job requiring human and technical resources as well as time. They get involved, openly, in defining, and sometimes driving, the Investor Relations program. They put high-potential staff in charge of Investor Relations and ensure that these IROs are closely and directly involved in strategic thinking. Indeed, they are able to understand that certain decisions involve anticipating market reactions in a way that IROs alone can predict. They see Investor Relations as an investment, returns on which can only be evaluated over time.

2.3 The Efficient Investor Relations Organization

Investor Relations is a central and centralizing function within the organization. It plays a key role in corporate strategy, which in turn helps determine the fair value of the listed company's shares. As the intermediary between the issuer and financial markets, Investor Relations has a decisive impact. Its core responsibility is to convey the firm's identity, establish its market position toward adequate valuation, and contribute to build corporate reputation. The development of the organization's Investor Relations strategy must, therefore, originate from the Investor Relations department (IR department). This department will also be held accountable for designing and implementing measurement techniques.

Investor Relations can be described as a two-way street, a dialogue. In this respect, it has a lot in common with marketing and with customer–supplier relationship management, as illustrated in the following diagrams (see Figures 2.1, 2.2, 2.3, 2.4, and 2.5).

The financial market is the first client of the Investor Relations department for information about the company, its various businesses, historical performance, prospects, and strategic directions. In parallel, it is also its leading supplier of intelligence about how the company is perceived and valued by the investment community. The Investor Relations department ensures that consistency is maintained in all financial communications messages. To achieve this, the Investor Relations team must consist of professionals who are competent and legitimate, whether they are in-house

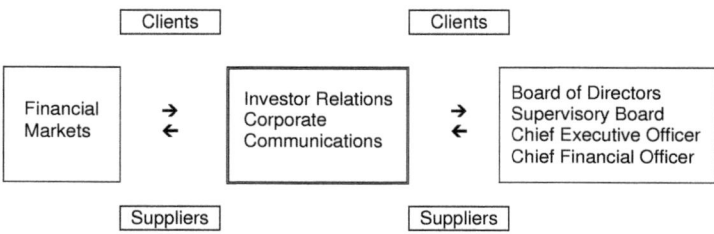

Figure 2.1 The Investor Relations Relationship Framework

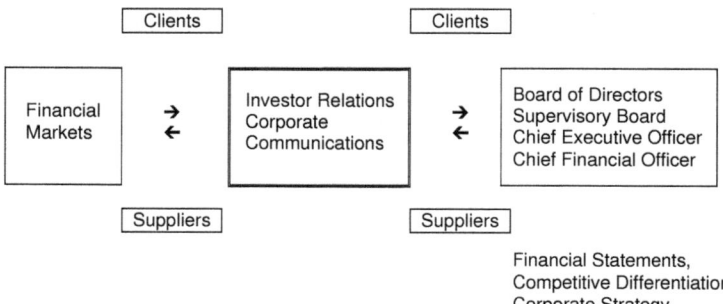

Figure 2.2 Company Management in the Role of the Supplier to the Capital Market

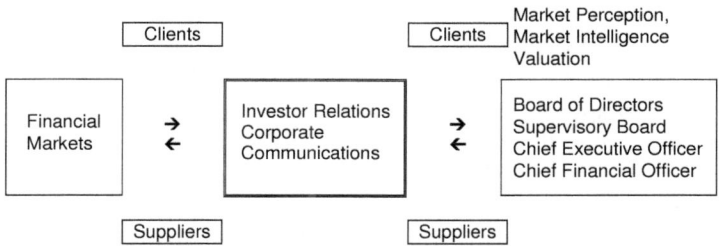

Figure 2.3 Company Management in the Role of a Client of the Capital Markets

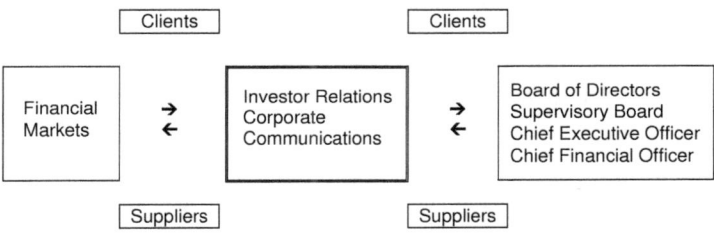

Financial Analysis
Presentation of the Company's Business
Activities, Prospects and Strategy
Marketing to the Investment Community

Figure 2.4 Capital Markets in the Role of Suppliers to Company Management

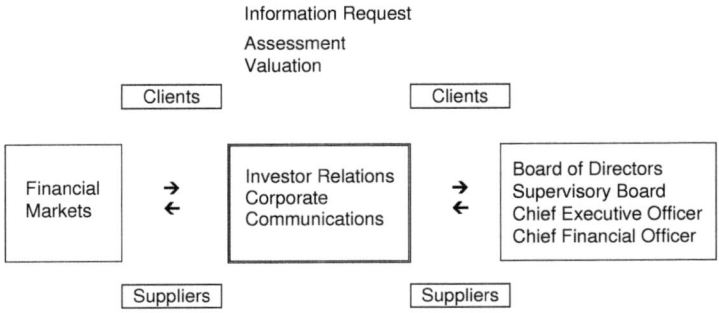

Figure 2.5 Capital Markets in the Role of Clients of Company Management

or working on a contract basis. This team needs to have access to all of the information it deems necessary to perform its task. It should be consulted as early on as possible before any financial or strategic messages are sent out to audiences it may not be directly reporting to: the board of directors, the audit committee, human resources handling employee share ownership schemes, the domestic or international economic, and financial press relations.

The company's management provides the IR department both with the resources it needs and with strategic and financial information. At the same time, it is a "client" of the department, from which it receives information about how it is perceived by the financial market, about analyst forecasts and recommendations, and about changes in the shareholder base. It is essential that the Investor Relations department head be permitted to give the highest levels of management an objective view of market sentiment toward the company.

In particular, the head of Investor Relations will focus on the following:

- Establishing, internally, the central role of the Investor Relations department in the "customer–supplier" relationship between the listed company and financial markets. The person's tasks will, among other things, include
  - Coordinating internally the editorial content of the company's financial and strategic vision;
  - Institutionalizing the flow of information about investor perception;
  - Implementing market intelligence–gathering methods and stock surveillance;
  - Gradually adapting the company's organizational structure to international best practices in Investor Relations.
- Developing means and methods to coordinate and integrate the company's Investor Relations efforts on all topics and to all audiences. Particular attention will be paid to the following:
  - Positioning Investor Relations with regard to: corporate communications, relations with the press and market authorities, corporate governance, and sustainable development;
  - Building awareness within the company of the strategic importance of Investor Relations. More specifically, this can imply ensuring compliance with legal obligations, consistency in terms of content and form of communications, and transformation of the annual report into a full-fledged Investor Relations tool rather than just a corporate communications or a legal document;
  - Developing tools for monitoring the company's Investor Relations activities with a view to measure the return on investment.

In addition to guaranteeing that information released to the outside world is consistent over time, the creation of a centralized and integrated Investor Relations department also enables companies to do the following:

- Speak with one voice;
- Make sure IROs and teams have the necessary in-depth and hands-on knowledge of the company they represent in the financial markets, make them aware of the obligations and risks associated with price-sensitive or privileged information, help them master a certain kind of vocabulary and communications skills, ensure that they reflect the company's corporate culture at all times. This definitely takes time and the perfect candidates are hard to find. In any case, they should have a robust financial background, along with experience in auditing, management control, or financial analysis;
- Ease the investigation process in the event of problems and inquiries by market authorities.

Let us now spend some time on assessing what makes a strong Investor Relations function and what are the pitfalls to avoid when setting up and staffing an IR department.

2.3.1 A Flexible and Scalable Investor Relations Organization

The size of a company, whether it is measured by its market capitalization, its free float, or its revenues, often directly impacts the size of the team and of the budget allocated to Investor Relations. It can also be a function of its capital market experience, of the complexity of its story, and of how global its Investor Relations program is. Financial information must consistently be of the same quality in terms of content and form, regardless of the circumstances. This requires an organizational structure that is flexible enough to be adapted to changing regulations, market expectations, and to the evolution of the corporate structure itself.

The effectiveness of a company's Investor Relations can only be evaluated over the long term. In the meantime, however, it is important to ensure that the company does not experience a sudden loss of visibility or credibility, as this would deteriorate, and possibly endanger, its ability to tap the capital markets in good conditions.

The volume, frequency, and quality of Investor Relations should be consistent over time, under all circumstances, including in the event of the following:

- Budget cuts;
- Major changes in the size and/or shape of the free float, including a secondary offering, a sharp increase in the number of retail shareholders,

an increasing internationalization of the institutional shareholder base, more employee shareholders;
- Coverage by an increasingly large number of analysts, including abroad;
- Listing on a foreign market, and so on. Flexibility will also mean being able to adapt to changes in the following;
- Regulations on the dissemination of financial and other information;
- The expectations and demands of the markets;
- Internal organization and change in the ownership of certain major Investor Relations projects such as the annual report, the annual general meetings.

Even if the size of the IR department changes, it must continue to play the same role in three key areas:

- Building internal awareness of the strategic importance of Investor Relations;
- Acting as the company's authorized spokesperson to speak to the investment community on behalf of the company;
- Adopting international best practices in Investor Relations.

2.3.2 Position in the Organization

The IR department must report directly to the highest levels of management.

As we have seen, management commitment is paramount to achieving superior Investor Relations. For instance, the IRO should be systematically allowed to participate in the executive committee meetings and not simply on an as-needed basis.

If the IR department does not report directly to the chief executive officer (CEO), it should have ready access to the latter and be able to count on his or her active support and participation in the Investor Relations program, as the IRO will deem appropriate. Positioning Investor Relations this high in the organization will allow the IRO to have easy access to information inside the company as well as to all price-sensitive information relating to its strategic plans, budgets, and so on. It is thus clearly in the company's interest to position the department, hierarchically, as close as possible to the level where strategic decisions are made. The company's credibility vis-à-vis the market depends on whether its IRO is regarded by the market as knowledgeable, trustworthy. There is no point appointing an IRO if management does not involve this person in the "operations" of the company.

It is quite common in larger companies for IROs to report directly to the chief financial officer (CFO), and less frequently, to the CEO. This is also better regarded by the investment community than if the IR department is part of corporate communications, for instance.

In some less frequent cases, the IRO actually has a seat on the executive committee and can be in direct liaison with the board of directors. It is surprising that this is not more commonplace, given the strategic importance of Investor Relations and the fact that the IRO should be their primary source of information about how the markets view the company, information that is essential to the mission of the board.

In medium-sized companies, however, Investor Relations is often directly handled by the CEO and CFO themselves, in some cases with support from communications or from marketing. Establishing a proper Investor Relations function sends a positive signal to the market that management is taking it seriously.

Therefore, setting up an Investor Relations team that is considered competent and legitimate, inside as well as outside the company, will allow the chairman and top executives to optimize the amount of time they spend on Investor Relations. What's more, the ability to bring together different executives, all of whom are approved spokespersons for the company and duly trained for this purpose, can prove crucial in times of crisis.

Capital markets will positively view this type of organization as a sign that the company is doing all it can to offer a professional response to the expectations of fund managers, financial analysts, retail investors, rating agencies, and the media. (This is true even if the company's media relations are officially handled by the press department.)

Within the company itself, the existence of an IR department will signal that management is eager to raise awareness and understanding of the challenges, constraints, and opportunities that come with being a listed company. All employees of the company should benefit from this policy, which aims to do the following:

- Promote the development and benefits of employee share ownership;
- Increase the chances of success of the company's strategy by aligning internal targets with the objectives communicated to the outside world.

Lastly, it can be quite trivial, but IROs' offices should be located in the immediate proximity of the other departments they are in daily contact with (ideally, on the same floor!): finance, controlling, press, legal, marketing.

It is a great way to ensure consistency, as it would help enrich the Investor Relations information content on an ongoing basis.

2.3.3 Responsibilities of the Investor Relations Department

The term Investor Relations covers a wide range of activities from logistical planning to intense periods of thinking. These activities are never set in stone, never completely repetitive, and hardly ever predictable. The main tasks consist of the following:

- Coordinating financial and strategic communications;
- Building internal awareness of Investor Relations;
- Being the company's spokesperson in the financial markets;
- Relaying information to top management and the board of directors.

Investor Relations is at the front line of whatever is happening at the company: changes in management, strategy, or the operating environment. Few jobs offer such a constant challenge. That is precisely what makes it unique as a professional career.

Although Investor Relations teams have tended to increase in size, the growing volume of investor enquiries and complexity of reporting is putting pressure on them. There are also more external and internal groups making demands on the center of large companies, and the Investor Relations team often finds itself responsible for coordinating everything.

Project management is becoming an increasingly important part of the Investor Relations role. The Investor Relations team must coordinate information between many different departments, including tax, legal, finance, treasury, socially responsible investment, and human resources.

2.3.3.1 *Coordinating financial and strategic communications*

The IRO is responsible for ensuring consistency across all Investor Relations in content and form and over time. To achieve this, it is essential that the Investor Relations team has access at all times to a solid internal network, and notably to the managers of the company's operations.

The IR department should be involved in shaping the company's messages and have their say in how they should evolve over time. Key responsibilities are twofold:

- *Alerting role.* The IRO informs management of changes in analysts' recommendations, discrepancies between analyst estimates and internal forecasts, rumors, modifications of the free float, introduction of new valuation criteria, and market intelligence reports on competition.

- *Proposing role.* IROs make suggestions for the content of financial and strategic communications as well as for commercial and industrial messages. They make recommendations as to which are the key performance indicators to be selected and communicated to the intended recipients based, for instance, on the types of financial models used by analysts. They will be associated with, or even better, initiate the drafting of Investor Relations disclosure policy as well as of the company's code of ethics. All of these internal rules, which are core to corporate governance principles, will be seen by third parties as proof that the company is serious and well run, especially if it becomes the subject of an inquiry by market authorities.

While there are no set rules on the IR department's involvement in day-to-day activities, it should consistently be consulted, as early as possible, before any financial or strategic communications are sent out to audiences that are not under its direct responsibility: board of directors, audit committee, employee shareholders, and the press.

It will closely work with the finance division: Together, they will ensure that the indicators used internally to measure performance and operating efficiency are consistent with those disclosed to the financial markets. This consistency is an essential parameter in assessing shareholder value.

2.3.3.2 Building internal awareness of investor relations

The IR department will also work with the finance, legal, personnel and employee relations, and internal communications divisions, among others, in the following areas:

- Maintaining awareness and understanding of, as well as compliance with, legal obligations governing the dissemination of information to third parties. It is particularly important that everyone within the company is aware of regulations set out by market authorities and laws on insider trading and price-sensitive information.
- Broadening executives' and operations managers' understanding of Investor Relations beyond the scope of financial and strategic information on account of the fact that regulations relative to price-sensitive information cover a much wider—and more volatile—range of data than just quantitative information as reported in the consolidated financial statements. IROs build solid internal networks by relaying to operations managers what they hear about the competition through discussions with financial analysts. Their awareness-building efforts will notably pay off when meetings are organized between operations

teams and analysts, as the former will know which information is appropriate for them to give to outside parties.
- Promoting public company behavior in the corporate culture. In particular, this involves adopting a proactive customer–supplier attitude in the relationships the company maintains with financial markets. This notably implies that internal communications—and particularly newsletters—are consistent with the messages delivered outside the company.
- Fostering the adoption of a more international approach to communications, particularly by promoting communication in English if it is not the company's official language. This may also lead to publishing Investor Relations documents in the languages of countries in which the company operates and where it may have or want to develop a specific shareholder base. The importance of the quality of the English used in Investor Relations should not be underestimated.
- Participating in defining local practices with regard to corporate governance, changes in regulations governing financial information, and the consequences of transitions to new accounting standards on financial communications. This is the lobbying role of Investor Relations.

Investor Relations message development will have to take into account the increasing importance of non-financial metrics in the appreciation of the company's performance and of its level of transparency.

Again, it is crucial that the person in charge of Investor Relations be able to freely discuss market sentiment with the highest levels of management.

2.3.3.3 Being the company's spokesperson in the financial markets

If we consider that Investor Relations is comparable to a customer–supplier relationship, we can say that target audiences, both existing and prospective, are obvious customers. They are divided into four main categories in the following table (Table 2.1).

- *Financial analysts.* A distinction is made between sell-side and buy-side analysts:
  - Sell-side analysts work for investment banks or brokers. They advice investors, produce valuations, earnings forecasts, set stock price targets, and issue investment recommendations: buy/add, sell/reduce, or hold/neutral. (A combination of two recommendations may also prevail: one with a short-term time horizon, one with a longer-term view.) These recommendations are to benefit their firm's clients. As you deal with sell-side analysts, it is worth remembering that institutional investors tend to work with an ever smaller number of brokerage firms. They will be keen to benefit from high-sector expertise

Table 2.1 The Target Audiences of Investor Relations

Shareholders and Bond Holders	Capital Market Participants
Individual shareholders	"Sell-side" financial analysts → brokerage firms
Institutional shareholders	"Buy-side" financial analysts → Institutions
Employee shareholders	Independent research analysts
Bond holders	Sales forces
	Bankers
	Rating agencies (credit, socially responsible investment, and corporate governance)
Journalists	*Business Partners and Other Stakeholders*
General press	Customers
Financial and economic press	Suppliers
Trade press	Local communities
	Trade associations

and from the ability to conduct project-based research, sometimes in cooperation with industry experts and consultants. Part of the broker's remuneration (and industry ranking) is linked not only to research but also to corporate access. It means that they get business if they take your company on roadshows or are able to organize one-on-one meetings with management. This business model could well change in the future.

- Research coverage is closely linked to market capitalization. It is extremely challenging for smaller companies to attract analyst coverage due to the limited amount of commissions that the stock brokerage firms employing the analysts can expect to generate through buying and selling these smaller companies' shares; these revenues are unlikely to cover the analysts' costs. If, indeed, you belong to the "small- and mid-cap" category, you should go out of your way to help sell-side analysts understand your company by providing a very high level of information and education on your industry, in order for you to become the primary source of information for them. Regardless of your company's size, they will remember you. Also, another differentiator for smaller companies is the fact that in the absence of an IRO, the analyst will meet directly with the CEO or the CFO.
- There is also a growing number of independent financial research companies who are not associated either with a brokerage firm or with a fund management entity.

- ○ Buy-side analysts establish recommendations solely for the portfolio managers of the institutions where they work. Therefore, companies do not have access to their valuation models.
- *Broker sales forces* (see also 2.3.6.2). IROs are usually not directly in contact with these institutional sales people. While sell-side analysts are increasingly called upon to speak with their institution's clients, salespeople are the primary contacts of portfolio managers for whom they execute buy and sell orders. Sales people often accompany company management on roadshows. It is also recommended to host company presentations for a broker's sales force as they can be a crucial source of information for IROs. For instance, they can provide insightful information on market trends, institutional investor behavior, and intelligence on market rumors.
- *Institutional investors*. This category corresponds to an insurance company, a pension fund, or a mutual fund, as well as to a speculative or hedge fund. Sovereign wealth funds are state-owned investment funds which fall under this category. Institutional investors manage their own proprietary funds or those of third parties. Funds that are managed by government investment vehicles are called sovereign funds and tend to grow in importance and visibility. Whether they own shares in the company or not, and regardless of where they are geographically located, institutional investors are the largest players in financial markets. As such, they can move share prices up or down, buy or sell substantial stakes in companies, and request to be present on boards of directors.
- *The press*. IR departments usually do not handle media relations. Many believe that it is because they require different technical and relational skill sets than Investor Relations. Typically, press and media relations are entrusted to the corporate communications department. Media relations cover a wide range of target audiences, which receive, sometimes indirectly, the company's financial communications: the business and financial press, including newspapers and magazines for retail investors, as well as journalists in the generalist, trade, and foreign press. Technology has dramatically multiplied the number and nature of target audiences with the advent of online media. Note that news agencies are nonetheless key targets for Investor Relations: press releases become real-time news for the entire investment community, once they hit the wire services. In addition, journalists often maintain close relationships with financial analysts. They are a good information channel for small- and medium-sized companies that are not widely covered by analysts. For that matter, it makes sense to invest time and resources in clear and comprehensive media relations. In addition, certain financial media play an important advisory role for

retail shareholders. Therefore, maintaining a good relationship with journalists is important for Investor Relations too, as journalists have a powerful influence in building or destroying corporate reputations.
- *Industry analysts, trade press.* Industry analysts are researching technology and market trends. They are increasingly a source of information for financial analysts and investors. Catering to them in a professional manner is another area where an integrated approach to communications is critical.
- *Bondholders* (see also debt Investor Relations Sections 1.5, 2.3.4.2, and 3.6.3.2). They have traditionally been served by treasury rather than by IR departments, but bonds are no longer seen as simply safe assets: investors now look to them to provide their portfolios with extra performance. Companies that issue debt securities must, therefore, get organized to meet the demands from debt investors: specific presentations that include ratios other than those used by equity analysts, dedicated meetings, or, at the very least, invitations to the meetings arranged for equity analysts. Integrated bond/equity Investor Relations programs are being built, with a knowledgeable fixed-income contact in the Investor Relations team. Debt Investor Relations can make a real difference for firms below investment grade.
- *Banks.* Financial information is the main "raw material" required to assess their clients' resources and needs, but also quite importantly, their risk level. Whatever aspect of the business the banker is involved in, the relationship and level of trust developed with the bank will depend in large part on the quality of the financial information that is disclosed. In most cases, good financial information is a reflection of good financial management. Banks use Investor Relations for their own purposes, for instance, for the funds they manage when they are shareholders of the company. This, however, is not the only aspect of this customer–supplier relationship they maintain with the company: They can act as advisors and/or as custodians for retail investors who own their stocks through financial institutions.
- *Rating agencies.* The agencies assign ratings to bonds at the issuer's request based on the default risk to investors, in other words, the chance that the debt will not be repaid. Equity markets usually pay more attention to these ratings when they are downgraded than when they are upgraded. These ratings help determine the financing terms available to issuers along with the interest rates they can offer to attract the largest possible number of subscribers. Given the costs involved, only large companies generally apply to be rated, devoting a substantial amount of time and information to this exercise. The criteria used to establish credit ratings have evolved over time. Today, there are agencies that evaluate companies' sustainable development policies and the quality

of their corporate governance standards. They may analyze the nature and quality of resolutions submitted to shareholders' meetings and provide their positive or negative opinion to the institutional investors who commission this type of analysis.
- *Clients and suppliers.* These are not typically considered as direct target audiences of Investor Relations but are nonetheless concerned by the financial information the listed company publishes. For instance, they may be proud to be associated with the company or become concerned by its financial health.
- *Competitors.* The importance of analyzing the financial communications of your competition should never be disregarded. They are more than likely to study yours too. And as mentioned earlier, this analysis can prove a valuable networking tool in your relationships with divisional managers or the marketing department of your organization.

All in all, the IRO is the exclusive manager of relationships with financial analysts, institutional investors, and also, if applicable, with individual shareholders. In this configuration, the IR department's mission consists of the following:

- Providing the wider target audience with objective assistance in interpreting the information disclosed by the listed company, in order for all to estimate its future value;
- Building positive investor understanding and sentiment for the company's strategy for the short, medium, and long terms.

2.3.3.4 Keeping management aware of the market's perception

Whether the interaction with the investment community is via email, on the telephone or in a one-to-one meeting, the IRO will leverage the value of these contacts to learn more about the needs and perception of the company's strategy and performance by investors and analysts.

The IRO should be prepared to report on the market's perception of the company not only to the top levels of management but also to the board of directors. This is an increasingly common standard in corporate governance. In this respect, certain boards of directors require that an independent perception study be conducted at least once a year.

The frequency with which this type of information is reported and the content of the reports vary from one company to another. In general, the following information is provided:

- Trends in markets and stock prices for the company and the competition, both in terms of absolute and relative performance;

- Equity research on the company (recommendations and earnings consensus);
- Periodic update on ongoing implementation of the Investor Relations program (participation in conferences, roadshows, meetings with large shareholders) together with the list of questions asked (by theme) and the feedback gathered;
- Changes in the shareholder base;
- Reminders of upcoming dates on the financial calendar;
- Findings of perception studies.

In this way, the IR department can play a proactive role in helping management shape its strategy and thus gain this much desired "seat at the table."

2.3.4 Investor Relations: Profiles and Job Descriptions

There are probably as many ways to organize an IR department as there are companies. In all cases, however, the main goals are the same

- Bring together the types of skills needed to produce quality Investor Relations;
- List all actions and tasks that are required to design and implement the Investor Relations program.

The suggested organizational chart (Figure 2.6) below aims chiefly to do the following:

- Describe in more detail how the work is to be divided;
- Give some ideas for describing the positions that might have to be created (relations with retail investors) or adapted (administrative assistants, logistics).

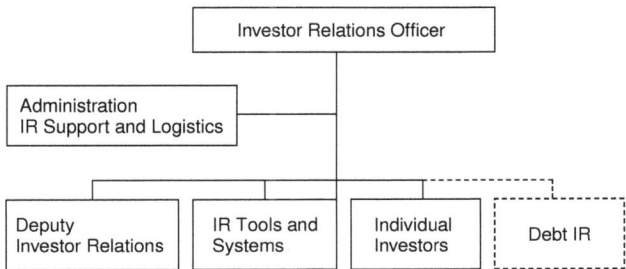

Figure 2.6 Investor Relations Organizational Chart

The structure and size of the team may evolve over time by bringing on board outside specialists or temporary staff, or by creating new positions. The need for more personnel will be chiefly determined by the following:

- The number of retail shareholders and whether a dedicated Investor Relations program is designed for them;
- How the issuer manages its relationships with the international financial community and the level of interaction required with analysts and investors outside the country;
- A decision to list the stock on a foreign market. While this does not necessarily require that Investor Relations staff be assigned to that country, in some cases, a position is created in this new market. It is not difficult to manage relations with local shareholders from a distance, provided that information can be distributed through adequate channels. However, it does not necessarily give the same image of commitment to this market place.

2.3.4.1 Profiles

The Investor Relations team need not be large, but it must be of the highest quality. Furthermore, Investor Relations is fundamentally a finance function. It is, therefore, essential that Investor Relations staff members do the following:

- Fully master the concepts associated with finance, equity markets and regulations;
- Have excellent writing and verbal skills;
- Speak and write English fluently if this is not the team's native language;
- Be proficient in most common word processing, spreadsheet and presentation software. For instance, computer graphics are typically outsourced but experience has shown that subcontracting is often time consuming—the contractors are not involved in developing the messages and may not immediately understand what they are being asked to do—and very risky in terms of confidentiality. It is much safer to develop a graphic charter using the most common software and then train staff to use this software, even if this means sending them to the graphics studio to supervise the final stages of the publishing process. This solution can make the company more efficient and responsive, and generate cost savings as well.

Relying on in-house resources is an efficient way to supervise the quality of the Investor Relations documents in terms of content and form throughout the production process, that is, from the time the message is validated by management through to when it is delivered to the public.

In many ways, Investor Relations can be compared to marketing: a quality client service is the first and most effective marketing tool, internally as well as externally. The Investor Relations team needs to be informed as early as possible about events that may impact the Investor Relations program that is underway to make sure that they provide their "customers" with timely and accurate information. For instance, any team member should be able to respond to a retail investor's questions or give the date of the next earnings release.

Such a combination of multiple resources and capabilities is going to be instrumental in making the company's Investor Relations more credible and efficient.

Diversity is also an asset. The breadth and diversity of staff in their professional backgrounds, workplaces, and past responsibilities is the greatest strength of any Investor Relations program. This should be kept in mind when selecting Investor Relations candidates.

The job descriptions below are solely for IR departments in a stand-alone manner. The goal is not to hire people and share them with other services, divisions or organizations, except when information needs to be coordinated, for instance, with the corporate communications and media relations.

2.3.4.2 Job descriptions

- *Investor Relations Officer (IRO).*

Company management appoints the IRO to interact with markets on a daily basis as its authorized spokesperson.

The IRO will typically have strong financial and analytical skills, with preferably a business administration education and more than 5 to 10 years of professional experience, failing which the company would be taking too much credibility risk. In most cases, IROs have a robust finance and accounting background, supplemented by education in sales and marketing or law. They are often former financial analysts or portfolio managers, but also have a talent for writing and public speaking, together with proven organizational skills.

Investor Relations has become a recognized profession; specialists are much sought after today, and salaries have increased accordingly, with a substantial performance-related pay in certain cases.

However, all too often, companies fail to provide these specialists with career advancement opportunities because they are usually not hired with this in mind. The job is not seen, as it could be, as a springboard to career success. Such an approach does not send the right signal to markets, as it may indicate that the company is compromising on expertise. It is unfortunate because the skills required to successfully perform this job are such that the IRO position should actually be promoted as a stepping stone to higher executive positions, in finance or in operations. IROs should, therefore, be selected accordingly.

It is also in the company's interest to promote someone to the IRO position internally, as analysts and investors will appreciate this person's familiarity with the company's products and services, and its competitive environment and growth drivers. By possessing an intimate knowledge of the company and its sector/in-depth industry and company knowledge, the IRO will be able to make the company memorable to investors who see countless numbers of presentations every week. The IRO will be able to supplement the presentation with stories and anecdotes and bring the company alive.

Medium-sized companies may choose the same person to act as head of Investor Relations and director of finance, strategy, or development, or to run both the IR department and corporate communications.

In all cases, the primary purpose of the executive appointed to handle Investor Relations will be to give the market ever-deeper insight into the company's businesses and strategy. As a consequence, the IRO's responsibilities are threefold:

- Interact with top management and the finance division on all aspects of financial communications and Investor Relations;
- Act as spokesperson in providing financial analysts and investors with information about the company. The IRO may also be contacted by or may deal with other audiences, including credit-rating agencies, the media, and so on;
- Proactively look for new shareholders and determine whether there is sufficient interest to justify management's time on future meetings.

The IRO's name should appear on press releases, together with that of the deputy IRO if applicable.

The IRO is the owner of the drafting process and coordinates the responses, comments, and corrections offered by the different parties involved in putting together financial and strategic press releases and financial presentations. The IRO's participation is actively involved in drafting the legal documents required for financial transactions and the annual report. The IRO may also be fully responsible for their production.

IROs help top management anticipate the questions and concerns institutional investors and financial analysts may express, following earnings releases or strategic announcements such as an acquisition.

Messages delivered to financial markets must be consistent among each other and over time; this is also the IRO's responsibility. Those in charge of relations with the media should, therefore, check their answers prior to responding, if they are asked for explanations or additional information on ongoing operations or on a recent financial press release.

The IRO identifies who shareholders are and constantly strives to learn more about them. This is a vital step in developing and implementing the Investor Relations strategy, as we shall see in Chapter 3.

The IRO helps select providers that will work directly with the IR department to develop the company website, organize conference calls, arrange printing, and logistics, and so on.

The IRO writes the job descriptions for the IR department staff, and coordinates and oversees the IR team.

The organizational ideas and recommendations are meant to convince management to develop an Investor Relations strategy that is innovative both in terms of content and form. Efforts should be geared, among other things, to improving transparency and creating new, easy-to-maintain, analyst- and investor-friendly tools.

The ethical standards set out by domestic or international Investor Relations associations shall be applied along with any regulations in effect. Within the company, the IRO will develop and promote policies for Investor Relations and corporate disclosure. In order to do so, the IRO must be able to become familiar with changes in regulations and make sure that a clear understanding exists as to what must be disclosed and when.

- *Deputy Investor Relations Officer (deputy IRO).*

The deputy IRO should be prepared to step in at any time to respond to questions asked by analysts, investors, or potential shareholders if the IRO is unavailable. The deputy IRO should know as much about the company as the IRO, be as knowledgeable and reliable, with a similar financial background. With a solid understanding of the company, the deputy IRO must be able to explain exposures, performance, and positions to the investment community.

The deputy IRO's name may appear on financial or strategic press releases, next to the IRO's. Certain organizations elect to have the IRO handle all relationships with fund managers, while the deputy IRO will be the primary contact for sell-side analysts. Others allocate contact responsibilities, depending on the region of origin of investors. Needless to say, the division of labor varies from one company to the next. Companies that are also listed on a foreign market may want to appoint an IRO in that country.

The deputy IRO helps to gather financial data, capital market intelligence as well as the industrial, technical, technological, commercial, and strategic information used to craft the company's Investor Relations program.

The job can be a testing ground to see whether the person is fit to become the IRO later on.

- *IR information systems manager.*

This position plays a key role in the success of the Investor Relations program, notably because it manages the tools with which the efficiency of the program will be measured. This person will identify and implement the technologies that will participate and aid in running a cost- and time-efficient Investor Relations.

The IR information systems manager will participate in developing and maintaining the tools used to keep track of Investor Relations actions, along with technical tools to monitor the share price and stock-market trends, set up contact databases, disseminate press releases, organize conference calls, analyze the shareholder base, and follow the IR department's budget.

The IR information systems manager is also responsible for updating and managing the Investor Relations section of the website, assuring that it complies with all regulations in effect. This includes identifying content in the different languages used, assuring that the same terminology is used in all languages, and that all information is authenticated and date and time stamped.

The IR information systems manager will also stay up to date on technological changes that allow the website to become a tool for the following:

- Relations with retail shareholders: electronic voting at annual general meetings and management of securities accounts;
- Relations with analysts and investors: downloading of spreadsheet programs, management of library archives, virtual roadshows, alerts and subscriptions to press releases, online conference calls; and so on;
- Compliance with legal obligations governing the reporting of financial information to the public.

For all these reasons, the information systems manager should also be involved in preparing calls for tenders and selecting service providers and specialized products such as software.

Finally, as part of the Investor Relations team, the information systems manager must also be involved in the preparation process of Investor

Relations messages and events, in order to assist in responding to information enquiries from the investment community.

- *Individual shareholder relations.*

Some IPOs, and particularly privatizations, are large-scale events that attract huge numbers of retail shareholders, usually hundreds of thousands of them. Retail investors can also be won over by the products or services the company offers, or its dividend policy. Retail investors are stakeholders who differ from analysts and institutional investors in terms of expectations and behavior. Because they tend to be much more stable shareholders than institutional investors, most large groups consider it is not only to their advantage to promote retail share ownership, but also to enhance their financial image. To this end, local regulations permitting, they often set up a myriad of services for this category of shareholders: free custody accounts, transactions services for company shares, organization of annual general meetings, and specific communications (shareholder letters, information meetings, fieldtrips, etc.). In these circumstances, and if it is the company's strategy to promote individual share ownership, it may make sense to appoint someone to handle these tasks specifically.

- *Debt IR.*

In companies that issue equity and debt, it can be an issue to try and efficiently deal with equity investors and analysts without understanding the debt story. Thus, it is not uncommon that all members of the Investor Relations team are exclusively focusing on the needs of fixed-income investors. This involves working closely with the corporate treasury department and credit-rating agencies and conducting regular debt investor roadshows.

A company that has a dedicated debt Investor Relations function will provide information about all its financial instruments in its financial statements and on its website under a specific tab, and notably including the following:

- Key debt ratios and credit ratings;
- Treasury accounting policies;
- Outstanding capital market issuance by currency, amount, interest coupon, and maturity date.

- *Investor Relations support and logistics.*

This is another key job, the performance of which will directly impact the image of Investor Relations. And in Investor Relations, as anywhere else, "The devil is in the detail." Except in small and medium-sized companies, where support can be part of services shared or mutualized with other

departments, it makes the IRO's life simpler to be able to rely on its own organization. The main responsibilities include the following:
- Administration of the IR department, and notably the management of Investor Relations planning and calendars;
- Contact databases maintenance, meetings, share-ownership identification exercises;
- Logistical support for Investor Relations. This is the backbone of the whole Investor Relations organization, covering the organization of events ranging from earnings presentation meetings, roadshows, and fieldtrips to investor days and conference calls.

When major events such as annual general meetings are scheduled, this logistics specialist may also rely on resources from others areas of the company, such as the corporate communications department, or on resources in other countries when the event is being held outside the company's domestic market.

2.3.4.3 Investor relations as a career

Investor Relations can be the job of a lifetime, a stepping stone to the executive suite ("the c-Suite"), or a dead end. Some will carry out Investor Relations roles their entire professional life in various companies, others will spend only a few years in the job before moving on to other functional or operational responsibilities, while a smaller, but yet meaningful, third group will become Chief Executive Officers or Chief Financial Officers.

It obviously very much depends on your personal career objectives, but also on the organization you belong to: only very few companies consider IR experience as 'a critical building block' and have created career paths which include an assignment to the Investor Relations department. Similarly, they have hardly ever developed proper succession plans to replace their current Investor Relations Officer.

- *Getting into IR.*

Based on the profiles and job descriptions provided in the previous section, sell-side analysts and investment bankers are often obvious candidates for the IR job. In this, they compete head to head with experienced Investor Relations officers for whom Investor Relations can be a career in and of itself. Other candidates may be Investor Relations consultants who decide to move 'in-house' and become the IR person for the company they had advised until then. Lastly, you may want to go into IR because of the "grooming role" it can help you play in your organization as you are keen to move up the ladder.

The number of business schools, universities and Investor Relations associations that offer some form of certification in Investor Relations is gradually growing. But, overall, you will not get into Investor Relations because you have a degree in this field. It will rather be because you have been in contact with IR professionals, with analysts and investors before, and you thought this might be an interesting job. And right you are! Below are some of the opportunities offered by the IR function:

- You get to work directly with and be visible to senior management;
- You have a bird's-eye view of what's going on in your company;
- You are involved in the strategy and operations and have input into critical decisions;
- You will develop robust financial skills;
- You are fairly autonomous in the job and can enjoy a certain amount of flexibility in the way you organize your work;
- You will become an expert at simplifying, clarifying and delivering a message with confidence, a skill set that will serve you well not only in investor relations but also for your career after IR.

Challenges should not be underestimated, such as:

- Dealing with a management team that does not understand the value of IR;
- The risks posed by increasingly severe regulatory environments and liability lawsuits;
- The ability to anticipate and adjust to changes in communications and securities trading technology;
- A hectic work schedule;
- The difficulty of setting goals that are measurable.

- *Staying in IR.*

There are several reasons why you might want to stay in IR:
- You got into the job in a junior role, have demonstrated your worth and want to add new skills to your résumé. Ultimately, you may be looking to fill the "head of IR" function when it becomes vacant
- You have decided that IR is what you excel at and what best fulfils your personal and professional expectations:
  o You will either want to remain in charge of IR at the same company, or try your skills at other ones. For instance: these may be in the same sector but of a bigger size; or where the Investor Relations Officer reports directly to the Chief Executive Officer, which was not your situation before; or you have demonstrated your ability to develop a successful IR program for an Initial Public Offering and can repeat the exercise elsewhere.

○ Another option for staying in the IR world may consist in becoming an IR consultant. This is actually a more radical change than it may seem: when working in a communications agency, Investor Relations differs substantially from the in-house IR role, in that business development (and profit-making) is at the heart of the job. If you feel you do not have this specific mindset, you should think twice before embarking on this new professional journey. Having said that, being an IR counselor can be very rewarding for those who are looking for intellectual stimulation, variety of clients and projects, and are prepared to take the financial risk: a sometimes substantial part of the remuneration can be tied to how much new business has been won.

- *Moving out of IR.*

Years of Investor Relations practice will have taught you how to think like an investor and really understand what long-term success drivers are about.

However, no matter how good and respected an Investor Relations Officer you are, this will not be enough: in order to advance to the highest levels of the corporate structure, within your company or outside, even possibly to a non-executive director role, you will have to prove yourself. This is especially true if your company does not consider IR as career prerequisite for holding senior executive positions and has secretly hoped that you would run the IR department for ever.

Whatever the direction you are taking, you will need a well thought-out plan, well in advance. In this respect, you should make sure that your IR reporting is also tailored to your personal goals. Hereafter are some examples:

- If you want to head up a finance or strategy or M&A, be on top of analysts' models and develop yours for the company, including valuation metrics;
- If you want to go to operations, be knowledgeable about your peers and competitors and provide market intelligence gathered through analysts' reports and investor meetings to the division you wish to join;
- If you want to manage corporate communications and IR as a single entity, focus your reporting on the interaction between IR, investors, media and customer communications, on the impact of reputation on valuation, in a holistic approach.

- Internal career move

While undoubtedly challenging, achieving this goal is, however, going to be facilitated by your proximity to the Chief Executive Officer, the Chief Financial Officer.

Those IR professionals who have made it to the executive suite have usually demonstrated their ability to think strategically, beyond the IR angle, when there have been transactions or crises, for instance. You will also need to have developed leadership and management skills. And you will have to advertise these skills by being visible, in order to catch management's eye in a different light.

If you want to move within your company, you will quite likely have to find the job yourself, and sometimes even create it. Your in-depth understanding of your company and the strong internal networking that you will have built over the years, have permitted you to identify:

- what is missing in terms of functions;
- what could be optimized in terms of responsibilities;
- the business area you are most interested in and believe you could add value to;
- the executives who will need to be replaced because they are retiring or are leaving, etc.

You may also consider suggesting that the scope of your current responsibilities be enlarged to areas that are close to IR. These can lead to the following combinations:

- IR + corporate communications;
- IR + corporate secretary;
- R + sustainable development, social, environmental, governance matters;
- IR + marketing;
- IR + strategy;
- IR + mergers and acquisitions.

Moving to operations can be even trickier: It will be difficult to move to manufacturing or production if you do not have an engineering background.

- External career move

It is quite likely that you will need to showcase your experience differently; by illustrating to prospective employers your career, your professional accomplishments and talents in the areas that you are targeting for your next career move. You will put your achievements in the context of corporate goals and will present your own profile as an individual, not only a seasoned corporate executive.

Just the same way as you will have developed strong relationships within your company, you will not have forgotten to do the same externally:

- Stay in touch with your usual IR contacts (buy-side, sell-side, advisors, service providers, and investment bankers), but also law firms, audit firms;
- Attend executive education programs and advance your skills;
- Be visible: speak at conferences, contribute articles, write books, teach, be an active member of professional associations;
- Think global.

Table 6.3 in the Resources section offers an Investor Relations resume sample.

2.3.5 External Investor Relations Service Providers and Advisors

Providing they are properly selected and integrated in the company's processes, external advisors can bring genuine results to companies: more information disclosure, press coverage, share-trading volume, institutional investor ownership, analyst following, and market valuation. Of course, it is more so with small companies that face particular problems in improving visibility and attracting investors. Because they have access to a much wider scope of cases, and have been associated with a variety of situations, the first task the Investor Relations firm usually undertakes is to improve the company's story and to train management. This may imply persuading management to be more transparent and, in particular, to release more information about the company's business prospects. Then the firm can arrange meetings between management, institutional investors, and financial analysts.

Media contacts are also seen to be important, for two reasons: It may prove easier for a smaller company to get media coverage than analyst following and, also, because media is an efficient means of communicating to retail investors. All of these may positively impact trading volumes. Ideally, these achievements may then be turned into greater institutional ownership and analyst coverage, and ultimately, into higher valuation. Let's be objective and admit that this is probably more the case for small caps that suffer from lack of liquidity and, therefore, lack of interest shown by institutional investors. If no one knows about your company, the price will not be set at an efficient level. By improving liquidity and increasing institutional interest, Investor Relations professionals can help establish a company's fair value.

What about large companies hiring external consultants, then? Although many of them have in-house Investor Relations teams, they do nonetheless use Investor Relations firms like other top-level company advisors. The scope of assignments may be identical to that required for smaller companies but they are more likely to be more used to investing in such services as perception studies.

2.3.5.1 Scope of assignments

Companies may rely upon external service providers to do the following:

- *Handle all or part of their financial communications and Investor Relations program.* This may include helping with incoming calls and inquiries from investors, retail shareholders or analysts. The portion of the activity outsourced will be determined notably by organizational structure, the internal resources available, and stockmarket performance. Outsourcing is often used for the logistics of Investor Relations, publishing, shareholder identification, and perception audits.
- *Target investors and organize roadshows.* Unlike investment banks and brokers, service providers do not receive a percentage of the transactions generated by the events organized. This will limit the temptation to set up meetings that benefit the provider more than the issuer. Investor Relations firms will assist in the investor outreach program by creating target lists and arranging meetings with existing and potential new analysts and investors, thus efficiently leveraging management's time.
- *Gain access to objective advice.* Independent experts often have more experience with a wider range of situations and can thus provide that much-needed "outsider's point of view." In many cases, they have successfully resolved challenges the company is facing for the first time. They can provide crucial input with regard to Investor Relations strategies, conducting perception studies and targeting new investors. When outside contractors are well integrated into the company, they can contribute to the quality of communications on strategy and finances.
- *Benefit from local expertise when engaging in cross-border transactions.* Successful Investor Relation professionals are mindful of the culture and practice of the country where they are operating or raising money.

External advisors can also temporarily act as spokespersons for newly listed small and medium-sized companies with no in-house Investor Relations team yet.

Whether your company is considering hiring outside Investor Relations support and counseling to prepare and take you through the IPO phase, or whether you have already been listed for a long time and are looking for an external opinion and extra resources, you will first and foremost have to draft the list of your needs and expectations. For instance, it will be useful to evaluate the following:

- Do you need ongoing support with administrative tasks such as press release distribution or Investor Relations infrastructure maintenance, or project-based assistance?
- Is gathering market intelligence and investor and analyst perceptions what you are interested in?
- Are you looking for sophisticated guidance and counsel on disclosure? In corporate governance? Crisis communications? Shareholder identification? Annual shareholders' meetings? Company positioning and message development? Annual report production?
- Does your search concern a specific transaction, such as an acquisition or a capital increase?
- Do you want the agency to have an international network of affiliates or partners?
- Is the agency staffed with former IROs, financial analysts, or portfolio managers?
- What is the agency's policy regarding conflict of interests?
- Does the agency have experience in your industry?
- How many IPOs has the firm been involved with?

2.3.5.2 Identification and selection process

There is a wide range of Investor Relations vendors and advisors to choose from. Some agencies offer comprehensive services, and certain consulting firms are more focused on specific areas. Determining which Investor Relations agencies to retain is similar to searching for any other top-level company advisors. You can go to:

- Resource directories for public companies;
- Internet search engines;
- Referrals from investment bankers, brokers, lawyers, or audit firms;
- Management at other listed companies you know by asking them about the firm they use.

Once you have done your background checks, and have come up with a list of potential candidates, you may consider launching a request for proposals process. Some key questions that should help you prequalify agencies for in-person meetings are as follows:

- How does the agency track client program results? What specific metrics do they use? For example, does the agency track volume, institutional ownership, and sell-side coverage?

- What kind of program reporting does the agency provide to clients?
- How many executive staff are dedicated full time to investor relations in the agency? How many accounts does the team handle? How much access will the company have to the agency's senior staff? What is the average number of years of experience of each team member?
- How can the agency demonstrate it has the established reputation and relationships that the company needs to achieve more visibility in the investment community?
- What is the agency's fee structure?

Request a sample of work completed by the agency that is relevant to your company's needs. You may also want to test—free of cost—the capabilities of the advisors by asking them to formally present their recommendations to solve a given issue the company is currently facing. ("What are the top five actions that we need to undertake to increase retail ownership of our stock?" "How should we improve our presentations to attract more European investors?") This will provide you not only with free advice, but more importantly, with direct insight into the firm's real competence.

A successful Investor Relations relationship is built upon a partnership between management and the advisory team, beyond simply financial considerations. This is particularly essential if you want the Investor Relations firm to help you build the bridge between management and the financial community.

The next step in the selection process is, therefore, to make sure that the proposed account team will attend the interviews and that management will participate as well. It is critical that they feel comfortable with the team and that honesty and dedication will prevail on both sides of the relationship. For this relationship to work best, it is important that you feel the firm can be your ally in the market, not your enemy. For instance, if you hire an outside spokesperson, you will want to make sure that he or she is competent and does not handle too many accounts at the same time. Indeed, no matter how large or well known the consultancy, the quality of advice will depend on the individual consultant.

At the end of this selection process, the written proposals you will receive should contain a detailed fee structure, but also references for you to contact and get feedback on your specific account team rather than on the agency at large. Also, ensure that the candidates apply a strict conflict of interest policy and that they have never been prosecuted in the past for using inside information.

2.3.5.3 Efficiency and performance assessment

One might argue that terminating or, on the contrary, maintaining the relations you have with an IR service provider, an IR advisor or any type of IR vendor may be the ultimate measurement of how satisfied you are with the services rendered.

Similarly, the need to measure this performance is widely acknowledged but few companies formally assess the performance of these IR advisors, vendors or agencies and the contribution they make to the company's IR program. It is not surprising given the difficulty of linking valuation performance metrics with advisor or vendor performance (and also the reluctance of some IR teams and agencies to do this).

Whether formally or informally conducted, the performance assessment exercise should cover the following areas:

– Service delivery;
– Strategic thinking;
– Creativity;
– Budget management;
– Innovation;
– Collaboration.

You may want to add more IR specific issues:

– Financial image shift;
– Investor/analyst recruitment.

The measures depend on the type of relationship being assessed. Hard metrics can be tricky to define and track.

This is probably why linking agency or vendor compensation to performance metrics is highly variable in IR. In the case of Initial Public Offerings or other financial transactions, the IR firm can agree to a "success fee" to be paid for the successful completion of the deal, on top of its retainer fees.

Therefore, performance is probably best measured with "soft" metrics in a varied and ad hoc approach which should reflect the type service provided, level of fee, volume of work, nature of the relationship (retained vs. project based). Benchmarking your practice with your IR peers can be quite valuable.

When it is effectively done, the evaluation process can be conducted regularly and rather informally, through discussion and ongoing feedback. An action plan can be shared to address performance issues on the part of the IR team and that of its IR firm or vendor, and to set measurable targets.

This is a list of questions the IR team should ask itself and its IR advisor or vendor to gauge the effectiveness of suppliers of all kinds in the IR value chain:

- Have deadlines been met? Has the budget been respected?
- Has the IR firm helped us met the right investors?
- Have roadshow logistics gone smoothly?
- Has the firm effectively helped us attain quorum at our Annual General Meeting (AGM)?
- What was the quality of feedback provided after our roadshow?
- Has our company received an award for its annual report? Website?
- Is our account or project manager in this firm stable or is it changing all the time?
- How often does the investment bank's corporate access team provide us with insight investor sentiment?
- Has the advisor effectively briefed management ahead of the earnings call or the investor day?
- How accurate is our stock surveillance program and shareholder identification?
- Is their data base user friendly or too complicated to master?
- How often do they proactively come to us with new ideas and suggestions?
- Could we have been able to manage this crisis without them?

This exercise should be viewed as beneficial to all and as a way to also elevate the IR profession internally and externally.

2.3.6 Investor Relations Tools

In today's digital world, it is important that all members of the IR department have access to the same IT tools (for example, the same versions of the software used). For instance, when working on a presentation, two different versions of the presentation software does create havoc! Make sure this applies to your service providers as well.

The list below summaries the most widely used tools in any Investor Relations program that is results oriented.

2.3.6.1 Contact database

The contact database (see Resources) is the primary tool used to develop and maintain an Investor Relations program. This all-important resource should be much more than just a sophisticated address book. It can be built in different ways, ranging from spreadsheets to shareholder relation management—SRM—software. It should in all cases be configured in such a way as to enable you to track Investor Relations actions, organize events, and integrate analysis of the shareholder base, among other things.

For instance, companies that issued bonds and/or started to organize earnings presentation meetings prior to getting listed should in theory have a preliminary contact list to work with. Their job will be to identify, within each institution in this initial database, the fund manager and/or analyst likely to cover the equity, in conjunction with the fixed income. Because of its origin and how it is put together, this "homemade" list is likely to be more up to date, independent, and targeted than those used by the investment banks or public relations agencies, or any that can be bought from outside vendors. This list of contacts can be managed and updated with user-friendly software. Further out, if the decision is made to target new analysts and investors to take an interest in the stock, the database can be expanded by acquiring specific Investor Relations information from specialist suppliers. When building your Investor Relations contact database, it is essential that you comply with regulations governing databases and data protection rights in your country (collection, use, processing, storage of and right of access to data).

To be as cost-effective as possible, the Investor Relations contact database and distribution list for press release distribution and meeting invitations should be maintained by regularly updating and cleaning contact lists through the following:

- Information gathered from individual meetings with sell-side analysts and portfolio managers about their special interests or concerns and the questions they have raised, especially when these are particularly challenging or relevant. This list will be supplemented by other important corporate contacts such as members of the board of directors, investment bankers, attorneys, etc.;
- Additions and deletions, in the same way that marketing departments keep track of active and prospective clients.

2.3.6.2 Monitoring tools

The tools described below are used to track both share prices and returns on investments in Investor Relations, as we shall see in more detail in Chapter 4 as we identify measures of the return on investment in Investor Relations. They should in all cases be adapted to the objectives set out in the Investor Relations strategy.

- *Stock data.* If anything is to be learnt from information gathered about the share, companies need to track more than trends in the stock price. They should also keep a record of the following:
  - Trading volumes;
  - Comparisons against:
    - the benchmark index or indices, whether the stock is included in them or not; and
    - the share prices of comparable companies and competitors' stocks.
  - The names of the largest buyers and sellers, when this information is made available and accessible to the issuer by the trading systems and networks.

Such daily statistics provide a good deal of information about the stock and allow the company to identify unusually sharp movements in prices or trading volumes. In addition, time differences are such that certain European stocks can be thinly traded throughout the morning and then see a flurry of activity once US investors are at their desks. This kind of information is particularly important, for instance, to companies with large shareholder bases in North America, which may decide to hold conference calls to discuss earnings releases in the afternoon to allow US investors to participate.

In some countries, market players are able to tell issuers how much of their capital is held by investment banks or which brokers are buying or selling their shares. This information can be particularly instructive when it comes time to organizing roadshows, or when it turns out that none of the analysts from institutions that are actively trading the stock actually cover it. IROs should be careful to stay on good terms with salespeople from these institutions, especially as they can provide valuable insight into trends in the share price. Top-quality information can often be obtained from these sources, as well as from market makers and any companies with which the issuer has signed liquidity agreements.

- *Financial research on the company.* The goal here is to monitor the following:
  - *The number and geographic location of the analysts that cover the stock.* (It may make sense to look at the breakdown by geographic location when your company is listed on several markets.) In the early days following a listing, issuers tend to be primarily covered by analysts working for the lead banks that managed the IPO. The smaller the company, the more difficult it will be to get other analysts to take an interest in the stock. Investment banks and independent equity-research firms need to generate some kind of revenue with

the work they do, and this is harder to accomplish when the stock is thinly traded, or when financial information on the company is minimal. There are intermediaries and analysts who are independent or who work with large global networks that specialize in "mid-cap" research. No matter how good their work, or how hard they try, however, perception is nowhere near what the large international firms or "blue chip companies" can achieve. Getting more analysts to cover the stock will often be a main goal of the issuer's marketing efforts. This is not the case for "large caps," which are often covered by between 10 and 30 analysts, depending, for instance, on how many markets they are traded on.

- *The consensus.* This represents the average analysts' earnings forecasts for periods ranging anywhere from one quarter to three years. It corresponds to the arithmetic mean—or to the median—of analyst estimates for certain aggregates: sales growth, operating income, operating margin, net earnings per share, cash flow, debt ratios, book value, etc.
- Monitoring the consensus, within the limits of regulatory constraints, involves keeping track of analyst estimates not only for these key indicators but also for other strategic targets set out by companies: customer retention, geographic breakdown of sales, breakdown of operating margin by business, and so on. Some research firms generate substantial revenue by selling earnings consensus reports that are not necessarily reliable. This may prompt certain issuers to calculate their own consensus and post it on their website, explaining the methodology used, giving the list of the sell-side analysts who are included in this consensus and also including all legal disclaimers. In particular, it should be expressly mentioned that any opinions, estimates, or forecasts regarding the performance of your company made by these analysts are theirs alone and do not represent opinions, forecasts, or predictions of your company or its management. Markets tend to appreciate this kind of initiative.
- *Stock recommendations.* The number of "buy," "sell," and "hold" ratings has a determining influence on the share's valuation. It is important to distinguish the recommendations that are based on fundamental analysis and those that reflect the current stock price. Analysts who like the company and have a good opinion of its managers and growth prospects may very well advise investors to take profits when the stock hits their price target. And while it may be flattering when all analysts have a buy rating, the risk is that any change in recommendation may trigger a sell-off.

- ○ *Price targets.* This is one variable that may reassure management when the stock is down, even though no bad news has been announced. Investors may take profits once the price target set by analysts has been reached or exceeded, unless, of course, support comes from upgrades and a new price target.
- *Share ownership identification.* This is, without doubt, the most costly undertaking in terms of time and money, but one that also delivers the most strategic benefits (see Section 3.1). The objective is for listed companies to find out exactly who owns them. Regulation can differ widely from one country to another, one of the few common requirements being that crossings of statutory thresholds be notified to issuers. The frequency of share-ownership identification and trend reports is left to the latter's discretion but once the free float reaches 40 percent level, companies that are developing Investor Relations strategies should schedule them at least once a year and make sure that the investigation process and the corresponding reports are consistent over time. This should guarantee optimal comparability of the data:
  - ○ *Q&A book.* This document brings together all of the questions raised by the financial community and responses provided by the company. It should be constantly updated, notably prior to important events like earnings releases. The topics should be classified by theme (finance, business, strategy, outlook being the main topics). The document helps to ensure that all those who speak on behalf of the company deliver the same message, internally and externally.
  - ○ *Perception studies.* One way for companies to manage their Investor Relations over the medium and long term is to assess their financial image at regular intervals and around specific themes. As we shall see in Section 4.2 below, this process also helps evaluate returns on investments in Investor Relations.

2.3.7 Investor Relations Budgets

Measuring the amounts spent on Investor Relations should help the company estimate whether the resources mobilized and actions undertaken are appropriate in terms of quality and quantity. Furthermore, Investor Relations budgets are not increasing, so it is a constant challenge to come up with new ideas that will increase efficiency.

From an accounting point of view, IR departments usually fall into the cost-center category, one that does not directly generate any revenues. That said, there should be no debate about their usefulness if we consider that an efficient Investor Relations strategy can considerably reduce a company's cost of capital.

There is no reliable data available on Investor Relations budgets, particularly because funds are allocated very differently between finance, legal, and corporate communications budgets in different companies. Nor is there a clear correlation between Investor Relations budgets and company size.

Budgets can climb quickly into the millions of euros or dollars when wide-scale advertising campaigns are planned or special policies are set up to build and manage relations with retail shareholders, an undertaking that requires significantly more resources than relations with analysts and institutional investors. It should also be said, however, that the resulting stability of the shareholder base can generate substantial returns on investment.

Traditionally, large amounts are allocated to the annual report, the annual general meeting, and listing fees.

In addition to personnel and administrative expenses, the main Investor Relations expenses usually include the following:

- Transportation (roadshows);
- Meetings (e.g., information meetings, annual general shareholders' meetings);
- Publishing (graphics, printing, and annual report production);
- Design and maintenance of dedicated section on Investor Relations in the company website;
- Subscriptions (databases and various publications or services such as stock surveillance);
- Information systems and telecommunications;
- Shareholder identification;
- Consulting fees.

The cost of these items may be reduced by relying on investment banks to promote the stock and by disseminating financial information via the Internet rather than via printed documents.

Detailed analysis of the shareholder base can also help save money by ensuring that roadshows target only investors that have a good chance of investing in the type of company in question. The cost of organizing annual meetings can also be substantially reduced when companies look into the number of shares held and the minimum required for a quorum. In the future, proxy soliciting and "virtual" annual general meetings via the Internet may grow in popularity as high-speed connections become mainstream and legal hurdles are overcome.

Yet regulatory requirements continue to grow such that companies now need to produce more legal documents than ever before, including annual reports and prospectuses that contain several hundred pages. The related budgets can be streamlined by investing to make these documents smartly interactive on the company's website, by shifting traditional paper documents and mailing to online information resources, thus substantially reducing the number of copies to be printed and mailed by traditional mail.

The savings can be spent on summary reports and booklets both for corporate and financial communications, with no compromise to the company's image.

Also, Investor Days (see Section 3.6.16) are one of the biggest expenses, but the rewards can be substantial.

Other sources of savings can be achieved by conducting surveys, for instance, asking your shareholders whether they want to continue and receive the annual report and other financial information in hard copies or in an electronic format. This may, however, be different between categories of investors. Current shareholders will be happy with the electronic information but prospective investors will want to do thorough research to get to know the company better. And in this case the annual report in hard copy is going to continue to be much appreciated.

2.4 Quality of Information and Reporting Systems

In order to assess the quality of a company's information and reporting systems before communicating with financial markets, the following questions should be raised:

- Is financial information reliable and available in time to comply with legal obligations?
- Does the content of the available information, financial as well as non-financial, correspond to market expectations? In other words, does the system track the right performance metrics?
- Does it compare favorably with the kind of information provided by listed competitors?
- Can the information systems deliver data at constant scope and/or constant exchange rates (important in the event of mergers, acquisitions, and disposals)?
- Can the systems handle different accounting standards, such as the international (IFRS) and American (US Generally Accepted Accounting Principles – GAAP) standards? Can it manage the transition from one to the other?
- Does the company have the internal resources and skills to upgrade the information systems? What kind of cost and time would the upgrade require? By how long could it delay the planned IPO?

The IRO should ensure that key consolidated figures are available within the legal deadlines that will apply once the company is listed. Indicators, which will be used to set targets for financial and operating performance over the short and medium term, should also be factored in budget reporting and in the business plan so that any discrepancies with market expectations can be anticipated and communications adjusted accordingly. It is also worth remembering that a company's budget is not known to the investment community, while historic data, past performance, and future objectives are at the heart of Investor Relations.

Just as it is essential that IROs and their staff have solid financial skills, financial information systems must also be organized to serve the purpose of the Investor Relations strategy.

Markets are frequently developing new ratios and concepts that require additional data. These new ideas must be expertly analyzed in-house before they can be used in the company's Investor Relations. It should be possible, for instance, to verify with the accounting department that the desired data exists, either in raw form or already included in a ratio. The IRO considers whether it is appropriate to use the ratio, and the impact it could have on market perception. It will then be decided, in conjunction with top management, whether the company should give in and deliver the information, explain why it is not providing it, or propose another indicator that is more meaningful from an operating standpoint and more flattering to the company over the long term.

In other words, the IR department should be in a position to do the following:

- Identify in time, or even anticipate, the new indicators investors will ask for;
- Coordinate between information-processing departments within the organization (accounting, controlling, consolidation, treasury, etc.);
- Provide restated historical data if the scope of consolidation changes or if the business portfolio is altered.

2.5 Understanding and Complying with Legal Requirements

The strict legal framework governing financial information and Investor Relations is based on widely accepted principles:

- Transparency;
- Equal access to information: all shareholders, regardless of their origin and the number of shares owned, have a right to the same information.

Lawmakers and market authorities in every country set out obligations applicable to issuers and those receiving information. Failure to comply with these obligations is punishable by law and can lead to prosecution.

Compliance is complex, and the regulatory burden can be particularly hard to manage for small and medium-sized companies. In addition, regulations tend to evolve over time and are not the same across the globe. The development of the European Union, the creation of new stock exchanges, and major financial scandals have imposed regulations that are more and more stringent. The Regulation for Fair Disclosure in the United States, implemented in 2001, and the Transparency and Market Abuse Directives in the European Union, effective since 2007, offer a bird's-eye view on the most common regulations on financial information currently effective in the world's leading capital markets, toward which other regulatory systems are converging.

Liability is increasingly an issue, and punishment can involve imprisonment and/or steep fines, sometimes levied against IROs themselves. Needless to say, lawsuits can do considerable damage to the image of the persons in question.

Simply put, Investor Relations practices are governed by rules that apply to all, and the only way to limit the risk of error or failure to comply is to be thoroughly familiar with them. Make sure you know exactly what applies in the country or countries where you are listed.

Company legal advisors and lawyers are not the only ones who need to know these rules. It is an absolute prerequisite that all those involved in financial communications and Investor Relations, including the management of listed companies, should be aware of the broad principles outlined below, first among them being the rules applicable to "sensitive" or "privileged" information.

2.5.1 Price-Sensitive Information

Price-sensitive information, also described as inside (or insider) information or privileged information, refers to information that is not in the public domain and that, if revealed, could have a significant impact on the share price or decisions to buy or sell the stock.

2.5.1.1 Main characteristics of price-sensitive or privileged information

This information must:

- be specific;
- be previously undisclosed;
- relate directly or indirectly to one or more issuers of financial instruments or one or more financial instruments.

It is not always easy to identify what qualifies as privileged information. Regulations provide some guidelines, but financial markets always want to know more than what has been officially disclosed by the issuer. The following types of information can be considered price sensitive:

- *Financial information.* A wide range of financial information is considered price sensitive:
    - Declaration of suspension of payments or court-ordered bankruptcy;
    - Establishment of mortgages or pledges, along with any other financial commitments affecting significant portions of the issuer's assets;
    - Substantial changes to the scope of consolidation (as is the case with mergers and acquisitions, or large asset disposals);
    - Changes to the shareholder base, notably involving significant changes to the holdings of one or more important shareholders;
    - Decisions affecting the company's capital structure such as capital increases or decreases, mergers, demergers, partial asset transfers, and public offers on equity markets;
    - Decisions relating to the allocation of earnings, particularly decisions to pay special dividends;
    - Decisions relating to stock splits or reverse stock splits;
    - The signature of shareholder agreements if notified to the company;
    - Earnings that are unusual compared with historic trends, company guidance, or the most recent consensus (based on information most recently disclosed by the issuer);
    - Updates of forward-looking statements previously provided by the issuer, including any substantial modification of previously announced targets;
    - Losses that correspond to a significant share of the company's equity;
    - Disputes that could have a significant impact on earnings or the company's financial situation or business, including labor disputes or disagreements between the company and one of its main clients or suppliers.
- *Organizational issues.* Examples include major changes to the issuer's internal organizational structure or management team, for instance, the death or resignation of an executive or disputes or major disagreements at the level of governance;
- *Commercial issues.* In this case, price-sensitive information will relate to the gain or loss of major contracts or developments involving important clients or suppliers;
- *Technological issues.* The development and launch of new products can have a significant impact on an issuer's business. This is notably true

in the pharmaceutical sector, where share prices are highly sensitive to marketing authorizations for new products or, conversely, the withdrawal of drugs from the market;
- *Strategic issues*. This can be any event outside the issuer's control, susceptible to substantially changing its positioning. One example would be the nationalization of businesses outside the domestic market when a new government assumes power. Along the same lines, any move resulting in a significant change to the company's strategy, for instance, a decision to refocus on one business and withdraw from others following major acquisitions or disposals, would be considered price-sensitive information.

In practical terms, unless it is can be legally justified not to, the company must immediately disclose price-sensitive information by means of a press release. Below is a non-exhaustive list of events that trigger a press release:

- Acquisitions or disposals: signature of letters of intent, confirmation that negotiations have begun or ended (acquisitions or disposals) and completion of the transaction;
- Signature of large contracts;
- Invitations to press conferences/meetings to discuss financial announcements;
- Company participation in conferences or trade shows;
- Results of votes on resolutions submitted to shareholders (notably approval of financial statements, dividends, board members' terms of office);
- Awards or prizes won;
- Appointments or resignations of key executives;
- Investigations launched by administrative authorities, regulators, or tax authorities;
- Significant disputes (beginning and resolution);
- Industrial accidents;
- All announcements involving products and services (launch, recall, termination);
- Changes to governance and management structures.

2.5.1.2 Insiders

Those who have knowledge of such sensitive information are considered insiders and are equally subject to specific obligations. Stock-market regulations may make a distinction between:

- persons working for the issuer, who, because of their position, have, on a regular basis, direct or indirect access to privileged information about

the issuer, either because they are employed by it or through their professional relations with it;
- those who occasionally have access to information directly or indirectly related to the company. For instance, this may correspond to lawyers, investment banks, and communications advisors who are involved in preparing a financial transaction for the issuer, and so on.

There are two obligations with which insiders must comply under all circumstances:

- *Abstention*. They may not use inside information in their possession to their own benefit or that of others before the information is made public. Specifically, this means they may not buy or sell the securities about which they have insider information.
- *Discretion*. Insiders are prohibited both from using the information they have to their benefit, and from disclosing it to third parties except in the performance of their profession or job duties.

Until the price-sensitive information has been publicly disclosed, the issuer has a duty to ensure that this information remains confidential and to inform concerned parties about the following:

- The legal and regulatory obligations governing access to inside information;
- The legal sanctions for the misuse or wrongful disclosure of inside information.

Most market regulations also stipulate that insiders must refrain from:

- knowingly disclosing or disseminating information that gives or could give inexact, imprecise, or misleading indications about listed companies;
- spreading rumors or disseminating inexact or misleading information.

The maintenance of constantly updated insider lists is mandatory in most countries. And if it is not, then it won't hurt to have one anyway.

2.5.1.3 Disclosure of price-sensitive information

Press releases (see Section 3.6.1) are the only proper way to disclose price-sensitive or privileged information.

Some countries require that press releases be officially registered or filed with the stock-market authorities for companies to effectively meet their legal obligations. Internet-based disclosure systems are gradually implemented.

Knowing that the wording and means of dissemination of press releases must meet very specific criteria, the main points to keep in mind are as follows:

- Press releases should be as clear, thorough, and precise as possible. They should include all information that can potentially have a significant impact on the share price or, according to certain legislations, prompt a decision to buy or sell;
- When drafting press releases, issuers should bear in mind that international news agencies, especially those whose networks feed directly through to market operators' screens, have very little time (no more than three minutes on average) to put the information into their systems. The journalists in question should be able to understand, by reading just a few lines, whether a press release is about a disposal or acquisition, an increase or decrease in revenues or margins, or other developments. The story will be elaborated upon in subsequent dispatches;
- There should be no doubt or ambiguity about the fact that the press release is indeed being issued by the company. The front page, title, and first paragraphs should include the full name of the company, and where possible show its logo. It should also include the name of an available and authorized contact person, for instance, the IRO or the press relations manager, with that person's direct contact information. It is inefficient and in poor taste to provide no contact, with the press release merely mentioning merely a website address and a main switchboard phone number. These may seem like small details but they are part of what creates a company's image;
- The distribution process should be tightly controlled (that is, the choice of medium and chronology) to ensure that market operators do not hear about the information from a source other than the company. Where the issuer is concerned, only one person should be authorized to "give the green light." Market authorities should be at the top of the list of recipients. Technological progress is such that, for a company with proper equipment (specialized service providers are often used), the information can be spread across the globe within a few minutes. Whole and effective distribution of an official press release is the normal way to disseminate information. The company cannot send out a summary of the release to a large number of people and send the full version only to a few;
- The press release must be sent out to the public in a timely manner and, where possible, outside of trading hours. Time frames are more

flexible in certain markets. In some cases, the only rule is that it be "as soon as possible," whereas other countries give the issuer five days to disclose the price-sensitive information. Time differences will also be a factor when the shares are listed on more than one exchange in various time zones. If the release is issued after a board meeting, shareholder meeting, press conference, or analysts' meeting, it must be distributed the same day, as early as possible, before or immediately after the end of the meeting. In extreme situations, for instance, if specific market rumors compromise the confidentiality of a deal being planned by the issuer, trading may have to be suspended when the company is not able to deliver a press release immediately. Even after a brief suspension, a preliminary or final release must still be sent out. The issuer must decide how much attention it wants to draw to the release in the morning or evening press, daily or weekly publications, or specialized magazines. Meanwhile, IROs know that financial analysts from investment banks meet, bright and early in the morning, with brokers and strategists who will ask them to comment and give their opinion on market and company developments, along with a recommendation to buy or sell. This is why earnings are often announced late in the evening or early morning, before financial markets open, with conference calls scheduled a few hours later. The main goal is to allow analysts to do their job properly by giving them enough time to prepare their questions. The meetings that follow will be all the more interesting. Some companies are against disclosing information in the evening because they say the news is in the print media before they have a chance to comment on it in detail. Each company has its own preferences. As we shall see in Section 3.6.1 (Chapter 3), a well-thought-out press release can satisfy all;
- Certain legislations make it mandatory to respond to market rumors if they are true.

The same information must be disclosed simultaneously throughout the world, in the company's domestic market and any other locations where its shares are listed. This means it must comply with the most stringent regulations in effect.

Many companies enforce embargoes, a controversial option. When texts are sent to press agencies or distributors under embargo, the latter subsequently has to be confirmed or lifted. This practice is not necessarily appreciated, or advised, because it presents a danger to company executives if the information is inadequately released to the media. There are many examples of embargoes being broken, intentionally or inadvertently, while the executives are still liable for the information, along with those in attendance at the meetings during which the sensitive information was disclosed.

2.5.2 Periodic Disclosure

Information disclosure is often broken down into the following categories:

- *Periodic disclosure requirements.* In general, periodic information refers to all documents which, according to regulations, must be published and registered at specific dates and intervals when companies announce earnings or financial transactions, and hold annual general meetings.
- *Ongoing disclosure requirements.* They correspond to any other information that can have a material impact on the price of securities, on the decision of an investor, and which must be made public in a continuous manner.

2.5.2.1 Financial accounting information

According to most laws and accounting standards, this includes objective data, facts, and figures relating to the company. These constitute the financial statements that will have to be audited, approved by the shareholders, and filed with the financial authorities. Their publication is subject to legal obligations and deadlines. Reference must always be made to previous comparable accounting periods, possibly covering two to five years. The main reporting periods in financial accounting information include the following:

- *Financial statements.* The figures presented, along with accounting aggregates from the income statement and balance sheet, often take into account changes in the scope of consolidation. In this case, a distinction must be made between sales at comparable structure and reported figures. Analysts also demand data at comparable exchange rates, if the company trades in various currencies. Companies may release preliminary earnings before the annual meeting gives final approval of the year's audited financial statements. In some countries, the law enables companies to release sales for the fiscal year before their full earnings. There may be a lag of several weeks or months between the two, reflecting the complexity of consolidating earnings across the company and the process of convening an annual general meeting.
- *Quarterly financial information.* Depending on the country or issuers' preferences, companies may provide quarterly information about trends in sales ("trading statement"), operations, or full consolidated

earnings. Many complain that reporting full consolidated earnings on a quarterly basis, originally a US feature, makes the market focus on the short term, whereas companies are run with a longer-term perspective.
- *Interim financial statements (six months)*. As with full-year earnings, reporting can be split into two parts with sales announced before earnings, depending on the country's legislation.

Typically, the first quarter or half year is compared to the same accounting period from the previous year, but analysts will also compare trends to the immediately preceding period ("sequential analysis"). Companies are not required to provide this comparison, and rarely do so in their press releases. However, simply subtracting the number from the previous full-year figure can be a source of error because it may not reflect year-end adjustments, provisions booked or written back, and so on. Companies may decide to compare first-half results with those of the second half of the previous year, to show that earnings are steadily improving or to highlight seasonal effects. However they choose to proceed, companies should at least anticipate such questions and possibly integrate this type of analysis into their internal reporting system. It is not standard practice in Investor Relations to compare actual results to budgets, because the latter are not made public. That said, targets and forecasts may be used as a basis of comparison when they have been provided to the market.

This type of financial accounting information is increasingly accompanied by guidance on the company's outlook. We shall see this in more detail in Section 3.5.3.

2.5.2.2 Annual general meetings

The annual general meeting (AGM) is a yearly opportunity to exercise shareholder democracy (see Section 3.6.19). Once companies issue securities to the public, they must, within specific deadlines, send notification of the meeting to shareholders along with the resolutions that will be submitted to their vote. There are ordinary, extraordinary, and special meetings. Shareholders are called upon to approve the audited statutory and consolidated financial statements and vote on the company's allocation of earnings, management organization and compensation, board members, and, in some cases, to approve transactions or change in the company's bylaws. Working within legal requirements, companies have a number of ways of convening meetings, depending on the structure of their shareholder base and the media attention they want to draw to the event.

- *Event driven by size of shareholder base*. Meetings can be more or less difficult and costly to organize depending on whether the issuer counts

hundreds or several millions of retail investors and if a quorum needs to be reached, which means that a minimum percentage of the voting rights needs to be in attendance or represented by proxy for the meeting to take place. Having detailed information about the structure of the shareholder base ahead of time is crucial. The company may decide to notify shareholders by letter, sending one to each investor owning at least one share. Depending on the country's market organization and legal framework, this information is obtained from its registrar, stock-transfer agent or broker, or its own securities services division. It may also decide to only convene a meeting of shareholders owning a certain amount of shares (more than 10, 15, 200, etc.) to ensure that a quorum is reached through shareholders in attendance and proxy voting. It can use all media channels (print, online, TV, and radio) to inform shareholders about how to participate in person or issue a proxy and obtain the necessary documents. Of course, any combination of these options can be used. For recently listed companies, the first annual meeting is in a way the final step to becoming a publicly traded enterprise. The process of convening the meeting can be an opportunity to gain highly useful information about the shareholder base.
- *Event driven by media coverage strategy.* Companies decide whether to hold a large or relatively small meeting, at their headquarters or in a conference center, depending on how the meeting is convened, of course, and also on how much media attention they want to draw to the event. They must consider the image they want to convey to their shareholders and the impression with which they want them to leave. Certain circumstances, such as proxy fights, will inevitably draw media attention, beyond the company's control, which requires specific preparation.

The annual general meeting being as much a legal obligation as a corporate image–driven event, some companies offer corporate gifts and a cocktail reception to their shareholders. Along with the annual report, annual meetings are usually the most significant items on Investor Relations budgets, especially factoring in related bank fees for proxy soliciting, dividend distribution, for instance.

2.5.2.3 Financial transactions

This can refer to capital increases, bond issues, public offers, takeover bids, delisting offers, public exchange offers, and so on. The legal documentation required by such transactions is ever more complex as the concerned parties must give details on more and more risk factors (see also

Section 3.5.2.7). This documentation provides investors with in-depth information about the issuer, free of charge. It must be approved by, and registered with, the competent market authorities before the transaction begins to show that there are no irregularities and that the issuer has fulfilled its obligations in terms of disclosure. The main documents are as follows:

- *An exhaustive description of the issuer.* This should include the legal status and object of the company, general information about the share capital (amount and breakdown between main shareholders), key businesses (structure, sectors, etc.), balance sheets and earnings over a minimum of three years in most jurisdictions, the names of the directors as well as recent business trends, and the outlook for the future;
- Details of the transaction under consideration: amount, time frame, conditions, guarantees, and so on;
- A description of the consequences of the transaction on the issuer's financial situation.

In some countries, annual reports that have been written with a view to support a financial transaction, and duly approved by market authorities, may be used to fulfill a portion of these cumbersome requirements. Where Investor Relations are concerned, however, there are at least two other advantages to preparing these documents:

- It shows institutional investors and financial analysts that the company offers quality and transparent financial information. When English versions are available, the documents can also appeal to foreign investors that may be interested in the company or seek to take part in the transaction;
- For IROs, this documentation will be an all-important tool. Indeed, it makes it easier for them to justify a negative answer to a financial analyst who requests more details not included in this documentation, which is very thorough by nature.

Some are put off by the cost of preparing this documentation and the time it requires to gather input from the financial, legal, operations, and communications divisions. Nonetheless, it seems clear that the benefits outweigh the drawbacks.

Financial transactions may involve financial advertising campaigns that are subject to strict regulations in terms of content and distribution channels. Advertisements must explain how to obtain documents pertaining to the transaction and say that these are available, free of charge, upon request. Only then can the issuer consider commencing the corporate advertising campaign. All disclosure requirements must be met before the company issues securities or receives subscription commitments.

Note that regulations can also require information from listed companies about the following:

- Standing offers;
- Internal control and corporate governance reports;
- Auditors' fees;
- Monthly information on the total number of voting rights and shares;
- Descriptions of share buyback programs and monthly overviews of buybacks;
- List of press releases issued in accordance with ongoing information disclosure requirements;
- Press releases indicating how prospectuses are to be distributed in the event of financial transactions;
- Press releases specifying how the legal documentation is to be made available prior to the annual general meeting.

Specific information is also required with regard to treasury stock, shareholder agreements, the crossing of thresholds, stock splits, reverse stock splits, and capital decreases.

The truth is that few people read every word in the hundreds of pages making up this legal document. It can thus be in a listed company's interest to simultaneously prepare other documents that are concise, informative, and practical. This can be done through a special section of the website, lists of frequently asked questions, press releases in the local language, or visual presentations.

In conclusion, ignorance of the law being no excuse, listed companies are advised to have their legal departments and IROs work together on a regular basis to build awareness of legal obligations relating to Investor Relations and to do the following:

- Update lists of insiders, which market authorities may request at any time;
- Inform those included on the lists of the obligations applicable to them;
- Rely exclusively on authorized spokespersons (top management, head of press or Investor Relations, in particular);
- Publish corporate disclosure guidelines and policies to outside parties;

- Establish a code of conduct to be shared with company representatives;
- Prepare Q&A for communicating on sensitive issues, enabling all to become "company ambassadors" and provide information that is exact and in compliance with law.

Companies are strongly advised to consult the legal documents made available by market authorities and to prepare in advance for any regulatory changes, knowing that these can be significant.

All in all, be sure you master legal obligations well enough to go beyond them and use this extra transparency lever as a differentiator.

2.6 Anticipating Changes in Investor Relations

Over time, various endogenous and exogenous factors may alter a company's profile and outlook. It is the duty of Investor Relations to ensure that these changes be properly anticipated and communicated.

2.6.1 Endogenous Factors

2.6.1.1 Time elapsed since listing

In the run-up to an IPO, a company must make a significant investment, on which it will capitalize in the following years, to establish its name and management's reputation with financial markets and present its business model. Less time will be spent describing activities in later earnings releases than at the time of the first information meeting, as the focus gradually shifts to the company's ability to meet its strategic objectives.

2.6.1.2 Size and breakdown of share capital

The market traditionally makes a distinction between listed companies based on their market capitalization, breaking them down into small caps, midcaps, large caps, and even mega caps in the United States in tens of billions of dollars. The portion of the capital owned by the public—referred to as the free float—is another variable that has a significant impact on the stock's liquidity. Potential investors will first look at daily trading volumes, that is, at how much of the company's equity is traded on average every day. With this in mind, Investor Relations at midcap companies may aim, for instance, to help prepare for an increase in the free float by promoting the share to more retail and institutional shareholders. Where large caps are concerned, the focus may be, for instance, on keeping a balance between domestic and foreign shareholders, or between retail and institutional investors.

2.6.1.3 Size, renown, and recognition

These factors can affect Investor Relations when new milestones are achieved in a company's growth, notably through acquisitions, or when the market capitalization increases enough to give the stock large-cap status. In this case, Investor Relations will target fund managers specializing in the category into which the stock has moved. Frequent media coverage will allow the company to establish its name and brand in the financial community rather than solely among its employees, clients, suppliers, and banks. This will be a time to introduce new messages to bolster the image of the company, its products and services, and financial performance.

2.6.1.4 Image and reputation

The increasing focus on sustainable development and corporate responsibility has added a whole new dimension to Investor Relations through corporate image and reputation, although at the end of the day, there are really only good images and bad ones. Reputations can be destroyed overnight and it can take years to rebuild them. It is considered a proven fact that, intelligently combined with corporate communications, Investor Relations can be efficient in restoring the image of companies and the reputations of their management. We are outside the realm of financial data here, in the world of the intangible. There are three key areas in which reputations are formed: governance, how environmental protection is factored into strategy, and labor relations. It is becoming increasingly clear that these criteria do indeed affect companies' valuations. The ever-growing number of funds and rating agencies focusing on socially responsible investment, combined with the requirement to provide more and more of this type of data with financial information included in social and environmental reports and safety and health performance reports (which is often termed non-financial disclosure), are opportunities to adapt the messages and media used in financial communications, with due regard to appropriate frequency and timing.

2.6.1.5 Sectors and countries in which the company does business

A company's Investor Relations will be all the more efficient if the information it delivers is highly instructive, regardless of whether it operates in well-known and documented markets, in nascent or polluting industries, or in what are considered to be high-risk countries. Informative communication is also an excellent way for medium-sized companies to draw attention. Those that do not have market leadership can still set the standard for their sectors in terms of Investor Relations by providing the public with general, macroeconomic, and technical information that takes time to gather. This will give the impression that the company has perfectly mastered its business sector, thereby adding to its credibility.

2.6.1.6 Internal organization

The appointment of a new CEO or director can be an opportunity to enrich the company's news flow. It will focus on the newly appointed person's reputation in business, track record, or knowledge of the company's activities. The message will thus depend on whether the appointee is known for turning around troubled companies, as an heir to a family business (in which case the appointee's credibility will have to be established with financial markets), or is appointed following merger with another company.

2.6.1.7 Expansion policy and strategic priorities

A company that intends to develop its business in the United States through acquisitions should spend a fair amount of time meeting with financial analysts and investors based in that country. The questions asked will help the company understand the environment into which it is venturing by providing information about the competition. It can subsequently rework its communication to include more relevant performance indicators and a better investment case. This expansion may also lead to a listing on a foreign market, in which case Investor Relations will have to be adapted to reflect new regulations and the specific expectations of domestic investors. If the company decides to diversify into new areas, or on the contrary, refocus on a core business, it will have to convince the markets that these major transformations are wise.

2.6.1.8 Financial structure and strategy funding

In the course of its development, a company may need to step up its capital expenditure or acquire or dispose of assets. These moves will impact its financial profile and earnings outlook, for better or for worse, over a given period of time. If such developments require a capital increase or debt financing, specific Investor Relations will be needed. For instance, listed companies that issue bonds will have to deliver specific information to credit analysts to enable them to calculate the myriad ratios they use. The priorities of equity and bond investors can sometimes differ, including on the topics of acquisition and debt reduction strategies, financing solutions, and share buyback and dividend policies. Companies must nonetheless present their strategic priorities exactly in the same way to all audiences.

2.6.1.9 Research and development

R&D expenses may be recorded in different ways depending on their nature and the accounting standards applied. Some companies book them as operating expenses, deducting them from operating income, while others record them as investments that are amortized over time. The IR department will seek to justify the levels of R&D expenditure announced and respond to any claims by analysts or investors that the issuer is investing too little or too much, notably compared with its competitors.

2.6.1.10   Shareholder returns

There are many ways for issuers to generate shareholder returns, and the decisions must be justified on the basis of whether the companies are paying dividends, allocating bonus shares, or making cash payments, sometimes or several times during the year. Very few issuers talk about their payout policies and commit to quantified targets. This is tricky issue for IR departments as issuers only give general guidelines, usually claiming that they need to remain flexible in allocating their resources.

2.6.1.11   Maintaining a positive image even if you delist your shares

'Delisting' corresponds to two types of circumstances:

- Going private again, with your shares not being traded anywhere any longer;
- Delisting from a foreign market. In this case, your shares will only trade on your home market again.

2.6.1.11.1   Going private again

In the course of your corporate life cycle, being a publicly traded company may, at some point in time, no longer be necessary or affordable:

- Your company is acquired and merged into another, with the buyer not wanting to maintain your listing;
- As the owner of the owner, you have been disappointed by the expected rewards of the stock market, you are keen to do away with listing costs and ever increasing disclosure and other regulatory requirements.

It would be a terrible mistake to think that there will therefore be little or no need for Investor Relations anymore: even if you will no longer be subject to regular information filings, your company will remain active in its own area of business. As such, it will continue to have an image, a reputation, and this will need to be protected.

As a consequence, the delisting process calls for a public relations and an Investor Relations plan to deal with how the company's employees, shareholders, creditors and other shareholders will react to the delisting. In particular, Investor Relations will keep all stakeholders and the public informed of what is happening throughout the delisting process.

Hopefully, the information discipline and governance principles adopted through the years of listing are there to stay. Nothing prevents your company from remaining visible on the financial markets' radar screens and it would be well advised to maintain some kind of Investor Relations activity and presence on the internet: for instance, keeping the habit of communicating on its annual results, explaining its performance and strategic directions. Who knows? You may go public again a few years down the road and, in the meantime, you may issue bonds or need bank loans or carry out a private placement of your equity.

2.6.1.11.2 Delisting from a foreign market

There used to be a time, in the 1980s and 1990s, when listing your shares on foreign stock exchanges was said to be the most effective means to access more investors, greater liquidity, a higher share price, and a lower cost of capital. Times have dramatically changed, with costs largely outweighing benefits, for most companies in the developed markets, at least. Consequently, a significant number of delistings have been registered, after (or in spite of, some will say) a delisting process that can be somewhat cumbersome and expensive.

But delisting from a foreign exchange does not automatically imply that you will lose all of the initial benefits in terms of shareholder base: shareholders that matter to large companies from developed countries invest globally anyway, directly via electronic trading platforms in their domestic markets. As long as there is enough liquidity in your home market, it is unlikely that your delisting will deter them from holding your shares if you have a good equity story.

Listing and governance requirements are also being strengthened in developing markets too, thus alleviating investors' investing apprehension. (An exception to this could, however, be large corporation from emerging markets whose home stock exchanges do not yet offer the liquidity, the regulatory, or governance framework required by global investors.)

Furthermore, with the globalization of capital markets, your company's valuation is likely to be primarily driven by your performance, rather than by your cross-border listing.

The role of IR will therefore consist in maintaining:

- the same presence with the investors in the country where it is delisted from;
- the same level of transparency and financial disclosure as before.

An active outreach program and a proper, corporate image-enhancing communication plan will help locally, while reaching out to new investors to replace those shareholders who may have left the share register upon the delisting, for some reason or another. Ultimately, having a solid, profitable equity story, and telling it over and over should take your company smoothly through delisting.

2.6.2 Exogenous Factors

2.6.2.1 *The competitive environment*

Investor Relations can also be impacted by the content and style of the messages sent out by competitors. Some will focus more on certain financial ratios than others; they may have different ways of describing the markets in which they operate, and fail to provide quantified targets or, on the contrary, give earnings targets for the following 3, 5, or even 10 years. Particular attention should be paid to how thorough and user friendly the competition's websites are when they release their earnings, and how far their disclosure goes.

2.6.2.2 *Macroeconomic and geopolitical environment*

The global financial crisis has seen investors shying away from companies which were headquartered in countries where it became very risky to invest: Spain, Greece, Portugal, to name only a few. Geographical turmoil such as wars or political instability may also cause severe disruption to a company's operations.

This can weigh quite significantly on the valuation of large groups originating from these regions, giving IROs a hard time in explaining the reality of the impact on their own company, based on an international footprint, or more diversified revenue and cash flow streams than investors might think.

Under those circumstances, IROs have also often spent more time describing their home country's macroeconomic environment than their own companies. Frustrating as it may be, this is nonetheless an opportunity for IROs to revisit the equity story.

2.6.2.3 *Technology changes*

The advent of electronic trading is having a dramatic impact on the business model of traditional stock exchanges: They are rapidly losing ground to electronic trading platforms and initial public offerings are no longer the large profit contributors they used to be. High-frequency trading where transactions are executed in microseconds, and dark pools," these equity trading systems that do not publicly display order flows, are capturing a rapidly growing portion of equity trading. Listed companies have only a very limited view left of who is actually trading their shares and it is becoming increasingly complex for IROs to identify who owns your shares in the most developed markets.

This, in turn, is triggering yet another series of regulations and profound changes in this industry as securities exchanges merge and demerge. Listed companies should brace themselves for more uncertainty...

2.6.2.4 Regulatory changes

Stock-market regulations may require the deadline for publishing financial statements to be shortened, or quarterly reporting may become mandatory. Such changes have a substantial impact on Investor Relations. IROs must keep abreast of changes in the pipeline and involve the company, where appropriate, in any lobbying efforts to limit, as much as possible, the negative impact of the new regulations on its organizational structure or, at least, to ensure that it has enough time to comply with the new rules. In most cases, any change in the regulatory environment boils down to understanding "what must be disclosed when?"

Some types of regulatory change can impact issuers' businesses and operations. Investor Relations must in this case explain how the costs associated with compliance will affect earnings, or possibly how the new regulations will boost demand for the company's products.

At the cross roads of technology and regulatory changes that are shaping the world of investors, analysts and IROs, we find XBRL and IFRS.

2.6.3 The Adoption of New Reporting Standards and Tools: XBRL, IFRS

2.6.3.1 XBRL

XBRL stands for eXtensible Business Reporting Language (XBRL). It is a global standard that enables the financial reporting process for both preparers and consumers on the web in an interactive manner. Its tagging allows for businesses' financial and accounting data to be electronically searched, extracted or downloaded.

In the US, the largest public companies have been reporting in XBRL since 2009 but the requirement became effective for the smallest companies in 2011. In China, XBRL data submission to the Shanghai stock market has been obligatory since 2004. In Europe, XBRL is used by various stock exchanges, bank supervisions, tax authorities and business registers.

Investor Relations need to stay abreast with developments in this area as demand from analysts, investors and other data users is strong.

2.6.3.2 Ensuring Smooth Migration to International Financial Reporting Standards (IFRS)

IFRS stands for International Financial Reporting Standards. It is a set of accounting standards developed by an independent, not-for-profit organization called the International Accounting Standards Board (IASB).

Table 2.2 Costs and Benefits of Migrating to IFRS

Short-Term Costs	Long-Term Benefits
• Identify and quantify the differences between your country's Generally Accepted Accounting principles (GAAP) and IFRS • Train staff • Implement new processes, accounting software and IT systems • Change policy manuals, training manuals, internal audit programs and systems	• One single set of financial statements accepted around the world • Provide financial analysts, investors and auditors with a cohesive view of finances • Enhance global competitiveness and domestic operations • Increase comparability and transparency of financial reporting • Facilitate access to international capital, funding and investment opportunities • Reduce cost of capital

The international standard-setting process began several decades ago as an effort by industrialized nations to create standards that could be used by developing and smaller nations unable to establish their own accounting standards. But as the business world became more global, regulators, investors, large companies and auditing firms began to realize the importance of having common standards in all areas of the financial reporting chain.

IFRS provides general guidance for the preparation of financial statements rather than setting rules for industry-specific reporting. The goal of IFRS is to provide a global framework for how public companies prepare and disclose their financial statements.

Currently, over 120 countries permit or require IFRS for public companies, with more countries considering the transition to IFRS in the medium term, including, potentially, the USA and Japan where the issue is hotly debated.

In the short term, the costs may outweigh the benefits; in the longer run, however, IFRS conversion just makes good business sense.

2.6.3.2.1 Challenges and opportunities for investor relations

In order to go as smoothly as possible, the transition needs to be properly prepared and communicated. This is where Investor Relations comes into play. Indeed, migrating to IFRS offers the Investor Relations team many challenges and opportunities.

Let's start with the challenges.

You will have to make sure that you are part of the IFRS project team from the very beginning. It will be critical in many ways: as Investor

Relations for your company, you have a unique understanding of the mindset and the working habits of financial analysts and investors. Only *you* know how they model and value your company.

In order to minimize as much as possible the risks of confusion that the adoption of IFRS could cause, you need to be fully aware of the impacts on your financial statements and overall disclosure. That may include the way your company provides forward-looking guidance to the financial markets. Is IFRS going to change anything to your financial objectives?

One of the other challenges that you could face is going to be your ability to convince management that the transition to IFRS requires an *ad hoc* Investor Relations communications plan.

This plan will help you manage the confusion that could arise from IFRS in earnings estimates, for instance.

On the other hand, IFRS represents a real opportunity for Investor Relations to "get a seat at the executive table." The transition itself is usually quite a daunting task because finance teams and management tends fear a potentially negative impact on how the market values the company. They will want to make sure that everything goes well in as predictable a manner as possible and IR is a prime beneficiary of this.

On this occasion, you will no doubt increase your financial skills as you will put together convincing messages that will simplify what can be viewed as an extremely complex change.

You should also take advantage of this transition to IFRS to work even more closely with your media relations and internal communications colleagues. Their own constituencies and target audience will need to understand what IFRS is all about and what the implications are.

As you plan and execute a best in class IR program around IFRS, you will help improve how the financial markets perceive your company. Education always pays off. It demonstrates that you are committed to providing quality information. Your own personal image as an IR professional should also benefit from "going the extra mile."

2.6.3.2.2 The European experience

Investor Relations officers who are going to have to manage a transition can benefit from the European experience in this regard: back in 2005, the European Union mandated that all listed companies adopt IFRS.

Most of the largest listed companies prepared specific IFRS-related presentations in a communications strategy that benefited from senior management and board support. This often included an explanation of their choice of options when adopting IFRS, together with sometimes precise and audited quantification of IFRS impacts. A smaller number actually started to report in IFRS one year before deadline.

Table 2.3 Communication Plan for IFRS Conversion

IFRS Ramp-Up Phase			IFRS Year One
Q2 ▷	Q3 ▷	Q4 ▷	Q1
• First presentation of transition roadmap • Announcement of Q3 investor & analyst roadmap • IFRS section built on corporate website • Development of support documents (fact sheets, FAQs, press releases)	• Investor & analyst workshop • Dedicate particular attention to impact of IFRS on outlook • Conduct post-workshop evaluation to identify areas requiring further analyst, investor and media education up to Q1 of following year • Integrate internal and external communications efforts on IFRS • IFRS section in place on corporate website • Fact sheet • CFO video interview	• Full year earnings impact of IFRS on Key Performance Indicators and outlook for the following year • Feed findings of post-investor workshop evaluation back into communications strategy • Update IR IFRS Toolkit • If available, provide reconciliation of full year earnings between local GAAP and IFRS on key financial performance indicators • Provide section on IFRS in Q4 earnings release and MD&A • Prepare a few slides dedicated to IFRS for the earnings call • Provide IFRS-based outlook for following year • Reiterate key message on IFRS • Ensure IFRS-based analyst estimates are	• First financial reporting under IFRS • Update IR toolkit • Downloadable Excel spreadsheets with historical data • Dedicate special effort on earnings call to ensure following year analyst estimates are properly factoring in IFRS changes • Consider posting consensus estimates on website

According to research, this significant communications effort paid off: only a minority of companies have seen their stock price move by more than 2 percent following IFRS disclosure.

What's more, those companies that organized a meeting or conference call on IFRS have seen their stock price go up or down by less than 1 percent.

All in all, increased information quality was a key success factor.

2.6.3.2.3 The investor relations roadmap for IFRS

One of the key success factors is advanced and thorough project planning with Investor Relations involvement from the very beginning.

The table below summarizes the key milestones of the Investor Relations program to ensure a smooth transition to the new financial standards.

2.6.3.2.4 The IFRS toolkit

The IR program can be supported by a series of events and tools designed to help the investment community understand that the transition to IFRS will impact accounting practices, not the company's strategy. This should be the key message of the communications effort.

In order to build the IFRS toolkit, the IR team can choose to include all or part of the following items:

- Presentation:
  - Develop a description of the IFRS project team and designate whom the team reports to within the executive committee.
  - Outline your key principles and definitions. You should not count on anyone else but your own company to explain IFRS to its stakeholders.
  - Implement and communicate your timetable. Explain when and how you started, who was in charge of what, and the progressive adaptation of the reporting system. This is also a way to make analysts aware of when your financial statements will no longer be available under your local GAAP.
  - Create effective graphic presentations. Avoid busy slides. Tables and waterfall charts tend to be the most effective way to explain the impacts of the migration to IFRS.
- Press releases. These will serve to announce the event (such as a short analyst and investor workshop and/or a conference call) where your company will present how it is going to adopt IFRS, but also highlight the main quantifiable consequences, if any, on your financial performance as it will be reported going forward. Needless to say, this could be price-sensitive information and should be reviewed by your legal department as well

- Analyst and investor workshop, conference call. The event should take place at least 6 months prior to first disclosure of full set of IFRS accounts. It will:
  - provide a general explanation of what is IFRS, in layman's terms, the transition timeline, and certain transitional considerations such as the principles elected by the company;
  - detail the key accounting differences with the local GAAP and how they will translate into the financial statements;
  - discuss business impacts, if any.

It is also recommended that a post-event survey be conducted to identify areas which may need further explanation. It will be particularly important to ensure that analysts and investors feel they have all the information they need to revise their financial estimates and valuation models to adjust for IFRS.

- A downloadable Excel spreadsheet providing one to three years of historical financial data reconciled under IFRS could well be popular with sell-side analysts;
- Frequently Asked Questions. From general to being more company-specific, these can include:
  - Why have we changed our accounting from GAAP to IFRS?
  - How long is GAAP accounting being continued?
  - What are the fundamental differences between GAAP and IFRS accounting?
  - What effects have the switch from GAAP to IFRS accounting had on the company's key performance indicators? On its outlook?
- A section dedicated to IFRS transition on your website. The following documents and information should be available: IFRS conversion and communication timeline, FAQ section, presentation, conference call archive. You might want to post an interview with your Chief Financial Officer highlighting what adopting IFRS is going to imply for your company.

2.7 Investor Relations and Cross-Border Listings

Competition for capital has definitely become global. Your company may want or need to look overseas to fund its expansion plans. The decision to list your shares on a foreign stock exchange could be driven by the following factors:

- Your growth profile;
- Your strategic directions;

- Your industry's competitive landscape;
- Your financial structure;
- The depth of your home stock market and its ability to sustain your capital requirements. This may, for instance, be the case for companies from emerging market listing their shares on the exchanges of more developed economies.

The same factors will also dictate the choice of the foreign exchange. The ongoing consolidation of stock exchanges worldwide makes it more complex.

The most frequently cited financial benefits of cross-border listings include:

- the ability to trade and list in a different currency from your home market:
  o Broadening your shareholder base. You will be better positioned to attract investors whose mandates only allow investing in shares that are denominated in a certain currency or who are restricted to investing in a given country by regulatory filings and mandate, such as corporate governance requirements and stock market regulations. If they have a limited command of your language, they will appreciate receiving your information flow in their own idiom.
  o Accessing diversified funding options. You may take advantage of discrepancies in interest rates, for instance, or of a stronger appetite for your industry or business model than in your home market. Being listed in another country may also allow you to raise your profile locally and identify acquisition opportunities.
- the potential for a lower cost of capital through higher valuation, itself driven by increased liquidity and analyst coverage. This can be especially true if you list your shares on a foreign market where your main competitors are also traded, at a premium, to your home market.

While the primary reasons for an IPO usually include raising equity or spinning off a business entity from its parent company, the strategy behind cross-border listings is often broader and more business driven. It is increasingly targeted at a specific country or region where your company has identified business opportunities. The cross-border listing then becomes:

- a marketing tool for your products and services in a target country or region;
- an international recruitment tool. Not only will your company be better positioned to attract local talent, but it will be able to retain executives with locally traded stock-based compensation;

- a communication tool that will enhance your image, both globally and locally, vis-à-vis your suppliers, your business partners, and the administrative and political authorities in the region.

If, after carefully weighing the costs and benefits of launching and maintain this secondary listing, you come to a decision to list your shares abroad, you will need to design a proper Investor Relations program. This will require you to:

- respect local disclosure and filing requirements, while ensuring shareholder equality at home and abroad and maintaining consistency across messages;
- enlist local support to help you navigate through the cultural differences between this new financial market and your home exchange. This may entail communicating in a foreign language, thus demanding additional work to make sure your messages are not simply translated, but tailored to the local audience. It is particularly critical if part of your strategy is to raise your visibility with a large retail (and potentially shareholder) customer base for your products and services. This support can be provided by a combination of your corporate team on the ground and a local investor relations and financial communications firm. If your cross-listing is really about building a strong image, it is strongly recommended to translate your financial documentation in the local language. Thinking that everybody understands English can be counter-productive;
- showing commitment and presence through regular trips and the availability of a local IR contact point. The size of your operations in the country where you are going to be newly listed may allow you to rely more or less heavily on your local teams. The challenge will then be to make sure they are as credible and knowledgeable as the IR team at head office;
- adapting your IR tools and organization. This will include:
  o revising your financial calendar to take local holidays and traditional reporting periods into consideration when planning your roadshows;
  o adding a section on your website to provide:
    - share price and trading data for the secondary listing;
    - local IR contact details.
  o learning how to work with difference time zones if necessary.

Because the objective of a secondary listing may be driven more by business goals than by traditional financial considerations, it is important that these goals be factored into the way you will develop you IR program.

As the listing targets a wider range of stakeholders, good cooperation with the corporate communications teams and the management in charge of your local operations will be essential.

2.8 The Convergence of Investor Relations and Corporate Communications

2.8.1 Convergence Is Here to Stay

Investor Relations has traditionally been the domain of ex-bankers, stockbrokers, or financial analysts who could read a balance sheet and know how to talk to the CFO of a listed company. It caused many problems. There was no single point of contact within the company and mixed messages issued from different areas of the organization. In addition, stakeholders and shareholders were considered mutually exclusive. Messages became blurred at best, or confused at worst.

In a world of globalization where transparent communication drives the value of a company's business, how companies manage consistent communication with the financial community, the media, shareholders, employees, customers, and other stakeholders, while tailoring their message to suit the interests of these groups, is putting Investor Relations and corporate communications professionals under pressure everywhere. The need for transparency, consistency, and equal disclosure, combined with the emergence of new technologies and new regulations are driving the convergence, not just of traditional Investor Relations and Press Relations, but of crisis communications as well.

2.8.2 Integrated Communications as a Value Driver

Reality is that there should be no hierarchy of needs as all are equally important. Employees are quite likely to be shareholders, and vice versa. And while the investment community might view a plant closure or restructuring plan at a listed company as a positive development and move up its share price, the employees losing their jobs are less likely to welcome the announcement.

The concept of convergence of Investor Relations and the other corporate communication functions should not be led by the organization chart. And Investor Relations and Press Relations can no longer afford to work in isolation. While the ideal situation may be to have all corporate communications functions managed by one person who reports to the CEO, the most frequent organization for Investor Relations to report to is the CFO's.

The next integration driver is for PR and IR departments to use the same communication tool to manage internal and external communication. These should be designed to facilitate the dissemination of information from any company, regardless of how they execute or define roles internally.

2.8.3 Ensuring Consistency across Communications

Integrated communications alone may not be sufficient—consistency is mission critical. You might see a PR—Press Relations or Public Relations—person—perhaps at divisional level—sending out a press release without realizing that there's a price-sensitive dimension to it. For instance, before you say that your company's latest product innovation will increase market shares by a given percentage, your safest rule is to have your press releases tested by the Investor Relations team and check whether the CFO and IRO agree with that view and its disclosure. In this respect, Investor Relations teams need to position themselves as integral to the communications strategy.

Companies that seamlessly communicate their business goals, and work to retain their brand identity and the loyalty of their audiences through integrated communications, are best placed to withstand a crisis and to call for understanding when it is needed most.

Altogether this may well enhance business objectives as well. This is the strength of the concept of strategic communications.

Key Principles to Remember

- Management's determination to make Investor Relations a competitive advantage is the main key to success. This involves establishing a long-term strategy and assuring the personal involvement of top management.
- The integration of communications has to be driven by the CEO to act as powerful strategic differentiator.
- Compliance with and full understanding of a steadily changing regulatory environment is a source of security and credibility.
- Investor Relations can only be successful if the Investor Relations teams have a robust financial background and solid communications skills.

International Best Practices

- Provide senior management with regular feedback from the market.
- Go out of your way to help analysts and media understand your company: They'll remember you!
- Build your Investor Relations tools so that they can help you measure the efficiency of your program.
- Be involved in educating employees on price-sensitive issues.
- Make sure press relations and Investor Relations work closely together.
- Investors and analysts are used to bad news. However, don't surprise them.

3
Implementing Best Practices in Investor Relations

Whether your organization is planning an initial public offering (IPO), a secondary offering, a bond issue, or you are an entrepreneur looking for venture capital to finance your growth, Investor Relations is a tool to be leveraged and a process to be mastered by anyone competing for capital.

This chapter contains many easy-to-use and reliable pedagogical features that can be applied in real business life to implement a world-class, best-practice-oriented Investor Relations strategy, in the following order:

- Know your new Investor Relations "customers"
- Attract and retain new shareholders
- Understand market expectations
- Develop the financial calendar
- Craft compelling messages
- Select and implement Investor Relations tools
- Enhance shareholder loyalty and retention
- Know how to deal with crisis communications in Investor Relations.

3.1 Identifying Shareholders

A listed company that does not seek to identify its shareholders runs the risk of not reaching its audience. Knowing precisely who owns your stock, and why, are the keys to building a secure shareholder base. At the same time, increasing investor activism is making shareholder identification more important and more difficult.

It is not an easy task, and sometimes a nearly impossible one, to draw up an exhaustive list, unless the stocks are held in a "registered" form. In this case, the shareholder's identity is recorded in a specific share registrar maintained by the issuer or a dedicated depositary bank. Yet the most common form of share ownership is the "anonymous" bearer form, as allowed under certain regulations, and in systems where shares have been dematerialized and are traded in an electronic form.

This makes the identification process all the more challenging and requires resources and systems that can do the following:

- Track and quantify holdings as well as categories of investors (individual shareholders, institutional investors) from a variety of sources;
- Provide senior management team with a strategic analysis of who actually owns the company's shares.

There are different legal and technical ways to discover your shareholder base. This high-cost and time-consuming effort is worth undertaking only if you have a clear idea of what your objectives are, if you conduct the analysis on a regular basis, and if you want to proactively manage your free float.

Furthermore, companies are not the only ones interested in knowing who owns their shares. Institutional investors are also very keen to be informed, as it gives them valuable insight into the potential evolution of the shares. For instance, the presence of many hedge funds as owners can result in higher risks of volatility, while a large portion of the shares held by employees can indicate long-term stability.

3.1.1 Legal Means

Share-ownership disclosure regulations vary from one country to another. For instance, some may require shareholders to officially declare their holdings in a company when they pass a certain threshold, expressed either in nominal value, as a percentage of the share capital, or as a percentage of the voting rights. There are also countries where no such obligation exists. Furthermore, in certain jurisdictions the power of investigation is given to the companies, while, in others, the nation's regulator has the power to dictate shareholder identification.

3.1.1.1 Notification of threshold crossing

Depending on applicable regulations in the country where the shares are listed and the company's bylaws, shareholders may be required to disclose the number of shares or voting rights they hold when threshold limits are crossed (generally fractions of 0.5 percent of the capital). Stock-market law strictly regulates the crossing of legal and statutory thresholds: the latter are approved by shareholders and included in the bylaws. Failure to make the required disclosure can result in lawsuits and deprivation of the voting rights attached to the shares. This, for instance, would prevent voting rights from being exercised in the event of a hostile takeover bid.

3.1.1.2 Identification by a central securities depositary

Securities have been dematerialized on the world's major stock markets, meaning they now exist in electronic rather than paper form. In a number of countries, central securities depositaries and clearing agencies exist which are responsible for maintaining register of securities, issuing international securities identification numbers (ISIN) for all issues of securities, and clearing and settlement of securities. In addition, they provide additional services to the issuers, such as securities ownership identification. This allows an issuer of bearer securities to request and obtain a list of all, or part of, the securities' holders registered on the custodians' books.

Issuers may regularly request (once a year or more) that the agency make inquiries based on thresholds as set out in their bylaws, for instance, upward of 10,000 shares per custodian bank and 500 shares per shareholder. They may also ask for full identification of all shareholders, even those with only one share, although this is a costly undertaking for companies with millions of shareholders, and the content analysis process is quite complex. In addition, while significant progress has been made over past years in certain legislations, there is still no way for companies to identify individual foreign shareholders as opposed to the custodian banks where these shares are deposited. This is an important factor if we consider that in certain markets, foreign or "non-resident" investors may hold more than half of an issuer's shares.

At the end of this process, the issuer obtains a file, which includes the name and address of all identified shareholders, be they corporations or individuals, along with the number of shares owned. While unique of its kind, the information contained there must be expanded through other searches, possibly via the acquisition of specialized databases.

3.1.1.3 Analysis of voting results

This type of analysis is much more varied and the findings depend, in large part, on the thresholds and means of convening shareholder meetings, as outlined in Section 2.5.2.2. The proxy ballot cards sent by mail, or brought in person by shareholders attending the annual general meeting (AGM), are legally the property of the company. To perform the analysis, these are captured and stored in a well-customized Investor Relations contact database and provide additional information about, or confirm the identity of, the shareholders identified by the issuer during the process described above.

The exercise is also very helpful when it comes to planning the annual meeting for the following year. You will want to compare the number of printed proxy ballots versus the number of shareholders who returned them and those who actually came to attend the AGM. Useful cross-analysis should also be conducted to do the following:

- Calculate the average number of shares held by retail investors: This is valuable information if the issuer plans a capital increase and wants to estimate the subscription rate for this category of shareholder;
- Assess the sensitivity of individual and institutional shareholders to different kinds of resolution based on how they vote;
- Adjust the size and, consequently, the budget of the event to actual presence of shareholders.

3.1.2 Technical Means

3.1.2.1 Free shareholder identification techniques

- *Questionnaires* (see Resources). Issuers may, for example, hand out short questionnaires after earnings presentations or roadshows to find out their audience's impressions of the meeting, and whether or not they are shareholders.
- *Resourcefulness.* There is nothing to prevent Investor Relations Officers (IROs) from directly asking the institutional or retail investors they talk with whether they own shares in the company and, if so, how many. Even if no specific answer is given, the question will rarely be dismissed outright. This can, in fact, be a valuable opportunity to discover what it would take to convince those who do not already own shares to invest. A shift in strategy? Lower valuation multiples? Any information thus gathered should be shared with company management.

3.1.2.2 Fee-based identification tools

- *Standard mailing techniques.* When a contact database already exists, there is no reason why issuers cannot rely on traditional investigation and marketing methods. For instance, they may send out questionnaires, anonymous if so desired, including questions about the number of shares owned. It is wise to plan this type of undertaking well in advance and to inform the relevant authorities in the country in question, ahead of time, of any plans to create a contact data base that will be used to this end.
- *Databases.* There are numerous databases that list international institutional investors and provide a breakdown of their portfolios by geography, size, and the nature of the holdings, investment policy, and so on. In some countries, institutional investors must disclose the content of certain portfolios such as the mutual funds, unit trusts, and

collective investment vehicles they manage on an annual, half-yearly, or quarterly basis. Many such databases are public information. They can also be developed specifically for issuers. Information is given about the number of shares held, changes made to the portfolio since the previous reporting period, the name and contact information of the fund manager, the buy-side analyst covering the country in which the shares are issued, specifically the one in charge of the sector in which the issuer is active. Moreover, databases also mention the rival companies in which shares are owned, the amount of funds under management, and a breakdown between domestic and foreign investments (this gives an indication of how familiar foreign investors are with the stock exchanges and economies of other countries). Issuers can only justify investing in this type of Investor Relations tools if they are targeting new institutional shareholders.

3.1.2.3 Financial intermediaries

Financial intermediaries have privileged access to knowledge about listed companies' shareholder bases:

- *Investment banks and brokers.* Through the transactions they execute for institutional clients and retail investors, these intermediaries can tell IROs whether particular fund managers own a large enough number of shares for the issuer to plan a meeting or whether they recently added to or liquidated their holdings. This information may not always be as accurate as the issuer would like, but it does nonetheless tend to be highly valuable.
- *Retail banks.* Large retail banking networks can provide a different kind of information. While issuers cannot gain access to the names of those who own shares through securities accounts, they can inquire about the possibility of obtaining a breakdown of the bank's customers by the number of shares owned (for instance, less than 5, 5–10, 10–20, and so on) along with other types of information, usually about the place of residence, socio-professional category, and age of stockholders. The results will depend on the degree of sophistication of the bank's information systems. Data pertaining to share ownership is particularly valuable for the issuer. For instance, understanding the average value of shareholders' investment in your company's shares can provide you with a valuable indication the amount of shares that could be subscribed in the event of a capital increase. It is also useful in planning meetings with retail investors in specific regions, which can in this case be substituted for the identification process described in Section 3.1.1.2 earlier.

3.2 Attracting and Retaining Shareholders

Rather than passively enduring an ineffective or hostile free-float structure, it should be part of the corporate strategy to define what could be the company's "ideal" shareholder base. There is no "one-size-fits-all" approach but, again, there is a clear analogy between Investor Relations and marketing activities.

Of course, the company also needs to be clear about which kinds of shareholders it does not want to attract, either because of the related maintenance costs or because market intelligence suggests that their management style goes against the company's interests.

Just as there are unquestionable advantages to having a broad customer base, an optimally diversified shareholder base has tangible benefits too.

One basic recipe for successful Investor Relations is to constantly maintain a pool of potential investors who will be there to buy shares sold by existing ones. This task is all the more complex and time consuming in that potential targets may be from very different sectors and geographic locations. It is nonetheless a valuable mission if the issuer knows from the beginning what it is looking for and why and how it should plan its profiling and segmentation.

But let's face it: some say that there is no such thing as long-term shareholders anymore and finding the "perfect" shareholder may well be the Holy Grail of Investor Relations (see Table 3.1).

It is therefore important to try and strike the right long-term balance between retail and institutional share ownership with some of the following criteria in mind (see Table 3.2):

- Having a fairly precise idea about your ideal free float structure will also help you choose the appropriate underwriter the next time you want to launch a capital increase: A bank with a balanced mix of retail and institutional clients can provide the shareholder diversity you are looking for. If your primary intent is to target individual investors, you should make sure that the underwriting syndicate includes not only global investment banks, but also a large retail bank with a nationwide network.
- Also, counting too many foreign institutional investors in your capital may cause considerable swing in the price of your stock the day they decide to sell, if a major macroeconomic crisis happens. It is traditional to sell off positions abroad and return to their home markets. This also explains why it is important to build a strong domestic investor base.

Table 3.1 The Benefits of a Diversified Shareholder Base

Diversity in Holding Periods	Diversity Across Shareholder Types	Diversity in Investment Styles
Long-term oriented shareholders can be expected to keep the shares for anywhere between several months and years.	The stock is more liquid.	There is little chance that shareholders with different strategies will buy or sell shares at the same time.
They support the company's long-term vision and strategy.	The buying or selling of large blocks of shares has a lesser impact on the stock price.	The stock price is less volatile.
They are less likely to be moved by quarterly earnings which could induce the company into "smoothing" reported earnings performance in the short-term.	Control of the company is more diluted, which may help facilitate governance.	
Various investment horizons provide additional liquidity.		

3.2.1 Intelligent Targeting

In order to go beyond identifying existing shareholders, initial targeting groundwork pays off and should be methodically conducted:

- Understand the market. Find out who is currently not an investor in your company and why you should want him or her to become a shareholder.
- Be specific with the brokers and investment banks who want to take you and your management on the road and make sure every meeting is justified from your perspective first.

Readymade institutional targeting tools with data-mining techniques can be purchased to identify investors whose investment style and criteria are compatible with your company's fundamentals and your free-float strategy. You will achieve positive return on investing in these tools as well as on developing your own custom database if you design a strategy to attract new shareholders. The process might be compared to

Table 3.2 Comparative Advantages of Shareholder Types

	Individual Shareholders	Institutional Shareholders
Pros	Strong sense of ownership. Strong loyalty, can be very instrumental in fending off hostile bids. Will easily participate in bonds or equity issues. Very good at creating "buzz" and popularity for smaller companies or companies that are not exactly households' names. Easy to mobilize for consumer related goods or service companies or utilities. Large retail shareholder base positively viewed by institutional investors.	Are less expensive to cater to. Add prestige and confer status. Can be large shareholders and efficiently ensure successful placement of shares. Provide geographical diversification. Investor meetings useful to strategic thinking.
Cons	Costly to maintain and retain (dedicated tools and staff in particular). Make small investments. Require specific financial policy (dividend distribution, gratis issue, etc).	Difficult and costly to identify. Potential increase in volatility fuelled by large hedge fund presence or activist shareholder groups. Growing tendency to ask for board seats and to try to influence company strategy as they increase their holdings. Demand substantial top management time. Discrepancy between management time horizon and short-term orientation of certain fund managers.

a marketing approach involving market studies. Below are a few ways to approach this strategy:

- List and make direct contact with foreign institutional investors that have shares in the your market but not in your company;
- Specifically identify those that have invested in securities issued by the competition but not your company. The idea is that the funds in question are interested in the issuer's sector and may decide at some point to take advantage of differences between valuation multiples. The criteria on which such decisions are based often include the following:
  - Market capitalization;
  - Free float;
  - Sector;
  - Business model and, within it, such factors as operating profitability, cash flow, payout ratios.

To make sure that the information obtained about institutional investors is exhaustive, issuers should also assess the following:

- *The origin of the funds under management.* The institution may manage assets for third parties such as pension funds, for instance, in its home country as well as abroad or for its own proprietary accounts.
- *Amounts under management.* This type of approach can allow issuers to target second-tier institutions that may be of medium size but have non-negligible investment potential.
- *Their organizational structure.* This refers to how investment decisions are made and whether teams are organized by economic sector or country. IROs should know ahead of time whether to prepare for an individual meeting with, and presentation to, analysts or decision makers. The type of questions asked will be very different depending on the organizational structure of the institution.
- *The valuation and decision-making criteria.* The IRO will also want to find out what their main sources of information are, how their buy-side analysts are ranked, and so on. As regards the latter point, investors often like to ask IROs which analyst or analysts they feel best cover their company.
- *Investment style and strategies.* Short-term or long-term focus, quantitative, index-based or relative performance, and so on. The main management styles are listed hereafter.
  - *Long-only funds:*
    - Growth: funds are invested in companies with above-average growth potential (it means those that operate in buoyant sectors).
    - Value: managers target companies that they deem to be undervalued and have rerating potential.
    - Growth at a reasonable price (GARP): GARP investors look for companies that are showing consistent earnings growth above market trends while excluding companies that have very high valuations. In other words, they are looking for growth-oriented stocks with relatively low price/earnings (P/E) multiples in normal market conditions.
    - Index funds: managers reproduce the structure of specific indices with their performances and risk levels.
    - Sovereign Wealth Funds (SWFs): these funds are state-owned entities, with states investing in any type of securities or assets. Their countries' financial wealth, derived, for instance, from large trade surpluses, high oil prices, or the foreign exchange that comes from currency transactions, gives them considerable investment power. They enjoy a mixed reputation, as their levels

of transparency differ widely from one fund to another. Given their size, they tend to favour very liquid investment opportunities and large market capitalizations.
  ○ Socially responsible investors (SRI): they favor companies that have outright corporate social responsibility policies, in terms of environmental and safety protection, corporate governance, labor management, taking a view that these companies tend to outperform the other categories in the long term.
- *Hedge funds.* They are divided into a number of subcategories, of which arbitrage, event-driven, and tactical strategies such as "long-short," which combine purchases or "long positions" with short sales. These funds primarily target absolute rather than relative performance. Unlike traditional "long-only" funds, they often rely on short selling and leverage, meaning they take on debt to increase their potential gains. Investment timeframes vary and can be extremely short. For instance, managers may bet on differences between guidance announced by a company, analyst expectations, and reported results. This means that they will not necessarily be too interested in companies that say exactly what they will do and do exactly what they say. Not as closely regulated as others (if regulated at all, some might argue), and at times rather opaque, these funds have considerable power.

This classification system is worth being aware of but has limitations insofar as the following are concerned:

- It does not show whether, within the same hedge fund, shares are held in "long-only" or "long-short" compartments, making profiling complex.
- Managers or departments may have different and more or less specialized investment styles within a given institution.

The above traditional investor segmentation has its limits and is insufficient to help efficiently prioritize management time. Other criteria should be taken into consideration, and even preferred such as:

- Typical holding period;
- Portfolio concentration;
- Decision-making process.

How long does the investor hold a position? How many stocks are held in the fund? How often do they rotate within one year? How many professionals are involved in the investment decision-making process? Responses to these questions will help the IRO understand whether the fund manager can spend enough time assessing a company's strategy and his or her ability to stand by management for the long term, without being deterred by short-term volatility. All in all, is it really worth the CEO meeting with this portfolio manager?

Many IROs should revisit their targeting process and make sure that their management no longer spends an inordinate amount of time with the wrong investors. Everyone will benefit from a more focused approach:

- The CEO will be able to spend less time in unfruitful Investor Relations meetings and more on running the company and implementing the long-term strategy;
- The IRO will be in a more visible and stronger role, internally and externally, as the indispensable bridge between the company and the investment community;
- The company valuation will, overtime, positively reflect this strategic approach.

3.2.1.1 Meeting with hedge funds

Issuers may demonize hedge funds, and quite justifiably so in certain cases, but they nonetheless constitute a separate category of investors. Their research is often extremely sophisticated, their knowledge of your industry impressive. This is why meeting with hedge funds can also help enhance management's strategic thinking. Having one or two good contacts in the hedge-fund community is useful, and discussions may be fruitful, albeit challenging, for all involved. Companies should not refuse to meet with such contacts on principle, but rather be vigilant about the ones that they do meet and by whom they are represented.

First of all, the IRO should list the reasons why they should be meeting with hedge funds. Is it to generate greater liquidity? Higher volatility? To remove uncertainty in the stock conveyed by market rumors?

Indeed, management time is incredibly valuable, and the IRO has the right to be selective about who in the company structure meets with which hedge fund, if at all. Dialogue with hedge funds should be a two-way street as with any other institution. In particular, you should insist on obtaining information about their holdings in your company directly from them.

3.2.1.2 Activist shareholders or the limitation of institutional targeting

Lastly, this inventory of potential shareholders would not be complete if it did not mention activist shareholders, although they can hardly be deemed to meet the criteria of the ideal shareholder.

Activist shareholders are known to discreetly build a position in a company, make a lot of noise, and ask for seats on the board of directors. In dealing with activist shareholders, management and the Investor Relations team should absolutely establish the view of the other shareholders. Are the activists alone in their thinking or are their views supported by other institutions in the investment community? All investors at some point in time take an active role. Listen to what they have to say because they have done a lot of work on which they have based their investment decision, as well as possibly their decision to become activists.

A basic rule is to try and keep the debate out of the public eye as much as possible, as it is less time consuming, more efficient, and more constructive.

3.2.2 The "Seed, Harvest and Lock" Approach to Investor Relations

Once the targeting exercise is complete, it is the IRO's job to initiate the "seeding" phase. The IRO will proactively contact analysts and investors who have been identified as potential buyers of the company's shares, in order to present its products, its business model, its strategy, and its growth prospects.

Hopefully, you will have successfully convinced the institution to consider building a position in your company. It will be time to "harvest" and the chief operating officer (COO) or the chief financial officer (CFO) may have to be involved to secure the fund manager's decision to invest in your company.

A meeting with the CEO is usually required to convert initial ownership into a larger stake. That is the "lock" phase of the process. By the way, the IRO should see to it that the CEO and the chairman have personal contacts with the chief investment officers at major institutions. Such relationships can prove useful if the company is under attack or needs to have specific resolutions approved at the shareholders' meeting.

This approach provides another reason why it is important to set out specific selection criteria during the targeting process. It will also optimize the amount of time management devotes to Investor Relations, which should in any case not exceed 20 percent.

The matrix below (Table 3.3) should help you implement this approach by allocating senior management and IR time where it can be best optimized ("whom goes where when" – See also section 3.6.10).

3.3 Understanding Market Expectations

A retail investor, who may be planning to buy a car, will want an idea of where the share price might stand at the end of the year so that he or she

Table 3.3 Roadshow Matrix

		CEO	CFO	IRO	Other (*e.g. Operations, directors*)
Q1	Roadshow				
	Conference				
	One-on-One				
	Other				
Q2	Roadshow				
	Conference				
	One-on-One				
	Other				
Q3	Roadshow				
	Conference				
	One-on-One				
	Other				
Q4	Roadshow				
	Conference				
	One-on-One				
	Other				

can sell shares at the highest price, whereas some analysts will seek to check the plausibility of earnings estimates for the next five years. All in all, listed companies must respond every day to a wide range of expectations and meet all of them in one way or another.

There are expectations about both the form and content of financial communications.

3.3.1 Form

- More and more people base their definition of accessibility on how easily information can be found on a company's website. They will also look at whether they have a specific contact within the company. The contact's information, with the person's name, should be clearly shown on the documents the company sends out. It may be the person in charge of relations with retail investors, an IRO, or a press officer. Rating agencies will usually look to the IRO (or the Debt IRO if there is one), the CFO, or the treasurer for information, while journalists will want to speak to the corporate communications and press relations team, saving any technical questions for the IR department. Clients and suppliers are likely to go through their usual contacts within the company. In short, easily identifiable contacts organized by audience contributes to a "customer-friendly" image.

Companies are legally required to release material information in a timely manner, and IROs may need to respond quickly to requests for information received by phone or e-mail. This is part of what defines a company's responsiveness.

Regularity is an asset when it comes to organizing the financial calendar. There should be no long intervals between announcements, but rather a steady flow of updates on developments within the company ("the news flow"). If your company only issues financial press releases at given intervals, it is likely to create peaks of volatility in your stock price around the announcement day. It is also wise to aim for regularity in meetings with existing or targeted priority shareholders and fund managers: Plan your meeting schedules accordingly, not every now and then.

3.3.2 Content

Clarity is a key asset when it comes to crafting convincing messages. In financial communications as in anything else, clearly expressed ideas have most power. IROs, hired in part because of their writing skills, will avoid using technical or financial jargon (or, worse, acronyms!) in their own communications. They will see to it that the prose of the legal department in documents or press releases for financial transactions is clear to all. The U.S. Securities and Exchange Commission (SEC) has even developed guidelines for companies to use in their filings, tellingly entitled, *A Plain English Handbook*.

Messages should be consistent over time and delivered via the same channels. Consistency is a key to successful financial communications, as described at length in the earlier sections of this book.

Regulations require that data be comparable, and companies must at the least make comparisons with the previous year possible. It is particularly difficult to describe a company's underlying performance when it has made acquisitions or disposals, or has booked restructuring charges. In response to the creation of numerous and varied bases of comparisons, the publication of pro forma statements is now regulated on most major stock exchanges. Markets will not be easily fooled by comparisons that have been deliberately forced to look as good as possible.

In other words, making information clear and accessible is in fact a way to generate more positive opinion on the stock.

When it comes to content, quality Investor Relations should be thorough and meet all of the criteria outlined above. Investor Relation messages should be as follows:

- *Objective.* Bad news should not be hidden, and press releases and annual reports should describe difficulties with objectivity and humility. A degree of frankness and integrity will always pay off in the long term.
- *Informative.* Issuers should bear in mind at all times that their Investor Relations target audiences need not necessarily know much about the sector or the company itself. This means that, if a press release announces that earnings are in line with guidance, it should also say what this guidance was. Bear in mind that every communication is an opportunity to raise awareness and trigger interest for your company.
- Lastly, announcements should reflect the company's overall strategy. For instance, each earnings release should be presented as a step toward the achievement of goals. The number of updates given on the progress toward this goal will depend on whether the targets in question cover the current year or several years. For instance, you do not necessarily need to put your quarterly performance in the perspective of your five-year strategic plan!

As popular as electronic communication has become, it will not replace meetings with executives or the publication of company documents. As they familiarize themselves with the expectations—or habits or requirements—of each type of audience, IROs will realize that the following:

- Certain non-specialized fund managers prefer to be invited to public meetings to hear the questions asked by those with more specific expertise, and in particular the sell-side analysts;
- Institutional investors that are swamped with e-mail may refuse to receive all of a company's press releases but will, on the other hand, expect its website to be well designed and regularly updated;
- Analysts and investors might be willing to participate in the same field trip but will not appreciate the presence of journalists. It is in the interest of issuers to plan separate outings;
- The press (online or offline) is still the best way to reach retail investors and build the company's reputation. This is particularly important for midcaps.

3.4 Developing the Financial Calendar

Financial calendars are planned to comply with legal deadlines for financial information disclosure, of which the main categories revolve around the following (see Table 3.4):

- Quarterly, interim, and full-year revenue and earnings announcements;
- Annual general shareholders meetings.

3.4.1 Who Prepares the Financial Calendar?

Listed companies must comply with certain regulatory deadlines for disclosing financial information, failing which they may get into trouble with market authorities: Indeed, these listed companies sometimes make a point in issuing a press release listing the companies that have not respected their obligations to release full-year earnings before a certain date. Bearing these deadlines in mind and knowing that they are more likely to be shortened than extended, companies can then develop their Investor Relations calendars. It is best to work backward and begin as far as possible in advance—ideally at least one year ahead of time.

Under the coordination of the IR department, different players must be involved in this planning process:

- *Internal legal department.* It knows what kind of information must be disclosed and by when, factoring in the board meetings held to approve the annual and half-yearly, in some cases quarterly, financial statements, convene the AGM, and so on.
- *Financial reporting and consolidation.* They will dictate by when consolidated data and financial statements will be available and validated by the statutory auditors.
- *Operations division managers.* The Investor Relations team will want to have enough of their time to discuss the past performances of their respective divisions, the outlook for the future, and possibly, involve them in Investor Relations events such as an analyst day.
- *Corporate communications.* This department will inform the Investor Relations team of its own schedule of events and media stories: management interviews, special features on technology, participation to major conferences, trade show appearances, etc.
- *The chief of staff, that is, the president or the CEO.* The IRO will be able to look at management's schedule and block out dates for earnings preparation and investor meetings, for instance.

Table 3.4 Sample Financial Calendar for Fiscal Year Ending December 31st

FIRST QUARTER

JANUARY

S	M	T	W	T	F	S
1	2	3	4	5	6	7
8	9	10	11	12	13	14
15	16	17	18	19	20	21
22	23	24	25	26	27	28
29	30	31				

FEBRUARY

S	M	T	W	T	F	S
			1	2	3	4
5	6	7	8	9	10	11
12	13	14	15	16	17	18
19	20	21	22	23	24	25
26	27	28				

MARCH

S	M	T	W	T	F	S
			1	2	3	4
5	6	7	8	9	10	11
12	13	14	15	16	17	18
19	20	21	22	23	24	25
26	27	28	29	30	31	

Event	Communication channels		Comments
Full-year earnings	Press release	☑	■ Depending on regulations and the amount of time required to produce consolidated financial statements, they company may report its full-year sales and earnings at the same time or separately
	Presentation		■ Depending on its IR strategy and legal requirements, the issuer may include financial advertising in its financial communications
	Conference call		
	Shareholder letter		
	Consolidated financial statements	☑	■ Some large groups publish their annual report at the same time as their consolidated financial statements
	Annual report		
	Roadshows	☑	■ Issuers that report quarterly earnings announce their fourth-quarterly results simultaneously with their full-year earnings
	Press conference	☑	■ Given the large number of companies that report their results close together, roadshows should not be organized immediately after the reporting season in order to avoid congested institutional investors' schedules.

SECOND QUARTER

APRIL						
S	M	T	W	T	F	S
						1
2	3	4	5	6	7	8
9	10	11	12	13	14	15
16	17	18	19	20	21	22
	24	25	26	27	28	29

MAY						
S	M	T	W	T	F	S
	1	2	3	4	5	6
7	8	9	10	11	12	13
14	15	16	17	18	19	20
21	22	23	24	25	26	27
28	29	30	31			

JUNE						
S	M	T	W	T	F	S
				1	2	3
4	5	6	7	8	9	10
11	12	13	14	15	16	17
18	19	20	21	22	23	24
25	26	27	28	29	30	

Event

Annual general meeting

Financial situation
First quarter

Communication Channels

	Press release	Presentation	Conference Call	Shareholder letter
Annual general meeting	☑	☑	☑	☑
Consolidated financial statements	☑			
Annual report	☑			
Roadshows	☑			
Press conference	☑			

Comments

- Public meetings are often held following full-year earnings releases but not for quarterly earnings. The latter are typically followed by conference calls, held after the press release has been sent out
- Annual general meetings are usually scheduled during the second quarter
  Annual reports are in most cases published for this occassion
- Besides the latter months of the year, June and November-December are good times to schedule:
  - Analyst Days
  - Strategy Roadshows

Continued

Table 3.4 Continued

THIRD QUARTER

JULY							AUGUST							SEPTEMBER						
S	M	T	W	T	F	S	S	M	T	W	T	F	S	S	M	T	W	T	F	S
						1			1	2	3	4	5						1	2
2	3	4	5	6	7	8	6	7	8	9	10	11	12	3	4	5	6	7	8	9
9	10	11	12	13	14	15	13	14	15	16	17	18	19	10	11	12	13	14	15	16
16	17	18	19	20	21	22	20	21	22	23	24	25	26	17	18	19	20	21	22	23
	25	26	27	28	29		27	28	29	30	31			24	25	26	27	28	29	30

Event	Communication Channels		Comments
First-half earnings	Press release	☑	■ Like the full-year results, interim earnings may be reported in stages and include commentson the financial statements for the second quarter
	Presentation	☑	
	Conference call	☑	■ To save on costs, companies are increasingly organizing conference calls Rather than public meetings to present their interim earnings
	Shareholder letter	☑	
	Consolidated financial statements	☑	
	Annual report	☑	
	Roadshows	☑	
	Press conference	☑	

FOURTH QUARTER

OCTOBER

S	M	T	W	T	F	S
1	2	3	4	5	6	7
8	9	10	11	12	13	14
15	16	17	18	19	20	21
22	23	24	25	26	27	28
29	30	31				

NOVEMBER

S	M	T	W	T	F	S
			1	2	3	4
5	6	7	8	9	10	11
12	13	14	15	16	17	18
19	20	21	22	23	24	25
26	27	28	29	30		

DECEMBER

S	M	T	W	T	F	S
					1	2
3	4	5	6	7	8	9
10	11	12	13	14	15	16
17	18	19	20	21	22	23
	25	26	27	28	29	30

Event

- Financial situation
- Third quarter
- Analyst Day

Communication Channels

- Press release ☑
- Presentation ☑
- Conference call ☑
- Shareholder letter ☑
- Consolidated financial statements ☑
- Annual report ☑
- Roadshows ☑
- Press conference ☑

Comments

- This is a good time of the year to organize an analyst day, but not during the quarterly earnings reporting period.
- The fourth quarter is when the IRO:
  – Prepared the budget for the following year
  – Launches calls for tenders to select service providers, particularly for the annual report
  – Updated the financial calendar
  – Measures the effectiveness of its IR program
  – Drafts its IR strategy proposal to senior management for the following year

The IRO will pay particular attention to seeing that the company has not only all of the relevant data and performance indicators, but also enough preparation time to develop content for the Investor Relations messages and strategy. The IRO will also want to find out about the competition's financial calendar to avoid any overlaps: earnings releases and conference call times, participation in broker-sponsored events, field trips, investor day, and so on. It is not unusual for the IRO to ask sell-side analysts for industry-wide calendars or to contact peers in other companies to find out about their respective schedules of events, if they are not available on their websites.

Timelines (see Resources) for each event can begin only after the calendar has been established. While designating owners of the event, it reduces the level of execution risk and helps identify potential productivity gains and savings. For instance, early advance planning and scheduling may help you obtain attractive prices on meeting rooms and venues or documentation mailing costs for the annual meeting. Furthermore, analysts will appreciate receiving a "save-the-day" before invitations arrive from the competition.

3.4.2 Financial Calendar Content

The calendar should include, at the very least, the regulatory disclosure deadlines for announcing sales and earnings and holding the AGM.

It is then going to be supplemented with additional internal dates (board of directors' meetings, insider-trading black-out periods, dividend payment date). Other events such as quiet periods as well as blackout periods, described below, should be factored in. And school holidays, too!

All these in turn determine the company's annual calendar and Investor Relations program. The Investor Relations department will add any events for shareholders, financial analysts, investors, and/or the media, which it will either be organizing on its own initiative or will be attending, such as:

- Earnings conference calls;
- Nonfinancial news releases (new business wins, corporate events, product launches);
- Investor conferences;
- Roadshows;
- Analyst and investor days;
- Site visits;
- Trade show appearances.

3.4.3 Publication of the Financial Calendar

It is considered best practice to post the annual financial calendar in an easy-to-find manner in the Investor Relations section of the company's

Website. Some companies make it a press release at the beginning of the fiscal year or send it to the investment community with their season's greetings. Upcoming Investor Relations dates should be mentioned in each financial press, in order to make analysts' life easier, when they want to mention them in their reports.

Companies usually specify that the dates are provisional and subject to change. This latter option should be enough to convince any company that is still reticent about providing the market with a financial calendar.

By making their financial calendar available to the public, companies demonstrate the following assets:

- *Discipline.* A calendar reflects the different phases in a company's annual cycle and offers a strong basis from which to anticipate each disclosure deadline.
- *Visibility.* A company that announces its financial communications and Investor Relations schedules differentiates itself from those that do not.
- *Credibility.* The market understands that the listed company has organized itself in such a way as to meet its obligations and facilitate the market's job.
- *Professionalism.* When an annual financial calendar is published, it shows that the company has aligned its Investor Relations with the best international standards.

Once a year, it is a good idea to analyze the past year's calendar to see, for instance, whether earnings were released before there was time for the results to be analyzed in-depth or whether work should have been started earlier on the annual report to ensure that it would be ready in time for the annual meeting.

3.4.4 Quiet Periods

Although not always regulated by lawmakers and market authorities, it is highly recommended that quiet periods be observed prior to regulatory disclosures, for instance, of sales and earnings.

The duration may range between two and four weeks, depending on the company, based on the following:

- *The sector in which it operates.* For instance, in industries where half of quarterly sales are generated within the last two weeks of the quarter, this information is particularly material and price sensitive. The IRO will thus refrain from any contact with the investment community

and avoid making any statements, even vague ones. This is a difficult situation to be in. Financial analysts will often press the IRO for clues and try to get a privileged indication of earnings trends to put in the "previews" or reports in which they will reiterate their earnings estimates for the company, a few days prior to the actual release.
- *The financial statement production schedule.* How quickly can the company consolidate its earnings after the end of the reporting period? For instance, if earnings are released one month after the end of the reporting period, the quiet period should begin no later than the 15th of the following month, that is, two weeks later. Likewise, if the results are published two months after the end of the first semester, the quiet period may start one month after the half-year ends.

This rule applies to all company spokespersons. The company will refrain (or actually abstain) from any interaction whatsoever, about any subject, with journalists, analysts, or investors during this period, unless it is to provide strictly factual or historical information. Beware of the investor who is going to promise you that he only wants to talk about strategy and not about the quarter's numbers. This is a risky game. Anything you might say, and the body language that goes with it, may be interpreted subjectively. The more closely companies follow this rule, the less risk there is that privileged information will be disclosed, even unintentionally. The enforcement of the Fair Disclosure Regulation in the United States or the Transparency Directive in Europe has led to the indictment of several CEOs and IROs. The risk is really not worth it.

The quiet period ends with the press release announcing the company's earnings.

3.4.5 Black-out Periods

While both black-out and quiet periods aim at preventing insider trading, the distinction between them is not always clear. Companies will often use either of them indifferently when they want to indicate that they are not available for comments on current trading or to update on prospects or any other price sensitive information. The length of the period which is voluntarily set by the company can last anywhere from three days to several weeks before it announces sales or results for the most recently closed accounting period. The black-out period usually ends a few days after the trigger event has occurred.

However, it is important to note that market authorities draw a distinction between quiet periods and black-out periods, with the latter specifically referring to a number of days or weeks immediately preceding an earnings release, the announcement of a merger, or the launch of a public offering. In that case, shares and related securities of the company cannot be traded by insiders such as company directors, officers and certain employees. An exception to this principle is when these trades are executed through an automated program.

The Investor Relations and the legal departments work closely on the elaboration and the observance of this company policy, which is part of the disclosure policy. As such, it can be posted on the company's website.

It is worth noting that black-out periods may also correspond to the period when analysts involved in a transaction, such as an Initial Public Offering, are banned from issuing investment recommendations on the offer.

3.5 Crafting Compelling Messages

Contrary to what some believe, Investor Relations are not solely about the following:

- Company finances, numbers, and consolidated financial statements, all of which become yesterday's news once they are published;
- Good news.

It is generally agreed today that between one-third and possibly more than half of a company's value is attributable to non-financial and intangible assets that cannot be found in financial statements. In addition, companies that demonstrate humility and honesty when they fail tend to fare better than those that only talk about what is going right.

The field of, and required expertise for, Investor Relations is expanding as portfolio managers increasingly include new variables in their valuation models and investment criteria: innovation in new product development, intellectual capital, research and development activities, use of technology, corporate brand, management reputation, corporate governance, sustainable development, and corporate social responsibility (see Table 3.5).

A company's strategy cannot be analyzed simply by looking at the figures, which are in reality just the tip of the iceberg.

The boundaries between financial, technical, operational, commercial, organizational, social, and environmental factors are thus blurrier than ever, making it more difficult, but also more necessary than ever, to achieve consistency over time, format, and channels of communications. With this in mind, the messages developed and delivered by Investor Relations should tell the audience the following about the company:

- Overall vision of the company;
- The good news and the bad news;

Table 3.5 Investor Relations Messages by Theme

Markets	Business model	Strategy	Organization	Teams	Performances
Competition Regulations, Macroeconomics	Clients Revenue streams Growth drivers	Strategic priorities Operational objectives Financial objectives	Brand awareness Reputation Brand equity, quality of products Human resources Intellectual capital Labor organization Culture Adaptability Corporate governance Environmental respect Processes Communications Transparency Risk factor management	CEO reputation Management team: – experience – compensation policy – credibility Ability to attract and retain key executive talents Alliances and networks	Financial statements Segment analysis Procurement Acquisitions Innovation Sensitivity analysis (exchange rates, interest rates, raw material prices, etc.)

- The company's competitive advantages;
- Its performances, as measured by the indicators that are used internally and by the financial market's favorite metrics.

It is essential that the company should seek to maintain the same level of transparency and of disclosure in terms of quality and quantity, as at the time of its IPO. As a principle, issuers must thus refrain from merely giving the most favorable picture.

In its efforts to educate financial markets about its business, the company will systematically provide a definition of acronyms as well as of financial ratios, and a glossary of technical terms.

3.5.1 Writing Clearly

Writing clearly is a "must-have" skill. It can really enhance reputation, or it can deter your target audiences from reading anything that your company writes. You should entice your readers, not overwhelm them. In certain countries, the regulator is requiring that texts be written in a clear and readily understandable style, given the excesses of "legalese" contained in financial documentation. Indeed, this is quite a challenge as the same document will be targeted at varied audiences, with varying levels of understanding, education, and knowledge.

The language used should be direct and simple, reflecting your company's personality. And it may be advisable to hire professional copywriters and native speakers. In this respect, never forget to take enough time to review translations, if you can. Translating texts is never enough: Rewriting is often a necessity to ensure it is going to be read with pleasure and understood by the reader and that it uses enough idiomatic and colloquial expressions.

3.5.2 Financial and Strategic Messages

3.5.2.1 The business environment

Listed companies must describe the business environment, the sector, the cycles in which they operate, specifying the following:

- Regulations that affect their activity in terms of obligations, business opportunities, and future performance;
- The economic environment as reflected in growth rates in the countries in which they are established, interest rates, exchanges rates, raw materials prices, climate trends, consumer spending patterns, and so

on. This description should include an analysis of a company's sensitivity to the key exogenous factors to which it is exposed and any seasonal aspects of their business;
- The competitive environment and their positioning with regard to their main competitors.

In addition to own company data or estimates, it is advisable to educate the investor or the analyst about your macroeconomic environment. Provide external information sources and list them.

Presenting the competitive environment requires objectivity and caution. Using abusive language about competitors will inevitably backfire on corporate reputation. Remember that investors and analysts can provide a wealth of information on the competitive environment, which makes the dialogue IROs have with them all the more interesting.

Among various skills, an IRO who is as knowledgeable as can be about the company's sector and cycle, will be able to do the following:

- *Identify and help develop sector-specific indicators.* For instance, the financial analysts for the software industry look at the number of existing customers compared to new customers and the breakdown of revenues between licence and maintenance. Telecom operators are asked to provide gross and net customer additions, customer acquisition costs, average revenue per line/product/user/employee/unit, just to name a few.
- *Anticipate upturns and downturns and develop effective messages.* These will notably highlight the company's strategy and actions to adjust to a changing environment. For instance, if your company has an international footprint, explain how regional differences may positively affect your business and product cycles.

In this respect, you should also be able to notice when investors are wary of lengthy explanations by management of the economic environment in which its company operates. The reason is simple: They are already well aware of it and overflowed with macroeconomic information.

3.5.2.2 Organization

Messages will focus on the legal structure of the company and the governance rules applied. Information about corporate governance is tightly regulated and is required by most of the world's major stock exchanges (see also Sections 3.5.6 and 3.5.7).

Analysts, investors, and journalists will partly evaluate the company's reputation on the basis of awards and positions in various rankings for product or service quality.

This is also an opportunity for a company to describe the quality of their human resources, labor policies, employment attractiveness, and sustainable development policy.

Corporate business vision and mission statements may also be published to create a framework of values adopted within and around the company, associating all the company's stakeholders, including the financial markets.

3.5.2.3 Human resources

Companies will focus on the experience, depth and diversity (gender, geographical origin, education) of staff's skills, providing all the information needed to allow markets to evaluate their renown and reputation.

This is one highly visible area in which dynamic interaction is required between financial, corporate, and internal communications.

3.5.2.4 Commercial, technological, and financial performance

Companies highlight their track record in terms of financial results as well as achievements in other fields: industrial, commercial, and technological achievements, for instance. Wherever and whenever possible, they provide the following:

- *Presentation of their different businesses and respective market positions.* In this respect, communicating on market shares and leadership is tricky, particularly when it comes to financial or transaction-related documentation: Market authorities may require that these message be supported by third-party evidence.
- *Historic trends and performance comparisons.* For instance, comparing results over a period of several years (such as in "Sales growth exceeded 5 per cent for the third year in a row"), and not simply with the previous one ("Sales were up 5 per cent compared to the previous year"), gives a sense of strength and credibility of management's ability to implement strategic directions.
- The breakdown of performance is given for each division and geographic area, in accordance with applicable accounting standards, and in a manner that is consistent with their overall organization.
- The business or sector-specific indicator is mentioned in the previous section.

These "extra efforts" will give corporate messages even more impact.

Reported performances should also be explained by the internal and external factors that helped make them possible: Successful price increases for the company's products compensating for inflation in raw materials, restructuring measures positively impacting the cost base, lower interest rates, and falls in indebtedness reducing financial charges, and so on. Here again, there is an educational role for Investor Relations to play.

Past performances should wherever possible be correlated with the objectives the company has communicated to the markets. This is an opportunity to discuss milestones in achieving its strategy and stress whether if it is ahead or behind schedule.

What company management in general and Investor Relations in particular should refrain from talking about is how they are viewed by the financial market. It is not for the CEO to voice an opinion on how cheap or undervalued he feels the company is.

3.5.2.5 Business model

The presentation of a company's business model is focused on the financial criteria and on the key performance indicators that are applied in strategic planning and in the setting up of realistic targets and credible objectives. Examples include the following:

- Compound annual growth rates;
- Revenue breakdowns by division (or product lines) and geographic area;
- Market shares;
- Annual research and development expenditure;
- Operating income as a percentage of sales;
- Dividend payout ratio;
- Cash flow as a percentage of sales, before and after capital expenditure ("free cash flow");
- The capital intensity of the business as expressed through capital expenditure as a percentage of sales;
- Net debt-to-equity ratios;
- Cash and cash equivalents.

The internal financial reporting systems must be structured to provide data that are relevant to the understanding of the company's business model. In this respect, international accounting standards require that financial reporting and internal organization match. For instance, if your business is organized by product lines as opposed to geographical regions, you will see to it that this is part of the presentation of your business model.

In certain cases, some corporate governance and socially responsible investment metrics are factored into the business model as well. All can serve as a basis for management compensation and for the attribution of performance-related pay, either in cash or in shares, when such remuneration policies are in place.

Companies must be vigilant not to give in to passing trends that favor one ratio over another. If they are in the process of launching a financial operation, they may also have to withstand pressure from investment banks that want to structure the business model to make it attractive to their own clients, possibly to the detriment of the ideal shareholder base targeted by the company, and away from the way management is actually running the company. Note that portfolio managers pay close attention to how robust a business model is in making their investment decisions.

The business model presented to the market should be stable over time except where significant events such as acquisitions cause it to change.

Companies that present their business models clearly show that visibility on their activity is good, even if they do not give targets. The simpler and clearer the business model, the easier it will be for analysts to build their models and determine the value of the company.

Lastly, do not exasperate analysts by reclassifying your financials too often. It means that they have to rewrite their entire valuation model. Try to keep your core presentation uniform year after year. If, for instance, you have changed the fundamentals of your business through a major acquisition, provide a detailed reconciliation and variance analysis. If this applies to your company, make sure you properly explain measures that contrast with Generally Accepted Accounting Principles (GAAP) and reconcile to the reported numbers.

3.5.2.6 Strategy

Companies should develop specific presentations for the senior management to talk about their longer-term strategy and not simply make it a part of their results announcements. The goal is to attract maximum attention and not be distracted by short-term achievements.

When discussing their strategy, companies should also provide performance indicators:

- that enable the market to evaluate how successfully a strategy is being implemented;
- for which management is accountable.

The following principles should apply:

- Align internal and external key performance indicators ("KPIs");
- 1 strategic objective → 1 key performance indicator;
- No key performance indicator available? No message.

In other words, management should exert extreme caution before it communicates a given strategic objective but has no metric to be held accountable for. It is wise to stay away from mainstream, generic messages that can apply to virtually every company ("profitable growth," "value creation" are good proxies of this) and become meaningless if not properly substantiated.

Strategic messages are particularly important when the goal is to prepare the market for changes resulting, for instance, from an acquisition or a move into a new geographic area. Such news will be readily understood, and maybe even endorsed by the market as soon as it is announced if it is consistent with the strategy the company has presented over time. Investors do not like surprises. This is another reason why communications too must be long-term oriented. The share may trend higher or lower in the two days that follow a strategic announcement, but the important thing is where it stands two years later.

A clear explanation of the strategy goes hand in hand with a clear explanation of the risks attached to it.

Strategy messages should be developed together with those supporting the business model. This can be done using the capital allocation approach: what can be invested? What can be returned to shareholders?

3.5.2.7 Risk and uncertainties

Risk disclosure statements are part of the documentation legally required from issuers. They are usually the subject of fierce negotiations between companies, lawyers, and market authorities. Some companies have been put under the spotlight for publishing risk statements too vaguely or for not updating them regularly. Once more, the IRO should closely monitor what lawyers may recommend and ensure that the excess of legalism is not counterproductive from the market understanding and company valuation standpoints.

These statements can come in the form of dozens of pages of legal language, enough to discourage any investors who take what they read literally.

In recent years, the SEC has started to require listed companies to discuss the effects of global warming and efforts to curb climate change when disclosing business risks to investors.

For instance, efforts to limit the impact of climate change may increase costs for plants that have high emissions of carbon dioxide. Global warming may contribute to floods and hurricanes that lead to increased claims for insurance companies.

What investors want to know is that your company has a map of issues presenting high risks and an organization in place to address them. It is up to the company to define what a material risk is that might influence investment decisions.

The difficulty for IROs, as well as for investors, lies in dealing with information that is not standardized and is often reported differently from one company to another.

The disclosure of risk factors (see Table 3.6) has also been expanded to include uncertainties that can affect business performance, with some companies going as far as dedicating a section to these issues on their website. This is actually a proactive approach to risk communications, which is evidence of good governance and regulatory compliance. It can facilitate better understanding of the legal documentation, while inspiring confidence.

The IRO should be prepared to talk about the factors that are not within the company's control as well as those that are. Furthermore, taking into consideration the fact that investors do not all have the same risk appetite, the IRO should help them classify these risks. In this respect, Investor Relations will provide instructive objective and reassuring information about:

- the risks inherent in the company's business and its industry (economic environment, competition, technology, management, financial situation, risk of default or bankruptcy, and so on);
- the prevention and protection strategies in place.

3.5.3 Outlook

Regulations do not usually require companies to provide quantified outlook and objectives—also known as "guidance"—as opposed to qualitative statements. But markets do: it is a key factor in determining valuations. In certain cases in Europe for instance, the provision of forecasts in the company's issue prospectus may be subject to statutory audit, thus increasingly deterring companies from committing to quantitative financial targets.

If the company decides to provide some form of indication of its future performance in a forward-looking statement, it is better to do it as efficiently as possible. This is an extremely strategic decision in which the IRO must necessarily be closely involved.

It is not within the scope of this book to recommend whether or not companies should provide more or less detailed guidance, or how often they should do so, if at all. Actually, some companies may avoid giving any kind of guidance by consistently providing quality information about their business and current performance, along with a thorough description of their business model. The important thing to remember is that providing the "long view" is a continuous dialogue.

Table 3.6 Risks and Uncertainties

External risks
Economic uncertainty
Demand
Availability and cost of finance
Catastrophic business event
Climate change
Commodity prices and supply continuity
Regulation and legislation
Political context and stakeholder relationships
Country risk
Internal strategic risks
Investment strategy
Evolving risk profile
Development
Income sustainability
Capital structure—gearing
Financing strategy execution (e.g. capital requirements, liquidity, interest rates, exchange rates and rating)
Asset integrity, safety, health and security
Delivery of projects
Insurance
Operational performance
Resources discovery, estimation and development
Corporate and compliance risks
Reputation
Communication
People
Corporate responsibility risks
Environmental
Community

Nonetheless, there are ways to offer guidance that fit with a company's own best interests and applicable regulations. Analysts, investors, and journalists legitimately want to know where a company is heading. Companies must make this highly sensitive information available to the public at large, and not to just a few select individuals. Selective disclosure is highly reprehensible, and the legal consequences can be rather serious and costly.

3.5.3.1   *Forecasts, objectives, outlook and guidance*

Depending on market regulations, these terms can have very different meanings and can imply legal obligations that it is better to be aware of ahead of time. In some cases, forecasts must be approved by statutory auditors and not simply calculated by management.

Objectives are a bit more flexible and can often be used to communicate approximate targets or ranges, although the latter must not be too wide if they are to be credible.

Outlooks leave a good deal of leeway, depending on the time horizon covered by the company's strategic objectives and the type of qualitative and/or quantitative indicators used.

The translation of these terms into other languages may not be without consequences, depending on the applicable regulations.

3.5.3.2 Selecting guidance indicators

As discussed above, companies should allow the market to evaluate their performance based on the same indicators used internally. The idea is to stay away from long-term goals that are too generic and to provide some kind of a dashboard, combining standard financial information (sales, profitability, cash flow, etc.) and operating data that are specific to the company (geographic footprint, new clients, utilization rates for industrial facilities, etc.). It is also an opportunity to give more explanation about the business model.

The IRO is the best person to identify the indicators analysts are following and to give this information back to accounting and reporting departments. Demand for this information will be met bearing in mind constraints relating to the internal information systems and the possibly strategic (therefore confidential) nature of the information being sought. It is recommended that companies study the analysts' valuation models when deciding on the indicators to be communicated to the outside world and guided upon. This analysis will allow the IRO to anticipate what consequences the selection of specific objectives may have on the company's share price.

Whatever objectives the company ends up using, it will in all cases need to provide factual information about the working assumptions behind, whether these relate to the macroeconomic environment or factors that are specific to its businesses ("Our projected guidance assumption of 90.3 million dollars in non-operating items, excluding the foreign operations, is contingent upon the final results of our 2008/2009 loan agreement."). It may also be necessary to review the key risk factors associated with the realization of these targets. This is, by the way, an additional opportunity to show that the management team is aware of a range of possible long-term scenarios and has a clear strategy for dealing with each.

Depending on their type and degree of reliability, objectives may be any of the following:

- Qualitative ("Net income for the current year should be slightly higher than in the previous year.");

- Quantitative ("Sales are expected to exceed 850 million euros in three years' time.");
- Ranges ("Management expects cash flow from operations to back to between 300 and 400 million dollars in the medium term.");
- Worst-case or best-case scenarios ("A 10 percent increase in oil prices would add some 300 million dollars to our cost structure." "Given the exposure that our large development pipeline gives us to short-term interest rate fluctuations, increases or decreases in short-term interest rates could have positive or negative impact on our financial results.").

Absolute values should be avoided and targets should always be expressed in the conditional.

The importance of the objectives delivered to the market should not be overestimated or underestimated. In the event of an inquiry by market authorities or lawsuit, listed companies may be required to justify their disclosure content and procedures. Targets should be as consistent as possible with the company's internal earnings forecasts and based on information available at the time the forward-looking statements are made.

3.5.3.3 Choice of time horizon

The market expects companies to provide earnings forecasts for the current quarter, half year, full year, and the following year, at least, as well as indications for the ensuing years. The level of precision that analysts, in particular, seem to be counting on is sometimes absurd. Indeed, companies are supposed to help analysts do their job efficiently, but not do it for them. Every IRO will tell you that these boundaries can be a source of misunderstanding between the issuer and the markets.

Financial markets and listed companies do not trade in the same time horizon, and it is truly difficult to reconcile them. It is always in the company's interest to align the targets it makes public with its management methods. For instance, firms that have five-year strategic plans should provide an outlook for that period.

On the contrary, if a company is going through difficult period, short-term news flow will be critical.

There are proven advantages to giving targets for the medium and long terms.

- There is less risk of repeated changes to the said targets over the period, meaning that:
  ○ earnings estimates are in a more narrow range;
  ○ the share price is less volatile;

- The stock is more attractive to long-term investors. University research tends to show that companies that provide objectives for longer periods have a better chance of attracting long-term investors;
- The targets are more consistent with the company's business model;
- It is easier to reconcile internal objectives and external guidance.

Companies that use longer time horizons for their strategic objectives can blend qualitative and quantitative targets, applying the former to the year underway and factoring them into the medium-term outlook. For example, they might say, "Operating margin should continue to expand at the same pace as last year. Management is reiterating its target of achieving a 10 percent operating margin by the end of its five-year strategic plan."

Research has shown, notably in the United States, that there is no negative impact on the valuation of companies that stop or fail to provide guidance for the following quarter and focus instead on the full year or a longer period.

3.5.3.4 Changing the way you provide outlook and guidance

Companies may have to revise their targets upward or downward to take into account the results they effectively report and/or a change in the underlying assumptions they made when they first gave guidance.

From a legal standpoint, such revisions constitute price-sensitive, insider information that must be made public by a press release, usually the one issued to report earnings. Yet particularly in the United States, the forward-looking statements included in the earnings releases or presentation frequently states that "the company undertakes no obligation to publicly update or revise any forward-looking statements, whether as a result of new information, future events, or otherwise." This type of statement does not comply with the regulations of other countries where, precisely, companies do have the obligation to update the markets in case of any material change to previously disclosed information.

Similarly, some legal advisors will argue that, in between two reporting periods, a company should not respond to the question, "Are you confirming your earnings objectives?" as this might be deemed to constitute price-sensitive information.

Companies that provide targets for the medium and long terms will not necessarily have to add one year to their guidance every year, except under special circumstances (if they have acquired or divested themselves of a major portion of their activities, for instance).

As we have seen, there are many ways for companies to keep market participants informed of their prospects, their strategic goals, their financial objectives. With time, these targets may become unachievable or irrelevant, whatever the reason may be. If there is a guidance policy in place, management, and the board of directors in most cases, can decide to revise it and even put an end to this practice.

Because the value of a share is largely based on the investor's expectations (for instance, dividend distribution, potential capital gain), it is therefore the company's duty, and quite often a strict legal requirement, to communicate this change. This is a highly price-sensitive information.

Elaborating on the reason for change is a challenging Investor Relations exercise, sometimes akin to a crisis communications exercise. For sure, it will not go unnoticed, but, over time, it can also be beneficial to the company, if it is properly crafted.

- Reasons for change

This evolution can be driven by external and internal causes such as the following:

- *Macroeconomic factors.* In this instance, you may want to avoid being penalized for not being able to factor into your guidance the impact of elements over which your company has no control and whose volatility may greatly affect your ability to achieve your target, for good or bad. These factors include taxes, interest rates, currency, raw material prices, government-administered prices and other arbitrary price-setting mechanisms.
- *The performance track record.* A company that has consistently missed its earnings targets (and analysts' estimates) will have undoubtedly been badly bruised, share price wise. It may have to do with the quality and the reliability of its information systems, the inability to accurately forecast performance, an overly optimistic new management, or the incapacity to anticipate and adjust to a volatile operating environment. It can take several quarters or reporting periods before these problems can be remedied and a more cautious stance taken.
- *The business model.* This can be the case when part of your profits becomes more heavily dependent on any of the above macroeconomic factors, following a large acquisition, a major asset disposal, the launch of a new product, or a large investment in a new country. Another example justifying a change in the guidance policy may have to do with increasingly longer term contracts, with actual profit generation scheduled towards the end of the period, or beyond the current guidance horizon. These elements may increase or, on the contrary, reduce the predictability of the objectives you have disclosed for a given period.

- *Management.* A new chief executive officer may not feel committed to the objectives set by its predecessor and want to discontinue the policy. Or, the company may have learnt the lesson from a history of profit warnings and want to rebuilt market trust and establish a reputation for reliability.
- *Competitive environment.* A change in the way the company's direct competitors and peer group communicate their prospects may prompt the decision to revisit the guidance policy. Indeed, guidance provision can be a differentiator in investors' decision–making process, and, as a consequence affect the company's valuation.
- *Share ownership.* A change in shareholder structure may well require guidance policies to be aligned within the same group of companies, when several of them are listed. New majority shareholders may also require that the communication of a business and financial outlook be updated to suit their own objectives.

- Nature of change

Revisiting a guidance policy implies setting goals differently. This can take various forms:

- Updating the current guidance;
- Moving from qualitative to quantified goals, or, the other way around;
- Using a different set of key performance indicators and financial metrics;
- Lengthening the time horizon (rather than shortening it, usually);
- Stopping guidance altogether.

With the exception of the last-named, most extreme, change, these forms can be combined as described earlier in this Section 3.5.3, in order to form the new guidance policy.

- Managing change in guidance policy

Giving the risks involved—increased volatility, reduced analyst coverage, poorer financial reputation, just to name a few—switching from one guidance policy to another has to be a well thought out decision. It requires that management, the board of directors and the Investor Relations team be fully aligned.

In order for it to go as smoothly as possible, the change needs to be articulated in a timely and credible manner. Timing is important when you consider changing your guidance policy, as investors will wonder why you do this now.

In particular, if the new guidance results in less transparency (or if it is perceived as such), analysts and investors are likely to resent the change and be vocal about it. They will argue that, from now on, it will be more difficult for them to come up with realistic earnings estimates and make a well-informed investment recommendation or decision.

As the primary contacts for data-hungry sell-side analysts and investors, Investor Relations officers have a very important role to play in conducting the change in guidance policy. This will involve

- working closely with management in order to list the pros and cons of changing earnings guidance;
- analyzing industry practices, considering if, when and how other companies have revised their guidance policy in the past, and what market reactions have been, both upon the announcement and in the longer run;
- writing the rationale for the change, possibly including stopping earnings guidance;
- identifying metrics that are core to the valuation of the company, consistent with the execution of the strategy over a more extended horizon, and for which some kind of outlook should therefore be provided;
- submitting the calendar and the content of a new guidance policy for discussion and approval.

Because developing an effective new guidance policy is often a question of "give" and "take," the "give" part is a critical success factor. If the company decides to limit the number of metrics it sets objectives for, or to move away from annual guidance and only communicate longer term, qualitative directions, it will be best advised to compensate for this perceived decrease in disclosure by

- enriching its messages with more facts and data that are relevant to understanding its business model and long-term strategy;
- providing more information on the drivers of its end-user markets;
- being more specific about the external constraints, the macroeconomic assumptions that can affect its performance.

3.5.3.5 Stopping earnings guidance

Providing guidance is hardly ever a legal requirement. Furthermore, academic research has yet to demonstrate that its benefits substantially outweigh its costs.

It can actually well be the opposite, given the costs incurred in preparing the guidance and managing the company towards those goals...and missing them.

The many benefits of guidance usually include transparency, an effective way to establish earnings consensus, achieve higher valuation, increased liquidity and lower volatility. It is also a powerful internal incentivization (and compensation) tool and illustrates management's commitment to meet or even exceed the objectives. Furthermore, it is supposed to simplify the life of Investor Relations officers as it satisfies the requests from sell-side analysts. Arguably, monitoring earnings consensus without any form of guidance can be a difficult exercise that requires skill, caution and a perfect understanding of the potential legal implications. These are extremely powerful reasons why companies that do provide guidance are not keen to move away from this practice. One could observe that these are the same companies that complain of the short-termism of the stock market.

Costs far exceed these benefits when guidance is missed, not to mention the impact on the company's reputation.

Yet, those that have made the leap and stopped providing guidance have not necessarily suffered from it over the longer term. They have made sure they were demonstrating performance and communicating progress. This is ultimately what investors are interested in. Where is the company heading? What are the metrics that matter? What type of performance is really sustainable? What is the time horizon that makes sense for a strategy to be fully implemented?

Lastly, there is no such thing as a perfect moment to announce a change to a guidance policy. In any case, the press release should make it clear and intelligible, with a substantiated rationale for doing so. The news should not be buried somewhere in the text, with the hope that nobody will notice. This would only make matters worse.

All in all, think twice before embarking on providing guidance.

3.5.3.6 Profit warnings and pre-announcements

There are three main situations in which companies can issue profit warnings and pre-announcements:

- When they realize that between the end of the reference period (for instance, the end of the quarter) and the scheduled earnings release date the actual results will be significantly below or above the targets announced to the market. In most cases, the overshoot or shortfall will relate to operating income, net income, or net earnings per share;
- When, in the course of the reference period, an event occurs that makes the targets announced obsolete;

- When companies realize that their actual earnings will fall short of the analyst consensus as published by specialized vendors or the company itself.

It is up to the company to decide whether the discrepancy between the actual figures and its own targets or analyst expectations justifies a profit warning. While such a warning will have an immediate impact on the stock price, failure to issue one will undermine the company's credibility, and investors may be even more disappointed.

The press release announcing the profit warning should contain enough explanations, in a straightforward and concise manner

- What exactly happened? Is this a one-time or a recurring issue?
- Are the causes internal to the company or external?
- What is the financial impact of the problem?
- What measures and action plan has the company implemented to remedy the situation?

The company may not readily offer revised targets, only if it is necessary to do so: These revised targets may be delivered to the market at a later date, for instance, upon the initially scheduled reporting date, once the company has gathered all the information it needs to revise them. This, however, is likely to create overhang in the stock until new objectives are made available.

In the vast majority of cases, warnings and preannouncements refer to a negative performance: results are not going to be what was expected. But positive pre-announcements do happen, though rarely (in other words, the company may decide to announce that its performance is going to exceed its initial projection, ahead of the initially scheduled reporting date). They are usually called earnings surprises. That says it all!

All in all, think twice before embarking on providing guidance.

3.5.4 Shareholder Value Creation

The concept of shareholder value creation has become one of the most widely endorsed messages in financial communications and Investor Relations. It is virtually every listed company's official goal to create value for its shareholders. Unfortunately, it has become far too generic to be as compelling as it may have been in its early days. The reason lies in the absence of substance attached to it.

Shareholder value creation as a strategic direction and as a message becomes relevant if and when it describes the levers used by management to achieve this much-desired ambition. Financial communications will then focus on communicating their respective characteristics, roles, and targets. Aiming at presenting the company's strategy as geared to creating shareholder value, these messages can be articulated around the following levers:

- Financial levers:
  - Increase earnings per share;
  - Improve total shareholder return;
  - Generate investor trust;
  - Raise return on equity (ROE), return on capital employed (ROCE);
  - Lower the cost of capital;
  - Offer attractive shareholder remuneration policy, via regular dividend payments, share buyback programs, rights issue, and other non-dilutive instruments.
- Operating and strategic levers:
  - Create value for customers;
  - Grow with mergers and acquisitions (M&A);
  - Steady organic revenue growth;
  - Tight cost control;
  - Best-practice–driven corporate governance;
  - Human resources and compensation policies.

In addition,

- The company will want to stress that it has developed proactive Investor Relations program and made shareholder value creation an intrinsic part of its corporate culture; and
- Communicating on shareholder value creation truly becomes powerful when quantified targets are associated: "We are increasing our return on equity (ROE) target, in the range of 33–36 percent."

In order to curb excessive communications in this area, certain legislators, in France, for instance, have decided to formally require that it be

- based on a consistently applied and clearly explained methodology;
- reviewed by the statutory auditors if the information is to be part of the issuer's legal documentation (in a prospectus, for instance).

Lastly, investors need to be able to reconcile indicators used to track shareholder value creation with the company's consolidated financial statements.

Because just about any company can claim it wants to create value, credibility lies in the respect of the following recommendations:

- Explain why you chose those value creation indicators in particular;
- Consider having them audited, if not already required by law;
- Post the definition of these metrics on your website;
- Be consistent through good times...and bad.

3.5.5 Mergers and Acquisitions

Mergers and acquisitions (M&A) must be announced in accordance with regulations governing sensitive and insider information.

Takeovers often catch the market off-guard. Announcements should be carefully prepared and the IRO duly organized, possibly with the assistance of advisors if the Investor Relations team has little or no experience in this field. In particular, provisional statements will have to be drafted for every eventuality, in case rumors of the deal are leaked early, the deal itself collapses or is pulled off.

M&A communications are conducted in accordance with the following principles:

- All parties should keep the transaction confidential until the last minute. At least one press release should nonetheless be kept on hand, for example, in case the press gets wind that a transaction is imminent.
- The justification given should be solid, credible, and perfectly in keeping with the company's strategic messages. You don't want to leave stakeholders to draw their own conclusions.
- The valuation applied should be clearly laid out, as should the projected financial impact and the anticipated benefits along with when they can be expected to feed through. A detailed integration roadmap should also be provided. These are the most challenging messages to prepare and the ones the market will be most interested in. Unfortunately, most press releases issued to announce acquisitions fail to provide this information. True, this may be because full details are not yet available because the completion of the transaction remains subject to a number of conditions. While quantifiable synergies are always a strong positive in this investment case, management may be reluctant to commit on precise numbers much before becoming actual owners of the business. In some cases, the evaluation process is still underway, or the working assumptions still contain too many variables. The financing terms may not be finalized. Be that as it may, the more quantitative data analysts have to assess the consequences of a transaction on the

company's future profitability, the better the chances that the market will welcome the deal.

Investor Relations should also address any impact in terms of human resources and corporate culture insofar as the deal can affect operations management, staff levels, or the values of the companies involved.

If not properly marketed, even acquisitions that are strategically beneficial for the buyer will put pressure on the share price for a long time. All communications relating to acquisitions should, therefore, be prepared in advance with the IRO, the person who can most effectively help management anticipate the market's reaction. Brought into the process as early on as possible, the IRO can offer crucial advice on shaping the messages that will be released to the market.

If the transaction is large enough, the press release may be followed by a conference call or information meeting with appropriate visuals and support materials, such as questions and answers (Q&A) documents.

The same timing and transparency apply when a key business is sold. Assuming the acquisition is not a hostile takeover, buyers and sellers should try to agree on their respective messages.

Below is a summary of other key recommendations for M&A communications

- Consider a dedicated section on your website for significant transactions;
- Educate the market about the 'new' business/geography;
- Provide a sustainable M&A rationale, how it fits your strategy and how it will create value over time;
- Be realistic about profit enhancement and integration challenges;
- Think twice before providing quantitative synergy targets;
- Be clear from the very beginning about what type of pro forma financial statements you will provide and for how long;
- Update on integration progress;
- If appropriate, provide an updated guidance;
- Reach out to the sell-side to ensure their models accurately reflect the change in the scope of consolidation.

3.5.6 Corporate Governance and Internal Control

Corporate governance is a separate legal requirement that must be addressed via financial communications. It covers the following areas:

- The organization, composition, role, and operations of the board of directors;

- Special committees (such as compensation, audit/accounts, nominations);
- Assessments of the board and committees' work.

Studies show that there is a correlation between strong governance and high profitability. Thus, some companies go beyond legal obligations and use Investor Relations to highlight the excellence of their corporate governance, notably focusing on the following:

- The high proportion and competence of independent board members;
- The existence of a code of ethics or code of conduct, notably governing the trading of company shares by directors and management;
- Executive compensation policy;
- How shareholders participate in the company's operations. Good corporate governance allows them to submit resolutions to the AGM, ask for representation on the board, and prevent a dilution of their holdings in the event of a hostile takeover bid.

IROs work closely with the company's legal department in this area. They may suggest, for example, that a press release be issued to announce the appointment of an independent board member. All are jointly involved in the preparation of the AGM.

3.5.7 Corporate Social Responsibility and Sustainable Development

3.5.7.1 From sustainable development to Environmental, Social, Governance (ESG)

Closely knit in with corporate governance, sustainable development is a political, social, and economic concept, defined by the United Nations as a development process that "meets the needs of the present without compromising the ability of future generations to meet their own needs'. Corporate social responsibility (CSR) has emerged as a major nonfinancial issue for companies to report on. It encompasses vast areas of corporate life

- Social and community-related issues, including philanthropy programs for certain companies;
- Sustainable development factors (environment, health, safety, for instance).

One result of the increasing popularity of sustainable development has been the development of socially responsible investing (SRI). The number of SRI funds and the amounts under management are growing, with SRI factors gaining in importance in the investment decision-making process. Special indices are being created, and rating agencies are dealing with Investor Relations teams on this subject, except where a separate department for sustainable development" has been set up. This trend has also led regulators to require specific reports, while dedicated SRI presentations and roadshows are developed by the company.

There is no doubt that communication around corporate social responsibility and sustainable development has become a vehicle for companies to enhance their image, reputation, and valuations, though there is a price tag. Stock-market regulations and specialized rating agencies are increasingly requiring that data be calculated with special reporting instruments, which has a cost and adds another reporting layer on top of already complex systems. This is an area where financial and nonfinancial disclosures meet and impact valuation. It only makes sense for issuers to go to this length if they plan to use the same information for their management and strategy.

Over the past few years, sustainable development has evolved into "Environmental, Social, Governance" or "ESG," as what was once considered a niche market among socially responsible investors is becoming more mainstream. Indeed, integrating ESG aspects is increasingly a part of asset managers' fiduciary responsibility. Furthermore, the significance of ESG issues has grown in importance, and their integration into financial analysis has become a significant performance driver for fund managers.

The reference for sustainability communication guidelines is the Global Reporting Initiative (GRI-www.globalreporting.org), "a long-term, multi-stakeholder, process whose mission is to develop and disseminate globally applicable Sustainability Reporting Guidelines for voluntary use by organizations reporting on the economic, environmental, and social dimensions of their activities, products and services."

It currently constitutes the world's most widely accepted, integrated reporting framework. While it originated in the United States, GRI has grown mostly in Europe where stringent regulations are imposed to address corporate governance and growing environmental challenges.

Many IROs will argue that most portfolio managers, unless they run an SRI fund, will hardly ever ask many ESG-related questions, if any at all. So why should your company need to communicate proactively a sustainability strategy? Through your sustainability strategy, you will engage with a wide range of stakeholders, beyond the investment community. This can positively impact your overall performance, and consequently, your valuation. Not being able to showcase your sustainability achievements may force you out of investors' radar screens in the competition for capital. After all, who would want to own a company that is poorly managed, treats its employees badly and pollutes?

If, from a corporate perspective, the benefits of sustainability reporting are rather easy to understand, especially in terms of reputation—with ESG information serving as a proxy for the quality of a company's management—this is less obvious seen from a pure IR angle. This is primarily because ESG issues do not seem to be at the top of the agenda for the investors and analysts they interact with daily. But this could well come faster than they think. So better get ready.

Here are some tips on how IR can successfully address ESG:

- Proactively address ESG issues on quarterly analyst calls, investor days, etc. It may simply be about presenting a couple of meaningful sustainability metrics every time on every occasion (safety improvement ratios, waste recycling ratios, number of independent directors, etc.). This will help support your growth strategy by talking about the processes in place to improve operating efficiency, reduce costs and minimize risks.
- Be involved in the creation of new, ESG metrics that can be specific to your company, your industry.
- Build the business case for sustainability with success stories and Returns On Investment on revenue and costs (resource efficiency and cost savings, employee productivity, innovation and growth, diversity.
- Highlight what makes your performance viable, sustainable, over the long term: discuss R&D expenses, customer retention, customer satisfaction, revenues from new products, etc.
- Engage with a broader set of stakeholders, including ESG fund managers and analysts. Ask them which ESG indices matter to them, share this information with other entities in your organization which deal with different stakeholders. Balance the pros and cons of seeking ESG rating.

Should you need one last reason, remember that investors are risk adverse and love sustainability. They are prepared to pay a premium for that predictability.

3.5.7.2 Integrated reporting: the future of financial reporting?

According to the International Integrated Reporting Council (IIRC – www.theiirc.org), a global coalition of regulators, investors, companies, standard setters, the accounting profession and Non Governmental Organizations (NGOs), which is leading the development of a global framework for Integrated Reporting, it is "a process that results in communication, most visibly a periodic "integrated report," about value creation over time. An integrated report is a concise communication about how an organization's strategy, governance, performance and prospects lead to the creation of value over the short, medium and long term. An integrated report should be prepared in accordance with the International Integrated Reporting Framework."

The integrated (annual) report may well represent the future of corporate reporting given the growing importance of extra-financial data in the investor's capital allocation process. Just as it may be another trend in corporate reporting. One that stock market legislators have yet to reach a consensus on.

Combining sustainability reporting and financial reporting all in one place therefore requires building bridges between different forms of corporate reporting... and the resources to do so.

Only a few companies worldwide publish their annual report in an "integrated report" form. Their decision reporting is then driven primarily by the following:

- Regulatory requirements in their home markets, as is the case in South Africa ("King III") which was the first country in the world to mandate integrated reporting, now part of the listing requirements, or in France (mandatory sustainability reporting required by "Grenelle II" legislation) , and mandatory reporting on climate change in the UK).
- The desire to achieve a specific market positioning because their products and services are contributing to the sustainable development of other stakeholders (consumers, communities, etc.).
- The growing awareness that business needs to be viewed in a more holistic way.

Integrated reporting is not only about ensuring the link between non-financial and financial performance. It is also about:

- connecting the strategy, performance and the social, environmental and economic context within which a company operates;
- illustrating how the non–financial performance contributes to business value;
- articulating all of the above in a credible and compelling way.

If opportunities for enhanced communication and valuation abound, challenges are plentiful as well:

- Which non-financial issues, among hundreds of ESG indicators, are 'material' to the business? Which stakeholder category are they relevant to?

- How do our stakeholders expect us to address sustainability issues? In one document, in a chapter in the annual report or in multiple reports?
- Who should be responsible for the integrated report: Investor Relations? Corporate Communications? An ad hoc department?
- How can we ensure that the non-financial, more subjective data is going to be as accurate and reliable as the financial figures?
- Is the integrated reporting going to replace the sustainability report?
- Can or should companies think about forward-looking non-financial data?
- How can we avoid too much information killing the information?

Regulations, best practices and guidelines are being gradually developed for Investor Relations teams. They should start getting familiar with the concept if they have not already done so. The key benefits of integrated reporting are worth keeping in mind:

- It provides the long-term perspective missing from most corporate communications;
- It Improves brand image & positioning;
- It allows for well-articulated risk management;
- It is a lever for increasing corporate reputation.

Figure 6.11 in the Resources section provides a list of the main ESG metrics that are of interest to investors and analysts.

3.5.8 Investor Relations for Employee Shareholders

Investor Relations also target employee shareholders, even if in most cases these are being taken care of by a dedicated department, quite often within the human resources department. Laws often promote employee savings plans with employees being offered company shares at particularly attractive prices. In this instance, Investor Relations should complement labor policy and focus on the following:

- Assuring real consistency—including in terms of regularity—between the external image (that presented to the press, for instance) and the internal one;
- Developing a specific communications strategy for these shareholders.

The tools applied specifically to this aspect of Investor Relations include the following:

- Internal roadshows;
- Intranet (possibly managed by the bank where the shares are deposited);
- Up-to-date share prices, models for personal portfolio management and valuation, and calculation of capital gains and losses;
- Regulatory information about insider trading, the conditions under which shares can be traded, and the issue of stock options.

The person in charge of employee shareholding schemes will work with the IRO to develop specific messages about the following:

- *Personal wealth management.* The long-term yields of stocks (usually higher than any other form of investment), different tax benefits, and changes in legal measures as well as tax incentives governing employee share ownership.
- *Strategy.* The risk–reward ratio of equity investments based on salary, convergence between the employee shareholders' interests and those of the company and its other shareholders, personal contributions to overall company performance and increase in the stock price.
- *Pedagogy.* Participation in promoting the company's image, brand, and values.

3.5.9 Bridging the Language Divide

Getting your message across multiple languages can be another IR challenge.

If your company's official language is not English, it is quite likely that you will need the services of a translator for some or all of your Investor Relations tools and documents. Not only should the translated document reflect the original document's content accurately and faithfully, it must also convey the same image of quality and be an easily intelligible and thoroughly pleasant read.

This is unfortunately not always the case. Part of the reason has to do with the fact that the relationship between IR and translators is not as optimal as it should be.

Sure enough, timing constraints cannot be ignored when it comes to translating an earnings release, whose content changes up until the last minute. Furthermore, English being the international language of finance, many IROs in non-English-speaking countries speak and write good enough English themselves to believe they can speed up the production of the English version by translating the original version on their own.

Yet, a better understanding of each other's constraints, needs and objectives can lead to a mutually beneficial relationship.

Here is a list of recommendations for IROs and translators on how to best work together:

- Identify what needs to be translated. Whether your shares are listed in a foreign country or not, the decision should not be driven by cost or regulatory considerations only. Your IR strategy may include catering to a large retail shareholder base or targeting investors in a country where the national language is not English. As a courtesy to this audience, you may want to have your slideshow translated or come to meetings with handouts in this region's language. This is particularly valid when your company has operations locally and you can use their brochures, for instance. Conversely, you need to be aware of the fact that investors in your home country may resent it if you do not bother using slides in your home language and use English slides instead.
- Choosing (and retaining) the right translator. It is possible that you may not find the perfect translator from day one and may need to shop around a bit. Ask your peers whom they work with and do not hesitate to ask your local teams abroad for advice or support.
- Work together more efficiently:
  - Talk to each other. Far too often, communication between IR and translators is done via email. Every now and then, you should talk to put the messages in context, to gather feedback on how previous translations have been perceived by their end-users such as analysts, investors, journalists, and how workflows between IR and translators can be further improved;
  - Brief your translator. Because translators are not machines but human beings, they have a work process and speed of their own. Discuss your project timeline with your translator and see how it is going to work out for both of you;
  - Provide him or her with as much supportive material or background Information as you can, such as analysts' reports, including a contact person in your IR organization;
  - Keep your translator regularly informed of what is going on at your company, by adding her or his name to your corporate mailing lists;
  - Help the translator develop and maintain a translation glossary that is specific to your company and industry.
- Protect yourselves legally:
  - If price-sensitive information is being translated, make sure the translator has signed a non-disclosure agreement and has the proper measures in place to store your information and exchange it with you safely;

- ○ You may want to mention that your earnings release or annual report is a translation from another language which is provided for information purposes only, and add that in the event of discrepancies between this and the original version, the latter will prevail.
- Write clearly. If the message in your home language is not easily understandable, you should not be surprised if it does not come out clearly in the translation either.
- "If you pay monkeys, you get peanuts." IROs should be careful with translation costs that are priced at a very low per-word rate. Yes, there exists software that provides automated translation very cheaply. (If you have never done so, try to translate any web page from your home language into another one and see the results. You don't want your earnings release to be that confusing). At present, this software is unable to actually rewrite your text. And this is precisely what is going to make or break the quality of your IR message in a foreign language. You need a professional translator for this and it has a price.
- Translation is not only about words and meanings. It is also about respecting typographical conventions. These can be industry, but also language or country specific (for instance, the use of comma decimal marks or of period decimal marks is not the same the world over). Make sure everyone involved is aware of and respects these.

3.6 Selecting and Implementing Investor Relations Tools

Once the organizational structure is in place and the targets have been identified and the messages shaped, the next step is to select and implement the right Investor Relations tools to disseminate information. There are three main communication channels: online, in print, and in person. Companies should invest time and money in scalable tools that can be used even if the Investor Relations budget needs to be cut.

These communication channels should be planned and produced dynamically. These must:

- be consistent over time and across communications (internal, corporate, Investor Relations);
- comply with legal constraints;
- allow for productivity gains;
- need low maintenance;
- meet the expectations and work habits of the target audiences;
- be designed for the long term.

3.6.1 Press and News Releases

The press release is the preferred method of disseminating financial information. It is often the primary channel used by companies to meet their legal obligations. The Internet makes it possible to disseminate the information instantaneously across the globe, including to those the company had not necessarily intended to reach in the first place.

The quality of a press release is not determined by its length or brevity, but rather by the fact that it is properly structured, clearly written, consistent with previous releases, and with content-rich information. It should include the names of company spokespersons and their direct contact details.

A well-designed earnings press release features the following:

- A first page that is intended for all, as it is the one that will be read by most. Parts of it may be used for other financial communications (summaries, shareholder letters, web pages, corporate newsletters), as long as readers are told how to obtain the full press release;
- Subsequent pages that are intended more for analysts and investors.

Below is a suggested outline. The first page may include the following:

- The title followed by three or four key messages presented in bullet points format;
- A table featuring the main figures and indicators for the previous and current years, highlighting any notable changes;
- A message from the CEO and/or a summary outlook.

Following pages may show the following elements:

- Comments on the performance achieved in the reported period, analysis of the main items of the income statement, balance sheet and cash flow statement, description of trends in environment, businesses and geographic areas where operations are located;
- Events occurring after the financial statements were closed, or "post close events";
- Outlook;
- Reminder of next publication date or financial calendar;
- Information about analysts' meeting and, where appropriate, conference call;
- A brief description of the company (also known as the "boiler plate").

Appendices will usually include the following:

- Consolidated financial statements: income statement, cash-flow statement, balance sheet, segment reporting;
- Supplemental information in the form of Q&A ordered by division ("What is the geographical revenue split?") or by topic ("What was the company's net debt at the end of the quarter?"). This is a highly differentiating way of providing information to the market. It does require additional work, but it demonstrates that the company is eager to facilitate the analysts' job and to enhance transparency. Another goal might be to ensure that the most frequently asked questions are covered before the analyst meeting or before the earnings conference call starts, and that management's time is best used to answer strategic questions.

When this format is applied, the first page can also be easily read on a mobile device such as a smartphone, a tablet computer or another hand-held device. The title becomes the subject of the e-mail ("XYZ reports 15 percent increase in net income in the first quarter") and the information contained on the first page of the press release is included in the body of the message, along with details of how to reach the spokespersons and about any meetings scheduled. The full press release is in this case sent as an attachment or is made available with a link to the company's website.

The recommendations below are designed to optimize efforts to produce quality press releases that relate to finance or strategy (announcements of earnings, M&A deals, or financial transactions):

- When writing the press release, bear in mind that it will be the first introduction to the company for a number of potential readers. It is unwise to assume that everyone who receives the release will already be familiar with the company;
- Readers are put off by press releases that are too long. Lengthy texts should be split into separate files, notably separating the appendices from the rest and specifying that the text and all attachments constitute the official press release;
- If visuals are used to support the meeting or the conference call, they should be structured around the same key messages that are listed in the press release. The announcement will gain in conviction and consistency.

3.6.2 Visuals, Presentations, and Slideshows

This is another key Investor Relations tool, one that also requires the ability to write clearly and concisely. Clear and insightful presentations can transform analysts' and investors' perception of the business and move the company valuation. It is also a tool by which investors can measure executives.

3.6.2.1 Form

Research has shown that the way people take in information during a presentation is 55 percent visual, compared to 38 percent vocal, and only 7 percent through text which plays only a small role in getting messages across. It is very basic, but nonetheless necessary, to reiterate that visuals must be pleasing to the eye and not too overloaded with text, diagrams, or curves. It should also be possible to read them from the back of the meeting room.

Graphics and animation are not used often enough to convey messages, for a simple reason. Presentations are unfortunately completed too late to allow for management to rehearse and adapt speeches to the animated flow of charts.

Before putting together any new presentation, the IROs must review the previous one. Any changes in form or messages will be noted by analysts, and their reactions should be anticipated and prepared for.

Most standard presentations should be relatively short, with no more than 35 slides. This usually results in the presentation not exceeding about 45 minutes and being straight to the point.

The outline should be shown to the audience with the name and title of each speaker. The title of the different slides may be worded as messages ("Introduction" could become "XYZ, a global leader in food processing"), and the same syntax should be used throughout (you have either bullet points or full sentences, but not a mix of both). Appendices are there to keep presentation short while ensuring that thorough information is available. Slides in the appendices may also be used in response to questions from the audience or to illustrate a complex issue.

3.6.2.2 Content

The presentation should combine strategy plans and progress, without forecasting numbers, unless they have been made public by way of a press release. The presentation should take investors and analysts from the start to the finish of the projects, enabling them to track performance against objectives.

Presentations are not to be wrapped up with a mere summary of the outlook for the current or following year. On the contrary, if the presentation is to be dynamic and the Q&A session fruitful, the key messages should be summarized at the end, in the same way sales pitches or equity stories are concluded. Impose your own conclusion.

It is good to have a written script on hand, even if it is not used, because one or more speakers may need to be replaced at the last minute. It cannot be emphasized enough that speeches should be rehearsed in full at least two times in each language if this is what the plan is. It also makes it easier to ensure professionalism during conference calls, because investors do not appreciate improvisation. The script should be compared to the press release to ensure that there are no inconsistencies and that the message is the same in all languages, if applicable.

Presentations should be updated as many times as necessary and adapted to each audience and circumstance. Earnings presentations are only useful on the day they are reported. By the time the roadshow is underway, the presentation should have been reformatted to concentrate on key numbers and issues. New information may have been added because audiences will have already seen the numbers. The presentations can be stored on the website in an "archives" section.

If you plan to hand out your presentation in a paper format, you need to know that investors seem to like smaller, A5-type size which they can easily put in their pockets or next to their plate at luncheon presentations. Remember to allow for enough note-taking space.

3.6.3 Online Investor Relations

Thanks to technological innovation and regulatory changes, the Investor Relations section of corporate websites has become

- an essential information platform for investment professionals, sometimes even their first port of call;
- a communication tool for companies that want to communicate widely;
- a legally recommended way to meet public disclosure requirements in a growing number of countries. However, unless the Internet is deemed to be a regulatory information channel in your country, you should by no means disclose price-sensitive information via the medium first. Only after it is in the public domain will you be allowed to post it on your website.

These Investor Relations pages have gone well beyond their initial purpose of being shop windows and online libraries for companies. They play an ever-important role in marketing shares by enhancing the company's visibility as well as showcasing its products and services. If properly designed and maintained, they will also prove to be a source of cost and time savings in information dissemination. And last but not the least, a website can lessen the Investor Relations workload, automatically answering analysts' and investors' questions and requests for information.

3.6.3.1 Basic principles for website construction

Investor information may be posted to a separate website or incorporated within the corporate website, but the following rules should be followed in all cases:

- Conduct a thorough peer review. Find out which companies have award-winning Investor Relations websites, in your sector or outside your industry as well;
- The website is not only a tool for disseminating information but also a vehicle for interacting with the company. It should provide specific instructions for contacting the company and subscribing to e-mail alerts lists for press releases. From the beginning, a system should also be set up to track usage and ask for user's feedback;
- The initial architecture should be designed simply, but also solidly enough to handle changes. Regulations may require that information be kept current at all times and time stamped, pages be translated into different languages be identified, and archives of historical information be stored for several years. There should be regular reviews about how the site can be upgraded in terms of content or navigability;
- Create microsites to keep the investment community and others updated about a bid, a transaction. The Internet is likely to be the most efficient way to get your story across as you want it told, to an audience that will increase exponentially during a deal or a crisis situation;
- Make the website user friendly, easy to navigate, comprehensive, and convenient, and as the ultimate information source about your company, in accordance with current regulations. It should help users understand more about the company's businesses and markets;
- This means that a glossary may be included, along with other features such as videos of field trips and sector analyses;
- Online Investor Relations are accessible to all, with no restrictions or password. This may apply to the blind, partially sighted, and hard of hearing, if you are planning on posting webcasts of Investor Relations events, for instance. Pages may be translated into several languages and currency converter are sometimes available too. The more accessible the site, the more likely people are to use it and understand the company. Viewing the website from the user's perspective will help you ensure that your information will never be more than just a few clicks away and that it features the most commonly used headings that make

sense to both professionals and the average visitor. Adequate programming will allow you to offer the possibility to print or e-mail pages
- Some sections may be devoted to certain categories of visitor (the analyst, the journalist, the individual shareholder, the industry analyst). The format used for a particular type of information should fit the audience's needs. In general, HTML and PDF will meet most users' needs. But extra care may be required so that your website can be copied, transferred, printed, and read from hand-held devices and tablet computers as well. Add interactive, graphics-based tools and a spreadsheet functionality for financial tables for analysts. They will take these data, feed them into their models, create charts, and make calculations. This is will often help differentiate your Investor Relations website from the crowd.

3.6.3.2 Site content

Websites and sections specifically devoted to analysts and investors are generally designed in the following way:

- *Homepage.* It should be possible to move directly to the "Investor Relations" section from the homepage of the corporate site. Headings should include, at the very least, a detailed section map, the last stock price, the title of the latest press release with a link to it, and access to information about contacting the company or subscribing to press releases and e-mail alerts. The Investor Relations policy can be introduced via a statement from the CEO.
- *Company information.* The idea is to use core messages to present the company's history, businesses, markets, and strategy. This page should include a list of key dates and figures along with biographies of key executives.
- *Calendar.* This page should include dates from the current year and the following one where possible, and mention the main meetings scheduled with the financial community, even if the dates are subject to change. It should be updated regularly.
- *Share data.* Users should find the stock symbol and quotes (usually in a delayed mode) as well as historic data (highs, lows, opening and closing price, trading volumes in number of shares and value) and information about dividends. If the company is listed on a foreign market, it will need to provide the same information in the local currency. The most sophisticated sites even provide an electronic calculator to enable shareholders to estimate the value of their investment and compare its performance to those of the major indices, also included on the site.

- *Financial data.* Information should be exhaustive, accessible in different formats, and where possible, downloadable into analysts' spreadsheets. There are often subsections with the annual report and a description of the accounting standards used as well as archives for at least the last three years. The key financial ratios should also be provided either in text or graph form with historical comparisons.
- *Press releases and other documents.* All releases issued by the company should be classified by date of publication or topic, with or without a search engine. This section should also include presentations given at the time of earnings announcements, strategic transactions, analyst days or conferences, and any legal documents filed with authorities for markets on which the shares trade. The annual report should be downloadable in several formats and feature a table of contents. It should be possible to select and print pages, interactivity should be easy.
- *Shareholder information.* Designed for retail and institutional investors alike, this section describes the share ownership structure and all information about the AGM, from the voting process to resolutions, broadcasts, and vote results. When legislations so allows, shareholders may register to vote directly through the website. Where such services exist, shareholders should also be informed about such things as the possibility of holding shares directly with the company, trading stocks, reinvesting dividends, or updates on corresponding tax laws.
- *Information for bondholders and credit analysts.* This Debt Investor Relations section notably features credit ratings, a list of bond issues and main characteristics (amount, coupon, and maturity), standard coverage ratios, covenants, presentations made during bond roadshows, issue prospectuses and contact information in Investor Relations, and finance or treasury departments.
- *Frequently asked questions.* This section is organized by theme and summarizes the questions most frequently asked about the stock or the company's organization, dividend policies, businesses, strategy, and outlook.
- *Corporate governance.* Here, the company describes its legal structure, management organization, and executive management with biographies of top executives, along with how they operate and how their work is evaluated. Company bylaws should be downloadable.
- *Sustainable development.* Company policy with regard to social affairs, environmental protection. Risk management is described and related benchmark indicators are given.
- *Contacts.* The names and complete contact information of those in charge of investor, shareholder, and press relations are found here. This creates a much more positive image than when the company hides

behind an anonymous department name with a general switchboard phone number and e-mail address for all inquiries. The list may also include contact information for service providers, authorized communications agencies, stock-transfer agent, and custodian banks.

In addition to press releases, presentations, and other Investor Relations supporting materials, you may consider developing content specifically for the website, such as interactive lements or video interviews of senior management.

It may also be useful to include the following information:

- A list of analysts who cover the stock;
- Consensus earnings and estimates;
- A tab to review acquisitions and asset disposals.

The website can also be divided up in sections addressing specific audiences: journalists, retail shareholders, industry analysts, and analysts/investors. (see Figure 6.12 in the Resources section for a basic IR site map template).

3.6.4 Blogs and Social Media

The Internet has given rise to the "blog" (for "web log") phenomenon. Beyond the traditional media, it is supposed to provide a means of connecting directly with investors or others interested in your company. Those in favor of blogging will say that it is an additional opportunity for Investor Relations to position their company to its best advantage, engage with online journalists, and develop relationships with the investment community. Opponents will argue that it is hard to monitor and carries considerable legal and image risks.

While social media are not yet typically investors' first port of call for news, they are an increasingly important corporate communications tool with media, customers and employees, and more generally speaking a wide range of stakeholders. In other words, after showing a great deal of reluctance, listed companies and IROs can no longer ignore them, as a growing number of sell-side analysts and investors are using social media as part of their research and investment process. They are looking for unofficial sources of information and insights on companies

- What your employees are saying about sales wins and losses, upcoming product launches, layoffs, restructuring or integration, internal communications from management, undisclosed details on the size of a business?

- How your customers, suppliers, competitors view your products & services, how new product deployment is progressing, what doctors are writing about drug efficacy or side-effects and how they comment on clinical trials?
- What safety issues your company might be facing. In today's environment, these are likely to be raised in social media forums before they reach 'official channels'?

This implies that an IRO, even if he or she does not actively use social media for IR purposes, needs monitor what is being said about his or her company on these platforms. It is essential to be aware and prepared to respond.

Hereafter is a step-by-step approach to developing your social medial policy for IR

- What goals are you looking to achieve from social media? These might include increasing analyst coverage, attracting new investors, participating in generating buzz / build brand awareness for your company or driving website traffic.
- What social media networks are your competitors peer group companies using?
- What resources do you need to achieve your goals? Is there a social media expert internally which could assist you in establishing an IR presence in social media?
- Does your company have formal social media guidelines for employees, executives, and directors in place?

Technology companies have been at the forefront of social media use by IR, with other industries more progressively embracing social media for investor and analyst engagement. It is therefore useful to draw from their experience. Here are a few tips that work:

- Start slowly, let experience build. Identify the platforms you want to be on and the resources you can dedicate to maintaining a social media presence in a sustainable manner. One of the most common practices among listed companies is to post their financial results, online annual reports, AGM details on social media with details and a link to their latest news web page, thus ensuring "bare minimum" social media presence. In other words, they do not add any new information to the legally approved and already disclosed content;
- Provide information that is incremental: it has to be new, short and interesting. Because material news will still require a press release, it is important to think "qualitative" versus "quantitative" when using

social media for IR. In order to do so, establish a partnership with other departments in your organization such as corporate communications or marketing. They will supply you with new ideas and information that you can digest and redirect to your audience. Furthermore, this is necessary to align internal and external messages on social media too;
- Social media is just another tool that younger generations grew up with. Look for a social media fan in your organization and entrust him or her with the development of your IR presence on social media. Chances are you will be better served at a much lower costs than if you were hiring outside;
- Always work closely with your legal team to establish and implement policies and procedures, these may include posting your social media "rules of engagement and commenting guidelines" on your social media platform;
- Organize internal social media training and awareness, especially regarding the disclosure of work related information;
- Monitor social media traffic;
- Solicit feedback and show a willingness to listen and engage.

Technology developments, and in particular of mobile devices, are also participating in the expansion of social media. Videos have become a popular way for companies to showcase their management or products in the form of "v-logs" for "video blogs" that are posted on social media platforms.

3.6.5 The Annual Report

From a legal standpoint, listed companies are required to publish annual reports, the content of which is tightly regulated. Over the years, annual reports and financial documentation have tended to become heavy documents with ever increasing details, while not necessarily making things clearer. This has led companies to produce summaries, abridged versions, and interactive online annual reports. But let us not be mistaken: the printed annual report is here to stay.

Together with the press release for ongoing information reporting, the annual report is, and will continue to be, the primary document for financial communications, although it is increasingly sharing the spotlight with corporate websites. The quality of both documents, in form and in content, shows when you have given consideration to the writing as well as the design.

Companies are nonetheless free to select any format they choose, depending on their budget, image, and how they intend to use the annual report. The latter can be divided into two or more documents including a summary report, full report, sustainable development report, financial statements, and so on.

One of the many challenges of the annual report is to make it interesting to a wide audience with very different concerns. This is why it is produced by a multidisciplinary project team from within the company, with help from outside specialists.

3.6.5.1 The purpose of the annual report

The main objectives of publishing an annual report are as follows:

- *Inform shareholders.* Copies should be distributed before the AGM according to a specific legal timetable that varies from country to country.
- *Create and reflect the company's image.* The annual report is in fact a corporate brochure and a tool for developing its reputation. It can help boost marketing efforts, for instance, by being displayed at the company stand at a trade show or recruitment fair on a university campus. It showcases and reflects corporate culture. In this sense, it is intended for employees as well, but should also be sent to clients and suppliers and will undoubtedly be analysed by competitors.
- *Present exhaustive information about the company.* Provide a service to analysts and investors by giving them exhaustive information about the company, presented in a timely fashion and in a format that suits them. Production processes and the content and form of the report must be constantly improved if these objectives are to be met.

3.6.5.2 Structure of the annual report

As a general rule, the annual report has the following outlines:

- *General information.* Readers should find a description of the company and its products and services. These are usually presented by business line, branch, division or sector, or in some cases the "lead company" (a brand, for instance) is presented separately from its subsidiaries, some of which may be listed themselves. Readers should also get an objective understanding of the company's competitive positioning and market shares with reference made to industry rankings established by independent third parties.
- *The chairman's statement.* Also referred to as the CEO letter, it is an invaluable vehicle for setting forth the core parts of the company's strategy. It should discuss the key events that occurred during the year, placing them within their broader economic context. Mention

should also be made of any acquisitions and divestments. The statement should address the company's outlook and objectives.
- *Financial information.* In general, the law requires companies to provide the following as a minimum: consolidated income statements, cash flow statements, balance sheets, resolutions approving the financial statements and allocation of earnings (dividend payments and additions to the reserves), sector information for each business line, and risk factors. The data required to analyse the financial statements are provided in notes and appendices, which are also audited by the company's statutory auditors as required by law. The statutory and consolidated financial statements can be presented in summary form.
- The annual report should also mention the accounting standards applied (International Financial Reporting Standards—IFRS; US Generally Accepted Accounting Principles—US GAAP, or other). Ideally, the company should also provide a definition of the ratios it uses the most, especially those featured prominently in its financial communications, as different firms can have different ways of calculating, for instance, net debt, cash flow and returns on investment.
- Stock-market data. Detailed information should be provided about the shareholder base, the number of shares in issue and potential dilution, and stock prices and securities traded by the issuer.
- Some regulations require that annual reports provide information about corporate governance, internal control, and all aspects of issuers' sustainable development policies.
- You should make sure that historical data comparisons are possible, especially when major changes are made from one year to the next; for instance, if the company moves to new accounting standards or makes major acquisitions or divestments, it will need to produce pro forma statements.
- If the issuer has been obliged to produce documents using accounting standards other than those applied in its country of origin, it must ensure that there are no differences vis-à-vis the annual report published in the original language and provide ad hoc reconciliation tables and methods.

3.6.5.3 *Distribution of annual reports*

Specific distribution requirements usually apply, depending on the country. Mandatory physical distribution of printed copies to every shareholder tends to be gradually replaced by posting a link or the complete file on the company's website, thus considerably reducing printing and mailing costs. In any case, the company must commit to deliver a paper copy of its complete audited annual reports free of charge to any shareholder who requests it.

The company's own mailing list is the primary distribution channel. Like many publications, there is a subscription list for the annual report, in this case, the Investor Relations targets described earlier and recorded as such. The list can be steadily expanded to include new contacts and requests received directly from students, libraries, prospective investors, and so on.

Depending on how long this list is and the kind of visibility it is seeking, the company may also rely on other tools borrowed from marketing techniques:

- *Standard mailing techniques.* Some financial media allow readers to order annual reports through them. Companies pay for the service through advertising expenses and the cost of printing additional copies. The publications should be carefully selected based on their readership and distribution. Nothing prevents companies from requesting additional information from the recipients, that is, asking whether they would like to receive the annual report the following year and/or whether they are shareholders:
- Where domestic and foreign institutional investors are concerned, as seen in Chapter 2, mailing lists can be purchased from specialized vendors.

Paper copies of annual reports must be printed, regardless of the number of documents they include, but here again the Internet is creating dramatic changes in financial communications; electronic versions generate real savings on printing and distribution expenses, notably because fewer copies have to be printed.

There are different ways to post annual reports to corporate websites, the most common being to upload PDF or HTML files. Other, more innovative techniques involve making the reports more interactive via the following:

- Dynamic menus and submenus;
- Search engines;
- Exportability of texts and tables into text and spreadsheet files;
- Ability to print the on-screen text at any time.

Such innovative features should be integrated into the design phase because creating a paper-only document is no longer an option, while remembering that the paper copy won't go away. Professional design and production companies for annual reports abound, which assist companies in this area.

Nonetheless, much remains to be done to further improve the production process:

- Publication dates need to be moved up. Annual reports tend to be published much too long after earnings have been disclosed to be of any real use to financial markets. Very few companies are able to publish their annual reports on the day they announce their full-year earnings;
- Information should be presented in a more similar format from one company to the next and one year to the next.

3.6.6 Shareholder Letter

Published at regular intervals, the shareholder letter is usually sent to retail stockholders by mail or e-mail or through financial advertising. The style should be easily understood by all and describe developments within the company, while also providing other information such as stockmarket data. Additional letters may be written to inform shareholders of financial transactions or other major events.

Companies that have large international shareholder bases, or are listed on different markets, may publish multilingual editions.

3.6.7 Financial Advertising

Depending on applicable regulations, there may be restrictions regarding format, content, frequency, and distribution channels. This is often a lucrative activity for the media that prints advertisements. Financial advertising is typically used to attract retail investors and may turn into wide-scale campaigns when companies are advertising major events like privatizations or capital increases. Financial advertising can be an excellent means for medium-sized companies to build their corporate reputation, provided that the ads

- are not too crowded with information and remain visually appealing;
- include the main messages and financial data as well as information about where and how to find the complete information;
- provide contact details for the IR department rather than just the corporate website address where additional information can be found.

When permitted by the local legislation, financial advertising via online banner ads is becoming increasingly popular. Users can in many cases merely click on interactive banners to go directly to a full press release, the issuer's website, or a presentation.

3.6.8 Press Kits

Press kits are prepared for media representatives during special events or as a basic documentation about the company. They usually include the following:

- The most recent press releases;
- Biographies of executives and, when appropriate, speakers;
- A brief history of the company along with key events and figures;
- A copy of a presentation that will be delivered;
- Visuals such as logos and photographs;
- Contact information for the press service and the press officers, internally and, if applicable, the appointed Press Relations agency.

The kits should also be archived on the company's website under the section intended for journalists.

3.6.9 Public Meetings

A company can organize information meetings in its home market where its shares are first listed to discuss, for instance, the IPO, an earnings release or a financial transaction. Depending on the Investor Relations strategy, additional meetings may subsequently be scheduled in other key financial markets, regardless of whether the company is listed locally. These meetings can be arranged by the company itself, by its Investor Relations advisory firm, and by stock brokers or investment banks. In any case, the IRO should have an informed opinion on which investor his or her company should see.

Groups with large retail shareholder bases may also hold information meetings in cities where large numbers of shareholders are living.

They can either invite the media, analysts, and investors to the same meetings or hold separate press conferences. In certain legislations, companies are not allowed to ban journalists from attending analysts' presentations.

Conference calls are increasingly commonplace and may one day replace such in-person meetings because there are obvious savings in terms of cost, time, and planning. Public meetings nonetheless offer real advantages:

- Those in attendance have an opportunity to see management in person, ask them questions, and possibly interpret their body language;

- They allow TV and radio media to deliver images and sound to their audiences.

Meetings typically begin with a presentation not exceeding 45 minutes followed by a Q&A session. The most successful meetings are those that are the most carefully planned and rehearsed. They offer clear visuals, well-trained public speakers, skilled interpreters if any are used, and a well-prepared Q&A session.

The following are some proven and tested tips to act on—dos and don'ts to help you manage Investor Relations meetings effectively and strategically:

- *Categorize your audience.* Adapt your presentation depending on whether you have new investors or analysts in front of you or whether these have been following your company for several years.
- *Be yourself and do what you are comfortable with.* Do you prefer to follow a script or, on contrary, dive straight into Q&A?
- *Look at your audience right in the eye and notice any change in investor body language.* For instance, realize why and when they are losing interest in what you are saying and move on to another worthwhile topic for them or start inviting questions.
- *Deliver a dynamic and concise speech*, well synchronized with what appears on the screen.
- *Maintain consistency* with what you may have been presenting in previous meetings.
- *Be open and candid in your dialogue*, talking about your company's weaknesses while, at the same time, never missing an opportunity to stress its strengths.
- *Use stories and anecdotes* to show how involved you are with your company's operations and to bring your company alive.

3.6.10 Solving the "Who Meets Who" Problem

As discussed before, the IRO is the investment community's primary point of contact in the company. For a medium-sized company with no IRO, the CEO or CFO plays this role.

In line with the "seed, harvest, and lock approach" described in Section 3.2.2., companies that have IR departments and IROs will want to organize the interaction along the main following guidelines:

- The IRO is the main contact for sell-side analysts who are initiating and maintaining coverage of the stock, and for portfolio managers

who have not yet bought stocks in the company. The IRO has the credibility and expertise to present the company single-handedly;
- The chief financial officer can meet with influential analysts on a case-by-case basis, and meet with institutions that know more about the company and its outlook, especially those that already own shares;
- The CEO may be called upon to meet with the large institutional shareholders and those mostly likely to increase their stakes significantly.

Of course, this "division of labor" should be flexible and change when strategic imperatives so require. Note that investors do not mind meeting separately with different people from the same company as this can allow them to obtain interesting additional information.

The IRO should attend all meetings, noting the questions raised and answers given, as most analysts and investors will compare what is said to their notes from the previous meeting. This type of detail is key to delivering the same messages consistently. The IRO's notes will also help in seeing how often the same questions are raised and how efficient the responses are. If a given question is asked less and less frequently over a period of time, it probably means that investors and analysts have been reassured and convinced.

Some portfolio managers only meet companies on a one-to-one basis and will turn down any invitation to attend public meetings.

3.6.11 Successful Investor Relations Meetings Tactics

The keys to successful Investor Relations meetings are not very different from those that generally make meetings memorable: advance planning and organization, taking care of details, adopting a positive attitude, keeping a sense of humor, knowing how to manage time, and so on. When it comes to Investor Relations, applying the following rules will not only make your life easier, but also convey an impression of professionalism:

- *Research thoroughly.* You should absolutely know a lot more about the investor you are going to meet than simply his or her name and that of the institution! Don't hesitate to use a consultancy to do so. Whether you conduct the meeting on your own or if it is your CEO, have the history of your contacts and, potentially, historical ownership data, find out about their investment policy and major areas of interest or concern, and prepare the meeting accordingly. For instance, if it is a first-time meeting, you may want to start with a brief presentation. On

the contrary, you will offer to go immediately into Q&A for an investor familiar with your past performance and strategic directions.
- *Don't trust your memory*
  - Have your back-up material ready (publicly available documents such as press releases, annual reports, and presentations)?
  - Write down their questions and your answers. These records of previous contacts with institutions will help you conduct more focused meetings, while keeping track, from a legal perspective about what was said to whom and when.
- *Prepare and rehearse the presentation as well as the Q&A session.* Have more than one way of explaining why you can't comment or respond to a question?
- *Commit to follow-up.* Make sure that you keep your promise to provide the investor with additional information that he requested.

3.6.12 One-to-One Meetings

Face-to-face meetings with investors or analysts are and will remain the most important form of communications for Investor Relations teams, with one-to-one meetings the favorite one, as they are the most irreplaceable source of information by far for both parties. One basic rule allows no exception: the IRO should always attend any meeting with members of the investment community. The IRO will provide additional information, reiterate the key messages, or avoid the CEO or CFO giving (intentionally or unintentionally) price-sensitive information by helping them to remain within the boundaries of publicly disclosed information.

IROs may schedule meetings close together to see as many people as possible in the shortest amount of time. In this instance, it is important that people of similar levels of understanding of the company's sector and business be brought together. Many nonetheless prefer one-on-one meetings

- *With sell-side or buy-side analysts.* Analysts are there to gather information about the company's development and especially its strategic and financial outlook. They will be comparing this data to information received about other sector companies they cover. One-on-one meetings are an opportunity for them to address questions they do not want to ask in a public setting for fear that it may give their competitors an insight into how they intend to value the company. They will subsequently update their earnings estimates, write multi-page reports or more fundamental research, and issue buy, sell, or hold recommendations on the stock, combined with price targets. This research will be sent to their clients or the portfolio managers for whom they work.

- IROs will not necessarily receive this research prior to publication, even to correct any factual errors. When they do, they can assess how the earnings consensus is evolving and adjust their messages accordingly. Be that as it may, analysts must remain free to establish their estimates and recommendations as they see fit. In no case should an IRO refuse to meet with an analyst because he or she has a sell recommendation on the stock.
- *With institutional investors.* Meetings with institutional investors are held at company offices or those of the investor, especially when the latter is based abroad. It is not always necessary to do a presentation of the company. If the investor so prefers, a Q&A session will provide more interaction and actually be more appropriate. It is important to provide, as soon as possible, responses to any questions that go unanswered during the session. It is also a good follow-up opportunity to try and find out how the meeting went, from the investor's perspective.
- Many executives and IROs are nervous about such meetings but they are often the first choice of portfolio managers. Even meeting experiences that are relatively unpleasant for company representatives always provide valuable information. IROs should see that meetings are scheduled between executives and analysts or investors whose questions can help them hone their strategic thinking, even if they have the impression that they are being held in custody in an interrogation room, as can sometimes be the case with hedge fund managers.
- When it comes to deciding whom to meet with and when, companies should recall that the market is more likely to warmly welcome strategic shifts or major acquisitions when representatives have met with all of the key shareholders in the recent past. Regularity of meeting is essential and a key Investor Relations success factor in the long run.
- *With the media.* Dealing with the media requires a more proactive approach to obtain the desired exposure. It is a job in itself in that it also requires professional skills and expertise that are not necessarily the same as for an IRO, which is why in most cases the job tends to be split in two. As previously mentioned, close coordination between Investor Relations and Press Relations is going to be mission critical in a number of instances.

Do bear in mind, however, that the same rules about price-sensitive information apply to all.

A strong recommendation is to avoid going off-the-record with a journalist with privileged information unless:

- you have both agreed beforehand;
- you have a good, lasting relationship with the journalist.

3.6.13 Roadshows

Roadshows were originally a series of meetings organized on the key financial markets to present financial deals. Much more commonplace today, the term now refers to any time management goes on the road to meet with the investment community.

3.6.13.1 Roadshow format

There are two main categories of roadshow:

- *Deal roadshows*, scheduled to prepare for transactions
  - IPOs;
  - Acquisitions;
  - Capital increases or secondary offerings.

These roadshows may last several weeks. When a financial transaction is being planned, the program is organized by investment banks and may include presentations specifically for their sales teams.

- *Nondeal roadshows.* These tend to be scheduled for just a few days but on a regular basis. They can be used to present past year's earnings, strategy, and future plans of a company. Issuers can handle logistics themselves or entrust this task to brokers, depending on their objectives and resources.

3.6.13.2 To go solo or to use an investment bank

IR departments should also know when and how to avoid going through the "corporate access" teams of brokers or investment banks. Here are a few suggestions to help you decide which route to go:

- If you decide to rely on a broker, make sure you take the lead in deciding who to see on roadshows. Banks and brokers are extremely efficient at steering you toward prolific traders such as hedge funds at the expense of longer-term investors. You should, therefore, select them very carefully. While not exactly a frequent (or popular) process, calling for tenders can help eliminate proposals with little value added. IROs will make their selection based on criteria such as the composition of the brokers' client portfolios, their geographic coverage, their trading market share in your stock, the quality of their equity research, and post-roadshow feedback. They may also look at the track record from previous roadshows in terms of profiling and smoothness of logistics.

- To be efficient, different brokers should be brought on board and used more than once, so that you can make you own judgment. What's more, comparing their opinions on which investors your company should meet in which city will provide you with free advice while also helping to spot potential bias.
- From a budget standpoint, this is the least-costly solution for the issuer. That said, it will send a different signal, and executives may well get a warmer welcome from investors and particularly large shareholders, if it is the listed company that takes the initiative to arrange and organize meetings. In this respect, an independent Investor Relations consultancy will assist you in targeting shareholders outside your home country or region. Market information databases can offer a second opinion on investment banks' recommendations.

3.6.13.3 Roadshow Participants

Depending on the type of roadshow, the IRO will travel with one or more of the following executives:

- The chairman;
- The CEO;
- The CFO;
- The marketing or research and development director when a new product is being launched, depending on how technical it is;
- An operating officer;
- The CEO of the company being acquired, except of course when the takeover is hostile;
- The most experienced IROs can also handle roadshows alone.

Targets for roadshows should be selected with care. For instance, it is more efficient to organize a luncheon between the CEO and several smaller ("Tier Two") investors together and to save one-on-one meetings for high-potential ("Tier One") portfolio managers.

On specific occasions (a transaction, a product launch, a major investment), it may be useful to bring the operations manager on board, providing certain conditions are met

- Their participation will bring significant added value and help investors improve their understanding of the business;
- They will be thoroughly briefed on what investors want to know, but also on what they won't be able to talk about;
- They will receive presentation training.

3.6.13.4 Ten rules for successful roadshows

All roadshows combine public and one-to-one meetings and involve seeing financial analysts and institutional investors. Success is achieved by delivering quality information to the right people and ensuring that logistics are planned down to the minutest detail, especially when two or three teams are traveling to several countries. In addition to the aforementioned recommendations, the following rules can be applied, including the selection of a broker if one is used for the roadshow

- *Rule No. 1.* Identify when a roadshow is a must and when it is not. There is no need to go on the road unless you've got something new to say. A press release and conference call may be enough at regular intervals.
- *Rule No. 2.* Begin the planning process as far ahead of time as possible, bearing in mind that investors are extremely busy during the earnings reporting season, during which it is much better to rely on conference calls and virtual online roadshows. This allows issuers to provide the market with complete information in a timely fashion (for instance, by sending your presentation via e-mail ahead of meetings to familiarize your audience with the company's story) and schedule meetings during quieter periods. It also enables executives to engage in higher-quality dialogue, focusing more on strategy, positioning, and management issues than on yesterday's numbers. In addition, fund managers tend to be more available outside the reporting season.
- *Rule No. 3.* Trips should be planned according to the analysis of the shareholder base and the targeting strategy. Decisions about whether to send the CEO or IRO to meet with a portfolio manager should be based not on the size of the fund but rather on the likelihood that the meeting will lead to the purchase of stock in the company. Cities with the most investment power are given top priority, with fewer executives traveling to those with less investment potential.
- *Rule No. 4.* Logistics must in all cases be smooth and flawless. Meetings held in the same city should take into account traffic patterns to ensure that the team will be on time for each meeting. You may want to meet with hedge funds first thing as it will provide good training for the rest of the day.
- *Rule No. 5.* Travel conditions should be comfortable. An experienced staff member or outside provider should ensure that executives do not have to worry about logistics, that the schedule is followed, and that debriefings are possible between meetings.

- *Rule No. 6.* Resist any pressure from your investment bankers to plan 10 one-on-one meetings back-to-back as executives are likely to lose their "punch" and ability to be convincing after five, if not before. It is better to add a day to the trip, or target the institutions more carefully.
- *Rule No. 7.* Brief participating executives ahead of time about who they are going to meet, and why, rather than simply being given the name of the institution and investor. They will need to have the following information at least a week before the show goes on the road.
  - The type and amount of funds managed and investment strategy followed;
  - Titles, backgrounds, and job descriptions of the investors they are meeting with, including information about how much they know about the company and sector, what they are most interested in and concerned about and, where possible, a list of the questions they raised during previous meetings;
  - Whether they already own shares in the company or in a competitor or if they have been shareholders in the past;
  - A clear understanding of the key messages to get across.
- *Rule No. 8.* When travelling abroad, be aware of cultural differences and of the level of awareness in your company:
  - Make sure you are aware of how the local press covers your sector:
  - If appropriate, consider having some documentation, such as a fact sheet, a corporate brochure, written in the local language. Translate your accounts into the local currency, at least the most important numbers. In that case, make sure you address the issue of currency volatility;
  - Have a native with you so that someone immediately near you can understand the questions. It can be the salesperson of the investment bank or of the broker who is taking you on the road. Should the need arise, select a good translator. If you have local management, take them with you, even if they are not used to Investor Relations. They can put your hosts at ease, and not only because they speak the local language;
  - Be aware of cultural differences. Certain investors expect modesty, as in Northern Europe, whereas US investors are used to a more upbeat speech.
- *Rule No. 9.* Arrange for feedback to find out from the investors you met how they appreciated the meeting:
  - The company's strengths, weaknesses, risks, and opportunities;
  - The quality of the presentation made, and particularly, their feelings about how executives responded to their questions;
  - The quality of the company's Investor Relations;

- Whether this meeting has changed their opinion about the company and, if yes, in which direction. Ideally, you will want to know whether shares were bought or sold following the meeting.
- *Rule No. 10.* Follow-up on meetings:
  - Send a 'thank you' note to each investor and possibly a short questionnaire to find out how the meeting was perceived Not all IROs think to do this, but it is a good way to differentiate the company and receive top-quality feedback for free;
  - Provide responses to any questions that went unanswered;
  - Update your contact database.

3.6.13.5 International roadshow checklist

In addition to the above recommendation, experience also suggests

- Not to forget (just to name a few)...
  - Your passport (and a copy of your passport);
  - Memory sticks with your presentation and other documentation;
  - Foreign currencies;
  - Aspirin, Vitamin C;
  - Business cards;
  - Cell phone chargers, batteries, electrical adapters;
  - At least one hard copy of your presentation.
- And to take into account
  - Time zones;
  - Languages;
  - Cultural differences;
  - Etiquette;
  - Holidays.

3.6.14 "Reverse Roadshow"

Imagination knowing no limits in Investor Relations as well, innovative forms of roadshows are emerging. For instance, the reverse roadshow is hosted by an investment bank. This involves a number of companies visiting a city for a day. Investors in that city will get to meet several companies in one day. Among the advantages of this format, one can cite the following:

- Sector-focused agenda;
- Efficient use of time;
- Lower travel and logistics costs.

3.6.15 Conferences

Investment banks and brokers organize thematic meetings throughout the year to present companies to their clients and allow them to meet management during brief one-to-ones and break-out sessions.

Such events, some of which are prestigious, can be a good way to make the company more visible to the international financial community. The IRO should closely examine whether the conference is a real opportunity for the company and assess the quality of the portfolio managers who will be in attendance. It is possible that the institutions in question do not correspond to the target profile, or that they will not be represented by decision makers, in which case top executives will not necessarily need to be present.

The participation of different issuers will on the other hand be an opportunity for IROs to see presentations given by the competition, to meet with their Investor Relations counterparts, and to get ideas on how to improve their financial communications.

Small and midcaps that are hardly or not covered at all by sell-side analysts are sometimes solicited by Investor Relations event–organizing specialists to participate in conferences for a fee.

3.6.16 Analyst and Investor Days

These events, also know as "capital market days," are catering to the sell-side and buy-side analysts and to portfolio managers. An important part of the Investor Relations program, they are typically organized at the issuer's initiative, without involving a broker and can be particularly rewarding when they are planned far enough in advance. Also, they have been proven to increase the number of analysts covering a stock.

Compared with the cost of a week-long roadshow with the CEO and CFO, they can be a cost-effective way of getting a message across to a wide group of investors and analysts.

3.6.16.1 Objectives

Companies do not organize as many analyst days as roadshows, but these events require at least as much work. Therefore, it is critical that you know what you want to achieve and what type of messages you want the investment community to take away, before you decide to go ahead with the analyst day preparation. The challenge will be to build "checks and balances" into the day's agenda, so that investors are happy with the details received about the issues that are concerning them, and you have put emphasis on the issues that you think are poorly understood by the market.

If you have no strong message to deliver, either you should find another topic or you give up the analyst day for this time.

The IRO, as project manager, identifies the main topics to be addressed during the event. These will revolve around a division, a region, a technology, combined with a strategic update. The event will also serve to demonstrate how the CEO's vision is implemented.

As they are a unique way to show management and corporate culture in action, priority should be given to informal exchanges rather than traditional presentations. Ideally, the time should be evenly split between presentations, Q&A sessions, and networking. Make sure you have allocated ample time for this in the schedule and that management will be available.

The events can be unique opportunities for analysts and investors to mingle with executives and operational managers in small groups and gauge them.

With this in mind, the IRO should take care not to allow a few investors to monopolize the time of the top management and ensure that they go from table to table if a dinner or luncheon is scheduled.

Lastly, an investor day is also an image-enhancing event. There again, particular attention should be given to quality logistics, clean documentation, and to the care with which analysts and investors will be received, while keeping things nonetheless simple.

3.6.16.2 *Planning*

Planning and timing can make or break an analyst day. Here is some useful advice on how to avoid the main pitfalls:

- Whether it is scheduled over half a day or several days, the timing of the event is important both to internal and external participants. The date should be set at least six months ahead of time, depending on their schedules, to ensure maximum commitment of time and resources of the executives and operational managers who will be participating and on the financial market's events calendar. The company is part of a broader sector, so it is important that the chosen date does not coincide with events organized by other listed companies from the sector and that it does not coincide with the earnings reporting season or during school holidays.
- Invitations should be sent out to the entire analyst and investor base, ahead of time, no less than a month before. A "save the day" notice will get your event into diaries even if all the details are not entirely finalized. If participants' numbers have to be limited, then it is best to mention this in your invitation, while being aware of the criticism about selective or preferential access this may entail.

3.6.16.3 Location

Site visits tend to be quite popular but demand complex logistics, significant planning and budgets for the listed company. The institutions represented by analysts and investors may not be willing to pay for travel expenses, especially abroad. Documentation should be made available to those who cannot attend, or a webcast may be organized.

Holding the event in your headquarters or in a hotel in a large financial city event will probably maximize attendance and reduce potential last-minute cancellations.

3.6.16.4 Content

The goal for the attendees is to have a better understanding of your business. Demonstrations are usually appreciated but you need to make sure that they do not take up too much time that could be better used with hard facts and data. Strategic presentations are a popular feature in analysts days. You know how much investors and analysts love models, so give them numbers or explain to them the relationships that will help them to enhance their models.

As with earnings presentations, AGMs or roadshows, executives and operational managers should be trained in public speaking and rehearse their presentations. In particular, operational managers should be updated on how to present the company's key messages so there is no confusion about what can and cannot be said. Allow for as much rehearsing as possible, invest into executive-speech coaching if necessary, and take this opportunity to remind everyone about the rules on disclosure (see Table 3.5).

3.6.16.5 Feedback and debriefing

- Consider issuing a post event press release, summarizing the topics discussed. In particular, this could potentially be required if additional information has been disclosed that could be considered price-sensitive (such as revised objectives, for instance, between two reporting periods).
- The IRO should take advantage of the "thank you" notes sent to participants to have them fill out feedback forms (see Table 6.6 in the Resources section). The finds of this survey will then be shared with executives in order to ensure that the next analyst day is even better.

3.6.17 Conference Calls

Companies are increasingly relying on conference calls as soon as important issues arise: earnings releases, strategic announcements, or accidents. This tool has the following advantages:

Table 3.7 Example of Analyst Day Agenda

Session	Speakers	Content
Welcome	IRO	Presentation of program and speakers Specifics ("housekeeping items"): communications, transportation, documentation
Strategic presentation	Chief Executive Officer	Markets: historic trends and outlook Sales and margin growth driver Threats and opportunities, strengths and weaknesses Strategic priorities and medium-term targets
Financial analysis	Chief Financial Officer	Presentation of business model, key ratios and performance indicators Financing strategy Financial outlook and guidance
Operational review	Division head(s)	Presentation of products and services Competitive position Sites visits or product demonstration
Questions and answers	Full management team	Organize questions by theme. Provide concluding remarks with your key take-away messages for the day

See Table 6.5 for analyst and investor day checklist and timeline.

- They enable companies to comment quickly on events after a press release is issued and before an information meeting is held in the following days. This is particularly important in times of crisis management;
- Events can be explained instantly to audiences across all time zones. This, together with archiving systems, makes the conference call an effective way to promote equal access to information and limits the number of incoming inquiries.

3.6.17.1 *Making the best use of technology*

Today, modern technology allows the IRO to do the following:

- Talk to several hundred people at the same time without noise levels becoming unmanageable;
- Know who is on the call and anticipate difficult questions in advance;

- Receive questions directly via e-mail;
- Control, to a large extent, the Q&A session. Indeed, the IRO can manage the Q&A session more proactively and carefully, through conferencing 'host-control' tools. The IRO will see a list of those requesting to ask a question via a web-based interface in advance of their introduction to the company. He or she then has the technical ability to bring forward the most important or relevant participants and push down or remove those who are less welcome. This is a very efficient way of ensuring that conference calls are run smoothly and deliver the correct message, leaving the CEO or CFO confident and able to concentrate on the content of the call. In any case, the Investor Relations team will have selected the conference-call vendor with maximum care and tested the selected system enough to have full confidence in its strength. Don't hesitate to have back up lines with the conference-call operator and proper equipment such as headsets if you feel more comfortable that way;
- Provide transcripts, including of the Q&A sessions on the website. Replays increase overall attendance by giving people who could not participate in the live event a chance to take part later.

3.6.17.2 Script and presentation

A conference call is a rather formal exercise that requires professional preparation to achieve its goal in the Investor Relations strategy.

Presentations given by management may be supported by visuals that can be downloaded from the website or sent to participants ahead of time. They should not:

- contain any price-sensitive information not disclosed in the press release; or
- exceed 30 minutes.

A script written for, approved, and rehearsed by management is an absolute prerequisite, failing which management may well give a sense of improvisation that will turn out to be counterproductive.

Here is a trusted method for drafting the script and preparing for an earnings call:

- Review the period's preliminary financial statements with corporate financial reporting, consolidation, and audit teams as well as with divisional managers and assess the progress to be reported against internal and external expectations. Compare this information with that of your company's publicly traded peers;

- Start developing messages and metrics from these analyses, with a particular emphasis on how to explain the period's performance, strategic development, achievements as well as challenges;
- Draft and edit the earnings releases and the conference-call scripts for all management speakers;
- Design Webcast slide content that will match the information disclosed in the press release and support the script;
- List potential questions that may be raised during the conference call, as well as answers to them;
- Rehearse the conference call with the management team. When reading from a script, it is extremely difficult to deliver your speech to your audience rather than just read it aloud. Management should be careful not to lapse into a monotonous recitation of speech. Appearing enthusiastic and energetic will engage the audience, while maintaining an upbeat tone over the air will efficiently convey confidence in the business. This is even more necessary if the call is delivered in a foreign language.
- Some companies have adopted the practice of pre-recording management's prepared comments. When technically possible, the stated objectives are to save time, allow for maximum focus on the Q&A session and avoid reading mistakes.

Best practice suggests that

- conference calls should be announced by way of an invitation, a press release and posted on the company website, specifying the time and number to call, even if it is not required by the issuer's regulations;
- companies listed on markets in different time zones should take this into account, along with the structure of the shareholder base, when setting the time of the conference call; for instance:
  - Conferences in Europe should be scheduled in the afternoon if US analysts are likely to participate. Many companies, however, are reluctant to let the market trade much prior to the call. A well-structured and really informative press release will help significantly reduce the risks of potential misinterpretation before the call begins;
  - When major events are being announced, conferences should be scheduled after the close of trading.
- enough time should be preserved for the Q&A session with a view to provide the most accurate responses possible. You may want to decide in advance who in the executive team will respond to which question. Here again, responses should not include any previously undisclosed price-sensitive information;

- each participant should be allowed only two questions in order not to monopolize air time unnecessarily;
- never abruptly bring a discussion to an end, alleging that time has run out, and always wrap up with a summary of the key messages;
- gather and analyse feedback on the conference call from call participants and communicate it to management. This report will also be based on a review of the research published after the call. It will help identify which messages were best perceived by analysts and investors, where messaging can be made clearer, and what opportunities can be captured during future calls.

3.6.18 Open Days

This type of event corresponds to opening company gates to the public, in a particular site or plant, for retail shareholders, for instance.

3.6.19 The Annual General Meeting (AGM)

The AGM plays a crucial role in shareholder democracy. It is a strictly regulated event, with schedules and legal requirements that vary from one country to another.

Dispute-free AGMs are a sign of good governance. However, there is sometimes verbal abuse or belligerent questioning or unintelligible questions from individual shareholders.

Every listed company will probably tell you that there is a difficult path to tread between showing respect for the shareholders and overdoing it from a commercial perspective. Companies should learn issues that are likely to cause problems and make a conscious effort to be proactive, raising difficult questions themselves rather than waiting for shareholders to do so.

Companies should try to make sure that any new information included in the CEO's speech should go out simultaneously as a press release as well, giving some flavor about an initiative or explaining a strategic point of view.

In certain countries, regulations are in place that set a time limit to the Q&A session. They are meant to avoid having to answer for hours on end questions that have little bearing on the meeting. The quality of answers relates to the CEO and chairman and how seriously they take the AGM.

In the longer run, AGMs could move online. In the meantime, they are likely to remain one of the IRO's most dreaded activities, time-consuming and demanding events.

AGMs offer a unique opportunity for dialogue. Regulations are widely changing to make it simpler and more attractive for shareholders to vote.

Listed companies that have large numbers of foreign shareholders or a significant free float should provide documents in English, if this is not their working language. They should opt for electronic dissemination of voting documents whenever regulations so permit or require.

Corporate and Investor Relations teams should work together throughout the event to convey the company's values and culture. The meeting is, in most cases, the only time shareholders can see and interact with the chairman and executives. It is an opportunity for the company to promote its image. While there can be some conviviality, there may also be fierce debates. The focus should consistently be on presenting the company's strategy. It is always a good idea for board members to be present, especially those whose appointment is submitted to a vote.

In more and more cases, larger companies are broadcasting live or rebroadcasting their AGMs on the Internet.

As with any Investor Relations initiative, the company should seek to be informative and to engage in a genuine dialogue not only with its shareholders, but also with other stakeholders, to raise corporate governance standards to new levels.

- *With retail shareholders.* Most of the time, the AGM is a formality, a process aimed at approving uncontroversial resolutions. Yet it is a mistake to consider the AGM as a mere formality. Where Investor Relations are concerned, it is an annual meeting between executives and the owners of the company. It should be planned with great care and significant attention to logistics for companies with large numbers of retail shareholders. The event can be a vehicle for learning much more about these very same shareholders and their expectations.
- *With analysts.* Due to regulatory schedules, the AGM often takes place in the middle of the year, making it also an ideal platform for the CEO to discuss developments of the first half. Analysts also anxiously anticipate this "update." If any previously undisclosed or insider information is to be discussed, the company should issue a press release before the meeting. Another one will be sent out afterward, notably to report on vote results, the approval of the financial statements, dividends, the re-election of the chairman, the nomination of new board members, and so on. The "post-AGM" news release is a good way to feed the company's news flow.
- *With institutional investors.* When a company has good relations with its institutional investors, it knows what it can and cannot do and can resolve issues before they come to the spotlight. Some will send the IRO and the company' general counsel to gather information from institutional investors about their voting policy before the agenda of the annual meeting is published. Getting familiar with the corporate

governance principles and guidelines published by leading institutional investors is also quite useful.

A global Investor Relations program will also need to take into account the habits of voting of non-resident shareholders and not limit the organization of the AGM to the strict respect of its home country rules:

- *With proxy advisory firms.* There is only a handful of proxy advisory firms in the world, and they can be extremely harmful if not properly handled. Their mission is to provide institutional investors, for a fee, with recommendations on how to vote on given types of resolutions that are submitted to shareholders' votes. When the institutional investors do not have in-house guidelines, they may systematically apply these firms' recommendations without any further analysis

It is therefore essential that the IRO and the company's general counsel work hand in hand to prevent any conflict on resolutions that could be controversial.

Together they will

- identify who at the proxy soliciting firms is covering the company and engage with them as much as possible, as early as possible, especially regarding resolutions that diverge from corporate governance;
- learn the corporate governance standards of these firms from their websites;
- ask institutional investors to explain if and how they use their recommendations;
- check whether these firms have their facts right about their company, and require corrections if appropriate.

It is worthwhile for listed companies to measure their Investor Relations against those of other groups to which they are, or would like to be, compared. Some lesser-known tools and documents can help set them apart and be made available online. Here are a few examples.

Thanks to innovation, it is now technically possible to hold online shareholder meetings, also known as virtual shareholder meetings. Legal restrictions may in some jurisdictions ban these virtual meetings but there is growing interest from shareholders and other interested parties to encourage the use of technology. The main goals are as follows:

- To increase shareholder meeting participation;
- To improve communication between companies and investors;
- To reduce costs for small companies with little to no participation.

In June 2012, CalSTRS, the California State Teachers' Retirement System, one of the largest public pension funds in the world, as part of the Best Practices Working Group for Online Shareholder Participation in Annual Meetings, issued a report titled, "Guidelines for Protecting and Enhancing Online Shareholder Participation in Annual Meetings."

Key recommendations are that companies should do the following:

- Adopt principles for online participation in shareholder meetings, just as they would for an in-person meeting;
- Publish those principles in a reasonable period of time in advance of the meeting;
- Establish procedures to validate online meeting participants as shareholders;
- Establish reasonable procedures to allow anyone to attend an online annual meeting and to determine whether non-shareholders may be permitted to participate on a view/listen-only basis;
- Establish procedures for shareholders to vote remotely and to have such votes properly recorded;
- Establish reasonable guidelines for questions from shareholders intending to participate online in shareholder meetings;
- Arrange for a shareholder to present his or her shareholder proposal in person or through a telephone or video connection, requiring a reasonable amount of time for a shareholder to make such a request in advance of the meeting;
- Add disclosure in the proxy materials that provides notice of the type of meeting to be used next year;
- Archive the meeting on a publicly available website for a specific and reasonable period of time.

One can reasonably assume that there will be a mix of traditional, virtual-only and hybrid meetings of shareholders in years to come.

3.6.20 Factbooks

The goal is to condense in a single document several years' worth of financial information about a listed company, including a description of its industry and businesses, and the macroeconomic environment in which it has operated (5 to 10 years).

3.6.21 Written Disclosure Policy

While not mandatory, this document is increasingly becoming a component of Investor Relations best practice. Firms use this document to inform employees about the regulations governing public companies, and markets about the rules and objectives of their Investor Relations policy. It is best practice in Investor Relations to establish a written disclosure policy that stipulates the following:

- Which audiences are targeted, internally and externally?
- Who the authorized spokespersons are?
- The rules and responsibilities entailed in working in a public company;
- The rules for employee behavior when it comes to communicating with reporters, family, friends, colleagues, and business contacts;
- The type and form of information disclosed to the public and at what intervals;
- The principles presiding over the disclosure and dissemination of price-sensitive information;
- Quiet periods;
- Blackout periods and insider-trading windows.

The company may elect to post its disclosure policy on its corporate website.

3.6.22 The Shareholder Guide

This educational guide provides the following:

- A definition of technical, financial, and stock-market terms;
- A description of shareholder rights;
- A response to the most frequently asked questions about stock and dividend taxation;
- A user's manual for the stock market;
- A description of the company;
- Historical trends in the share price;
- The list and contact details of shareholder services (direct purchases, special meetings, information letters, and shareholder clubs and committees).

It will exist as a printed document as well as one that can be downloaded from the company's website.

3.6.23 Corporate Social Responsibility Report

In a majority of markets, publishing a CSR report is not a legally required document (some specific disclosure may be mandatory in other documents, though), but increasingly, a strongly recommended one. It is targeted not only at a wider audience that encompasses the investment community, but also at key stakeholders such as customers, partners, governments, regulators, local communities, and employees.

As previously discussed (see Section 3.5.7.), socially responsible investors and sustainability factors are playing a growing role in investment decision-making. Therefore, CSR reports focus on the company's values, its environment, workplace, diversity of employees, relationships with suppliers, and key communities.

3.6.24 Fact Sheets

A fact sheet (see Table 6.10 in the Resources section) is an attractively designed and presented one-page snapshot of a company. It states the investment case and lays out key facts and figures and other statistics vital to the investment decision-making process.

This document is intended to be updated as often as needed, in order to reflect any significant event (such as an acquisition or change in senior management).

3.6.25 Deploying Technological Innovation in Investor Relations

Online Investor Relations is certainly gathering pace. When used intelligently, technological innovation can be a powerful tool for promoting a company's Investor Relations and differentiating it from the competition. It can help convey the image of a company that, at the same time, offers state-of-the-art, cutting-edge Investor Relations tools and transparency.

The Internet enables firms to disseminate financial information through an ever larger number of channels, including the following:

- Live broadcasts or rebroadcasts of public events like earnings presentations, AGMs, and analyst days, with sound, video or both, and possibly simultaneous translation into a second language;
- Downloading of these files to personal digital assistants, hand-held devices like latest generation mobile phones;
- Uploading of virtual site visits, roadshows, or conferences ("webinars");
- Interviews with executives discussing important announcements;
- Ever-greater interactivity of documents posted to the website, with different means of viewing and extracting data.

Optimal use of technology can also allow companies to reduce:

- Production and distribution costs (particularly for the annual report), especially now that changes in regulations and accounting standards are requiring companies to provide an ever-larger quantity of information;
- Lead time for making information available;
- Asymmetric information.

Mobile apps and tablets are becoming increasingly commonplace in the IR world. IR departments are adapting their websites to be supported by smart phones and tablets ("IR apps"). The expansion of social media is also benefitting from these devices, while IROs can stay connected to their offices and to market news or stock quotes since all of the major and most of the minor financial news services now have apps on the market. IR vendors are also selling subscription-based services for IROs to check certain information on the road (investor profile, shareholding history, etc.)

3.7 Enhancing Shareholder Loyalty and Retention

Just as customer relationship management (CRM) helps companies understand and anticipate customers' needs, a core aspect of Investor Relations can well be compared to a shareholder relationship management (SRM). The goal there is to improve shareholder trust, loyalty, and retention. Most shareholder relationship management tools that are developed by certain software companies seem to be primarily used at companies with a large base of individual shareholders. Yet SRM should apply to institutional shareholder relations as well.

3.7.1 Extracting Value from the Shareholder Base

Companies can extract value from their shareholder base in several ways:

- *Cost savings and efficiencies.* For example, they will be able to promote and accelerate take-up for online shareholder communications, which will undoubtedly reduce printing, mailing, and telecommunications costs. Also, by better educating shareholders and turning them into dedicated followers, the company may be able to rationalize the number of smaller shareholders and see an increase in their average position in the stock. This will result in more efficiencies.

- *Increased shareholder loyalty.* Faithful shareholders are more likely to participate in a capital increase, to help drive positive change in the company or to help withstand a crisis.
- *Brand loyalty.* Research indicates that most private shareholders tend to show preference for the goods and services of companies in which they own shares.

3.7.2 Combining Financial and Corporate Communications Strategies

To continue the CRM analogy, it costs less to keep an existing customer than to acquire a new one. It is, therefore, worth developing a strong Investor Relations program that will inform, educate existing shareholders, and possibly convince them to increase their holdings in the company.

Investor Relations efforts alone will not be sufficient to improve shareholder loyalty and retention, and they should be backed by the following:

- An attractive shareholder remuneration policy (bonus shares, increased dividends, preferential subscription rights, dividend reinvestment plans, etc.);
- Consistent financial performance;
- Access to some of their services or products on preferential terms, when regulations so allow. The goal, in this case, is to make the shareholder an advocate of the company's brand, products and services.

Companies seeking to build and maintain a strong base of retail shareholders may set up shareholder clubs or shareholders' benefit programs. These offer dedicated information channels, events, and services. Membership or participation may be contingent upon a minimum number of shares.

3.8 Dealing with Crisis Communication in Investor Relations

Any crisis affecting a listed company will directly and immediately affect Investor Relations, whether it is:

- a financial crisis (a profit warning, a hostile bid, a class action launched by disgruntled shareholders, a change of strategy requested by activist

shareholders, financial bankruptcy, investigations by market authorities, etc.);
- a business crisis (a major industrial accident, a massive product recall, nationalization of assets, injuries or death caused by defective products, damage to management reputation, the theft of key data, CEO departure, transformational change through heavy restructuring, etc.);
- an external crisis (terrorism, wars, natural disasters, etc.);
- a major change in the industry, driven by regulation or technology, new players.

There are two main issues:

– One for the entire organization: no one knows when the crisis is going to be over;
– One for IROs more specifically: most IR people are not used to handling the media. They are best advised to hire a PR firm and should actually be the ones bringing them in. It can prove to be a powerful tool to have a "seat at the table."

It is important to recognize that crisis management and risk management are joined at the hip. This is why risk management should start with an exercise to initiate the process and get IR, PR, legal and public affairs teams thinking what might happen and what is the process to go about it. Scenario rehearsals can be quiet effective.

All crisis management manuals will say that nothing can help more in the event of a crisis than proper planning. While this book certainly does not claim to be exhaustive about crisis management techniques, it aims to provide some useful hints for a professional handling of Investor Relations under such circumstances.

Bad news does happen, and financial markets are used to it, but if there is one thing they do not like, it is surprises.

Crises have consequences, some of which are:

- Immediately after they are announced, for instance, the share price will adjust or could collapse dramatically;
- Longer term; this will affect the market-risk premium assigned to the company, making its financing more costly.

Yet the media and the potentially negative news coverage, the financial markets, and the likely hit to the stock prices are, by far, not the only stakeholders to target. While engaging in a genuine dialogue with their own target audiences, Investor Relations should see to it that the

Implementing Best Practices in Investor Relations 183

stakeholders that are most directly affected by the crisis are prioritized. From the very beginning of any crisis, management should think ahead to the future of the organization. Unless it is a disaster that may result in property damage and/or casualties, the news media should be a secondary consideration.

3.8.1 Anticipating, Just in Case...

Knowing that it is never too late to mend, top management will have to do more than put in place alert systems, crisis management teams, and procedures. Their work will also involve looking beyond the crisis to see how it can help the company learn and grow from the experience.

All of this implies that efforts have been made well in advance, at the highest levels, to identify potential risks, occurrence probabilities, and their potential impact on the company's future. This is actually part of strategic planning insofar as it forces companies to identify their most vital and vulnerable areas and to create alert signals. The value of systematically investing in quality information systems cannot be emphasized enough. These systems should reflect the reality of companies' operations, obligations incorporated in their bylaws, and the expectations of financial markets.

Even the best efforts can fall short however, if the company has not striven over time to build a strong relationship with financial markets that is based on credibility, trust, transparency, and consistency. Markets typically consider that "confidence comes by foot and goes by horse." In this sense, one of the main reasons Investor Relations exists is to proactively prevent crises or effectively ensure proper damage control.

If a company has interacted regularly with analysts, investors, and journalists, and consistently provided them with reliable and exhaustive information that is adapted to their work methods, it should be able to anticipate the market's reaction to nearly any kind of crisis. If executives have made themselves available over time, they will have earned the trust of markets, during good times and bad. This process is the foundation of the Investor Relations strategy, the one without which crisis communication cannot be effective.

3.8.2 Joining Press Relations and Investor Relations forces

A critical success factor will be to effectively join Press Relations and Investor Relations strengths in the crisis management task force.

IROs should imperatively be involved in this entire process and not be seen merely as disseminators of regulation-compliant information. They know more than anyone about the market's sensitivities and how to identify key audiences based on how important their contributions are to the future of the company. They know when and how to use the right tools to keep shareholders, analysts, and even the business press up to date. IROs are also responsible for letting management know in real time how the company is perceived by the market in such circumstances. The chain of command may be such that the IRO does not feel free to speak freely and objectively, in which case an outside advisor, who must be legitimate and given the same priority access to internal and external information, may also be brought into this "inner circle."

The IRO and the Investor Relations team should have access to all the information needed to understand what is at stake, sparing no details. This will enable them to

- develop Q&A documents that are shared with the entire crisis management team;
- deliver messages that
  - are truly informative and as objective as can be,
  - describe business continuity plan for the crisis,
  - reach the key stakeholders before they hear about it second hand from the media or someone else;
- make sure the company speaks with one voice.

They should all be fully integrated within the crisis communication team and benefit from intensive involvement from the executive team. In many cases, the IRO will be among the first two or three spokespersons selected, sometimes before the CEO, to help resolve a crisis efficiently. Incidentally, this eventuality should be borne in mind when hiring an IRO. Successful crisis management also reflects the strength—and not just the size—of the Investor Relations team. Providing its contact databases are up-to-date, the company knows how to reach its key shareholders quickly. Both permanent staff and advisors and contractors should be highly experienced professionals and fully mobilized. Companies should not hesitate to expand their teams and may seek to add complementary skills, as is done during takeover wars.

In times of crisis, Investor Relations should not be relied upon to resolve the problem on its own but rather to assure that any information delivered is accurate and appropriate. Part of the team's job is to help maintain the company's reputation and retain the trust of consumers, shareholders, employees, and more generally speaking, all stakeholders.

Without delay, the company must come up with messages that are credible and can withstand in-depth analysis. Yet, let's face it: compelling messages and powerful talking points will only gradually appear.

Once this is done, the approach can move from a responsive to a proactive one, mobilizing the right people and resources depending on the nature and magnitude of the crisis. Bearing in mind that investors, the media, employees, and market authorities can be its closest allies or worst critics, the company should in all cases engage in a dialogue that will avoid seeming arrogant, indifferent, unprepared, or lacking credibility, as these attitudes could make the crisis worse. On the contrary, the circumstances can be turned into an opportunity for a firm to reiterate its fundamental strengths and long-term strategy. It is always much more difficult to regain credibility than it is to improve an income statement.

Key Principles to Remember

- There is much more to Investor Relations than about presenting financial statements. Companies' valuations are increasingly shaped by the transparency with which they disclose information, management's reputation, and the quality of corporate governance and sustainable development policies.
- Communications strategies must, from beginning to end, combine fieldwork, planning marketing and flawless logistics.
- Investor relations target different audiences with different expectations and timing strategies. The resources mobilized to reach and convince them and their retain their loyalty must be flexible. The Internet and technological innovations are providing companies with ways to optimize their investments and differentiate themselves from other companies that are competing for capital as well;
- Management should think twice before embarking on provifing guidance.

International Best Practices

- Use every opportunity to identify your shareholders.
- Don't forget school holidays when you plan your annual financial calendar, in your home country as well as in your target cities for roadshows.
- When you go road showing abroad, make sure your presentation is adapted to the local habits and culture. Give main orders of magnitude in the local currency.
- Always remember to send out a "thank you" note after meeting with and investor. This is an effective way to get direct and valuable feedback for free.
- Make sure your Investor Relations website is your Number One information platform.
- Structure your earnings presentation around the same key messages as those in your press release.
- Avoid giving your opinion on how cheap you think your stock is.
- Put crisis-proof procedures in place.

4
Measuring the Value of Investor Relations

Yes, Investor Relations can and should be measured, and the payoff of a strategic Investor Relations program demonstrated.

As discussed in Chapter 1, an Investor Relations strategy requires investment and translates into a series of realistic objectives, in line with a company's budget, philosophy, and environment. These will, in turn, become as many performance indicators. The actual performance of the Investor Relations strategy will then be measurable against these objectives. While not an exact science—many factors affect the share price of course—performance evaluation can indeed be applied to Investor Relations, providing:

- Investor Relations is considered more like a profit center, not a cost center concentrating on administrative on compliance tasks;
- as such, its contributions to the company's strategy and valuation can be demonstrated (and even incentivized).

In order to try and meet this challenge, it is necessary to have developed the appropriate performance evaluation framework, one that tracks strategic metrics, not simply the number of meetings, conferences, or press releases.

Yet there certainly are as many measurements as there are Investor Relations programs, confirming that no single standard applies across the profession. Furthermore, the growing importance of intangibles like brand strength, or quality of management in the valuation of companies further increases the difficulty in coming up with a clear and accurate measurement technique. In addition, it is an iterative process, one that needs to be ongoing and integrated into the Investor Relations program.

The following key questions however apply to every company and transcend boundaries:

- What will make investors invest?
- What is the right level of investment, measured both in cash expenditure and in valuable senior management time, to achieve the highest sustainable valuation?

It makes sense to go by the following principles and ask yourself some simple questions, when developing an IR measurement framework:

- Measure what you can control;
- Why do you measure? Why not?
- To what extent is IR effectively supporting the company's strategy?
- Is your shareholder base supportive through crisis?

There should be different measures for different reasons, and the size of the company will also matter in the measurement.

4.1 Quantitative Factors

Calculating returns on investment in Investor Relations involves the analysis of five categories of quantitative measurements.

4.1.1 Stock-Market Criteria

The main examples are as follows:

- Share prices are largely outside the IRO's control and should definitely not be the one and only measure of Investor Relations;
- Valuation multiples, both in absolute terms and in relation to one or more indices, and a sample of comparable companies;
- Trading volumes;
- Low share price volatility is a good measure of effective Investor Relations;
- Inclusion in one or more indices, including sustainable development and corporate governance indices;
- Evolution of ratings, such as credit, sustainable development, and corporate governance.

4.1.2 Equity Research on the Company

IROs should monitor developments in the following areas:

- Number and geographic origin of sell-side analysts;
- The consensus of earnings estimates;

- The percentage of buy, sell, and hold recommendations;
- Target prices.

4.1.3 The Shareholder Base

Investor Relations is a marketing function, a strictly regulated but also a strategic one. Therefore, evaluating the returns on investment in Investor Relations can, in many ways, be compared to measuring customer satisfaction retention. Which were kept, won over, or lost?

If proper Investor Relations action–tracking tools and shareholder relations management (SRM) techniques have been implemented and maintained over time, it will be possible for Investor Relations to identify the following:

- Who are our analysts and investors?
- What do they want in terms of information? Investor Relations products and services?

The more you know about your target audience and about what "works" with it, the better equipped Investor Relations is to fulfill its mission and develop efficiency, focus, and effectiveness in marketing its stock.

The shareholder base can be analyzed, based on the following:

- Categories of investor (institutional or retail);
- Investment styles (institutional investors);
- Geographic or regional breakdown;
- Average portfolio size in terms of shares held and values;
- Average holding period;
- Subscription rates for equity—and debt-raising transactions and concentration of shares. For instance, how many institutional investors own a quarter or half of the free float? What percentage do the top 5 or 10 shareholders own?
- Distribution and concentration of shareholder base, by category of investors (retail vs. institutional investors), and by average number of shares held. Too much stock in the hands of any one investor, or for that matter, in the hands of a single class of investors, leads to significant risk.

Taken together and analyzed at least once a year, these factors allow the company to do the following:

- See how efficient it was in targeting and meeting investors compared with its strategy for attracting shareholders. Has overseas investment increased? Have you been able to reduce dependence on a few investors?
- Plan its roadshows, without neglecting smaller markets that may be home to potentially large shareholders.
- Evaluate the real investment potential of certain countries or institutional investors, possibly leading it to plan a foreign listing.
- Use management's and the Investor Relations team's time optimally.
- Eliminate or reducing the need for investment banks and brokers in targeting shareholders and organizing Investor Relations events.

4.1.4 Financial Criteria

These primarily relate to the following:

- Cost of capital and, more generally, the company's financing costs;
- Size of financial deals and take-up rates;
- Company's valuation multiples compared with the competition;
- Total shareholder returns generated and other shareholder value creation metrics.

4.1.5 The Investor Relations Program

Records should be kept of the number of

- one-to-one meetings;
- days of roadshows;
- conferences attended;
- cities and countries visited;
- e-mails, requests for information, mail, and telephone calls received;
- participants in conference calls (number and geographic origin).

These different factors should subsequently be compared to one another and then to the objectives of the Investor Relations strategy. Questions may include the following:

- Was the percentage of foreign investors higher after two annual roadshows were organized abroad?

- By what percentage the meetings in the past 12 months with institutional investors have increased (or decreased) their stakes?
- How many analysts have a buy (or sell) recommendation on the stock compared to last year?
- How do the consensus earnings estimates for next year compare to the company's own guidance and budgets?
- Has the number of retail shareholders increased, thanks to information meetings held specifically for them?
- How much did the last capital increase cost compared with the previous one?

4.2 Qualitative Factors

There are times when a new director is coming on board, a major financial deal is being planned or executed, a crisis is being resolved, or a company simply wants to inquire about how the market perceives it and its Investor Relations strategy. These can be opportunities to evaluate the company's image and reputation. Executives, including board members, should be kept abreast of all developments in these areas.

While the quantitative metrics listed above may serve, among others, to determine the variable part of an IRO compensation, top management is said to favor qualitative, not quantitative, means or metrics to measure the effectiveness of the Investor Relations function at their companies.

4.2.1 Perception Studies

Similar to analyses of shareholder bases, efforts to obtain accurate and objective information about how companies are perceived require considerable work and must be repeated over time to see how Investor Relations have improved since the previous survey. The survey should thus be seen as a highly value-added investment that will only bear fruit if the results are taken into account and relevant recommendations are followed.

There is no point in conducting a perception study if the company does not intend to:

- share it with management, and possibly with the board as well;
- use the conclusions to improve or make adjustments to its Investor Relations program. Inquiries into how the financial community sees a

company will also reveal the former's perception of management, their credibility, their integrity, and trustworthiness—information not everyone wants to hear. Be that as it may, analysts and investors interpret the effort as a sign that the company is interested in its opinions. This can also help boost the issuer's financial image;
- conduct a similar study every 18 months or 2 years.

4.2.1.1 Areas of focus

The most popular topics are as follows:

- An ongoing analysis of perceived transparency, reliability of information, and accessibility of management;
- The perception of management's long-term objectives. Are they realistic? Too ambitious or not enough? Do investors trust management's ability to achieve them?
- A benchmark of the company's Investor Relations program with the competition and best practices both in terms of content and form. Is the company using the right metrics to communicate its strategy?
- Comprehension of the strategy as reflected in the messages delivered;
- The relevance of the financial results and outlook reported;
- Perception of management, corporate governance, and sustainable development.

4.2.1.2 Methodology

Whatever the topics addressed, the success of perception studies always depends on the following:

- The method applied and, in particular, the quality of the questionnaire or interview outlines. These should be precise enough to guarantee that the information gathered corresponds not only to what the company wants to know, but also leave room for dialogue between the interviewer and interviewee.
- The combination of quantitative and qualitative responses.
- The interviewer's experience and familiarity with the subject. The IRO should be involved in preparing the questionnaire and ensuring that the person conducting the interview knows the company well.
- The selection of participants. Depending on the study's focus, the list will include existing and former shareholders, individual shareholders or institutional investors, and existing buy- and sell-side analysts and journalists.

- The guarantee that responses will be transcribed in full and objectively. In most cases, the responses are not attributed, but the nominative list of investors or analysts polled is provided.

The decision to conduct research internally or externally depends on your goals and resources. If your company cannot afford to hire a consultant, put together a list of questions yourself and call targets.

You may also want to consider hiring a third party to provide objectivity and external validation when dealing with management, obtain blunt answers from respondents, and to benefit from a consultant's expertise.

4.2.2 Awards

Honors, awards, and distinctions are all testimony to the quality of a company's financial communications, from a benchmarking perspective or as a recognition of achievements in IR. These tend to be given by the media, IR associations or and specialized firms for the best annual report, best IRO in the sector, and so on.

Being recognized for excellence in Investor Relations should be on every IRO's mind.

4.2.3 Investor Relations Organizational Structure

During each phase of its development, the company should ask itself whether

- The Investor Relations team is of the right size and includes the right profiles;
- All tools—websites, computer systems, and databases—are up-to-date;
- Investor Relations channels (notably the annual report and website) correspond to users' expectations;
- Production processes are efficient;
- Regulatory changes are being anticipated;
- Service providers are duly fulfilling their missions;
- Budgets are sufficient to implement the Investor Relations strategy, factoring in potential productivity gains and savings.

4.2.4 Assessment by Senior Management

IROs should participate in the goals that are set for IR. Here are areas that senior management will want to assess the following:

- How effectively has IR implemented the IR program of the year?
- To what extent is IR effectively supporting the company's strategy?
- Has the shareholder base supportive through crisis?
- Has senior management time been optimized?

Key Principles to Remember

- Investor Relations are an investment, not an expense. Their efficiency should be evaluated based on objectives determined at the outset and regularly monitored over time.
- The share price is the most visible but not the only way to measure returns on investment. Changes in tool for assessing and improving the company's financial image over the long term.

International Best Practices

- Develop your own measurement tools to track the efficiency of your Investor Relations program, before you think of investing in specific software.
- Set measurable and realistic targets for your Investor Relations strategy, not just the increase of the stock price.
- Make sure management and the board of directors are being regularly kept informed of the company's perception by the market.
- Be prepared to take action and reassess your priorities based on the evolution of your return on investment on Investor Relations.

5
Conclusion

The dynamic and complex nature of the capital markets may challenge management to isolate the impact of effective Investor Relations and corporate communications from broader market forces. In addition, there is the deeply rooted belief that results will "speak for themselves" and that Investor Relations are costs that can easily be done without.

However, research is providing sufficient evidence to support the idea that the quality and frequency of disclosure has a significant impact on a company's valuation.

There are thousands of companies seeking to raise money on financial markets globally. Despite the increasingly large number of electronic markets, some of which are more tightly regulated than others, companies will still have to deliver information that is impartial and accessible to all, without discrimination. This guarantees that values can be accurately assessed by markets.

As technologies and business models continue to evolve, historical financials will become less reliable indicators of future performance. Increasingly, those companies that do not want, or are not adequately equipped, to communicate how they plan to create shareholder value will be at a strong competitive disadvantage.

In this highly competitive environment, Investor Relations are as much a part of companies' overall vision as their development strategy. When a proactive approach is taken, the quality of Investor Relations can prove a real competitive edge: If two firms have comparable financial and economic results, the one with the better Investor Relations can very well be more generously valued.

6
Resources

6.1 The CEO Investor Relations Checklist

Ten basic questions any CEO should always know the answer to

1. Who are your top five shareholders?
2. What is your next earnings release date?
3. What is your shareholder remuneration policy?
4. What are your three most important competitive differentiators?
5. What keeps you awake at night?
6. What is your optimal capital structure?
7. What are the performance criteria in executive compensation packages at your company?
8. Is there a written succession plan in place?
9. What is your objective for return on investment?
10. How would you describe your company's values?
11. What are the metrics on your company's dashboard?

6.2 Daily Stock Trading Datasheet

Issuer		Index	
Price		Price	
% Change		% Change	
Volume		Since January 1	
Open		1 year	
High			
Low			
Previous close			
Volume			
Market capitalization			
Historical Data	*Change*	*High*	*Low*
Since January 1			
1 year			
Peer Group	*Company A*	*Company B*	*Company C*
% change/ previous close			
Since January 1			
1 year			
Market capitalization			
Comments			

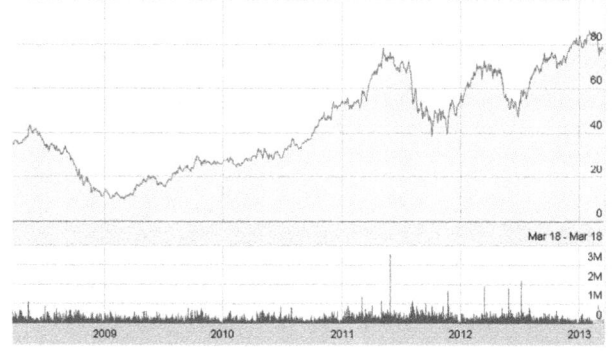

6.3 Sample Investor Relations Resume

Your name [Certification: e.g. CFA, PhD] Address Telephone E-mail	Citizenship: Born: 27/05/1969 Mobility: international	 Your photograph

Expert in Investor Relations

Award-winning international finance professional with proven track-record of building and managing profitable financial operations in the US and Europe. Excellent financial analysis and communication skills used effectively to convey market value creation propositions and motivate personnel to achieve challenging profitability targets. Highly disciplined business unit manager with extensive experience in operational efficiency improvement and cost control.

CAREER HIGHLIGHTS

Company A *An $15 billion IT service provider* **Senior Vice-President Investor Relations**	New York, New York, USA 2009–present

- Developed and executed a comprehensive Investor Relations strategy designed to provide financial analysts and global investors with a thorough understanding of the company's earnings dynamics.
- Developed a close appreciation for the models utilized by analysts to value/evaluate the organization's performance and communicate this information to the board, senior management and the international investment community.
- Actively promoted transparency and fair disclosure. Managed the NYSE listing relationship.

Main Achievements

- Company A Investor Relations team was voted best in the Computer Services & IT Consulting category in Institutional Investor's "America's Best Investor Relations" 2011 survey.
- Market capitalization tripled within 3 years.
- Expansion of sell-side analysts coverage and global diversification of shareholder base.

Company B *An $8 billion automotive component manufacturer* **Vice-President, Investor Relations**	San Francisco, USA 2005–2009

- Developed and executed core investor strategies and messages, ensuring that these were driven consistently through all internal and external communications.

- Conducted financial presentations at international investor conferences and one-on-one meetings.
- Recommendations to manage the "guidance" levels provided to the street.

Main Achievements

- 2006 Investor Relations Magazine Awards: Best IR Program.
- Enhanced external communications of corporate brand positioning/identity to strengthen Company B investment story. Advised senior management of expectations and feedback from Wall Street.
- Increased sell-side research coverage from 7 to 17 analysts in 14 months.

Company C	London (UK)
A $25 billion global leader in retail industry, listed on the London and New York Stock Exchanges	1995–2006
2002–2006: Senior Vice President, Investor Relations – Corporate Communications	

- Responsible for Corporate IR and PR functions, including all relationships with stockholders and the financial community as well as the media and community relations (staff: 10).
- Served as principal Company spokesperson to the financial community and the business media.
- Assisted HR department in creating employee communications.
- Member of the Company's Disclosure Committee which ensured Company compliance with regulatory and stock exchange requirements.

October 1999 to August 2002 Vice President, Marketing Communications, and Investor Relations

- Established the Corporate Communications/Investor Relations group.
- Primary corporate spokesperson.
- Developed Company D's brand strategy.

Main Achievements

- IPO December 2004.
- Lead investor relations officer and Company spokesperson through nine acquisitions, one secondary stock offering, one major lawsuit, three CEO transitions, three CFO transitions, two Chairman transitions and 36 quarterly earnings cycles

Additional experience

Vice President, Corporate Finance Salomon Brothers International, London, 1990–1995.

Equity Analyst, Robert Fleming Inc, New York, 1986–1990.

Fixed Income Senior Portfolio Analyst, London, RBC Financial Group, 1984–1986.

Education

CFA Institute

Chartered Financial Analyst – awarded CFA designation in 2000

YALE SCHOOL OF MANAGEMENT, New Haven, Connecticut (USA)

M.B.A., Finance

Named to Dean's Honor Roll as one of the top students in Business Administration

STANFORD UNIVERSITY, Palo Alto, California (USA)

B.A., Latin American Studies

Languages

English: native speaker

French and Spanish: fluent (oral & written)

Italian: conversational

Affiliations

Member of the National Investor Relations Institute (US), the Investor Relations Society (UK) and the CFA Institute

6.4 Earnings Presentation Evaluation Form

I. Presentation

1: Excellent;   2: Good;   3: Don't know;   4: Poor

Your overall impression:
1. The organization of the meeting?
   ☐ 1   ☐ 2   ☐ 3   ☐ 4
2. The length of the presentation?
   ☐ Good   ☐ Too short   ☐ Too long
3. If support materials were insufficient, indicate which documents were missing:
4. Is the annual earnings presentation enough?
   ☐ Yes   ☐ No
5. If no, what other types of meetings would you like the company to hold and with which frequency?
   ☐ Conference call
   ☐ Quarterly   ☐ Every 6 month
   ☐ Plant tour
   ☐ Analyst day

II. Presentation Content

6. Did you receive enough information?

   On the Company's operations
   ☐ Excellent   ☐ Good
   ☐ Average   ☐ Poor

   On the Company's outlook
   ☐ Excellent   ☐ Good
   ☐ Average   ☐ Poor

7. Which topics would you have liked to see discussed?

III. Perception of the Company

8. Do you think that presentations can impact investment decisions?
   ☐ Yes   ☐ No   ☐ Don't know
9. Are you a shareholder?
   ☐ Yes   ☐ No

   Why?
   Liquidity ☐
   Industry ☐
   Country ☐
   Currency ☐
   Other (please elaborate) ☐

10. Which are the most important factors in you investment decision-making? (you may tick up to 5 boxes)
    Industry ☐
    Profitability ☐
    Strategy ☐
    Financial structure ☐
    Global presence ☐
    Stock performance ☐
    Other (please elaborate) ☐

11. What is your opinion on the stock?
    Short-term
    Positive ☐
    Negative ☐
    Don't know ☐
    Long-term

    Positive ☐
    Negative ☐
    Don't know ☐

12. Has today's presentation modified your opinion?
    Positive change ☐
    Negative change ☐
    No change ☐

6.5 Analyst and Investor Day Checklist and Timeline

D-Day Minus...	
12 to 6 months	• Presentation to management of list of potential Investor day themes • Project validation, confirmation of day and location, RFP sent to vendors • Speakers confirmed, rehearsals scheduled, "liaison officers" designated • Checklist & timeline distributed to project team • "Save-the-Date" sent out to analysts and investors
3 to 6 months	• Full program and formal invitation • Online registration, vendor selection, budget and logistics • Bi-monthly progress reports/meetings
1 to 3 months	• Preliminary list of participants, including in-house executives • Second draft of presentations and scripts, draft pre (post) Analyst Day press release(s) • Website update, binders, covers, bags, name tags ordered • Weekly progress reports/meetings
1 month to 15 days	• Registration deadline • Presentations, scripts, press release(s), post-event evaluation form, participants' list & logistics details provided to management • Logistics explained to management • Bi-weekly progress reports/meetings • First rehearsals and media training sessions
1 week to 2 days	• All presentations, scripts and Q&A final • Second round of rehearsals • Translation of documents, if applicable, distribution to interprets • Website update • On-site logistics tests, incl. back-ups • Handouts final, incl. « briefing book » for speakers and management
1 day	• Dress rehearsal » • Logistics, incl.: presentations uploaded on website and on external hard disk, all audio-visual equipment in order • List of participants final, distributed to management and speakers • Back-up phone line in IR department • Informal dinner / cocktail reception
D-day	
	• If informal dinner held on previous evening, keep management and speakers informed of what you've heard before Analyst Day starts • Presentations uploaded, webcast ready • Post-Analyst Day press release, if applicable
D-Day Plus...	
1 day	• Send evaluation survey to all participants with "Thank You" note • Follow-up with additional information as promised • Provide management and speakers with executive summary of analysts' reports
2 days	• Update • Contact data base and mailing list • Q&A document
7 days	• Debrief with IR team and vendors • Send executive summary of evaluations of analyst day to management and speakers • Compare actual costs against budget

6.6 Analyst and Investor Day Evaluation Form

Please provide us with your feedback. It will help us improve the next session.

What was your overall impression of investor day			
Excellent	Good	Fair	Poor

Organization

What would be your favorite investor day frequency?			
Every 6 months	Once a year	Every 18 months	Every two years

What would be the ideal investor day length?			
Half day	One day	One and a half day	Two days

What would be the best period of the year to hold an investor day?

Should an investor day include a site visit?	
Yes	No

Where would you like the next investor day to take place?	
In the group home country	Abroad

Content

What would you like to have in the next investor day?		
A Group overall presentation	A focus on one business segment	A focus on several business segments

Please specify the business segments you would like the focus to be on:

Which member of the management would you like to meet during the investor day?			
CEO	CFO	Marketing officer	Operation officer

Today's investor day

How would you rate the quality of today's investor day?			
Excellent	Good	Fair	Poor

How would you rate the segment presentation (organization, key highlights, and figures)?			
Excellent	Good	Fair	Poor

How would you rate the presentation of fundamentals and main trends of our industry?			
Excellent	Good	Fair	Poor

How would you rate the presentation of our competitive advantages?			
Excellent	Good	Fair	Poor

How would you rate the presentation of our offering?			
Excellent	Good	Fair	Poor

How would you rate the presentation of our business model?			
Excellent	Good	Fair	Poor

How would you rate the presentation of our risk control policy?			
Excellent	Good	Fair	Poor

How would you rate the presentation of outlook and strategy?			
Excellent	Good	Fair	Poor

How would you rate the quality of today's handouts?			
Excellent	Good	Fair	Poor

Investor Relations

How would you rate the company's financial communications?			
Excellent	Good	Fair	Poor

How would you rate the company's transparency?			
Excellent	Good	Fair	Poor

How would you rate the accessibility of information within our Group?			
Excellent	Good	Fair	Poor

How would you rate the access to management?			
Excellent	Good	Fair	Poor

How would you rate the access to the Investor Relations team?			
Excellent	Good	Fair	Poor

Do you have any comments to add?

Optional
Name: _____
Company: _____
E-mail: _____

6.7 Investor Relations Contact Form

Mr/Ms/Mrs Name First name Company Title Department Telephone (switchboard) Telephone (direct) Cellular Fax (switchboard) Fax (direct) E-mail Address Zip code City Country	Industry	Meetings (dates and location)
Notes	Sell-side analyst ☐ Buy-side analyst ☐ Fund manager ☐ Journalist ☐ Private individual ☐ Other ☐	
Event 1 Invitation ☐ Fax ☐ E-mail ☐ Mail Response ☐ Yes ☐ No ☐ Pending	Shareholder No ☐ Yes ☐	
Event 2 Invitation ☐ Fax ☐ E-mail ☐ Mail Response ☐ Yes ☐ No ☐ Pending	Holding Record date Number of shares Change	
Press release distribution list ☐ Fax ☐ E-mail ☐ Mail ☐ Home country language ☐ English	Annual general meeting proxy distribution list Fax E-mail Mail Home country language English Ballot	
Annul report distribution list ☐ Yes ☐ No ☐ Home country language ☐ English	Received ☐ Pending ☐ Negative response ☐	

6.8 Request for Roadshow Proposal

Dear Sir or Madam,
We are contemplating a roadshow to present our full-year earnings, scheduled to be announced next 1 February. The exact timing of the roadshow is yet to be finalized but we are currently working on an end of February – beginning of March timeline.
  We are targeting the following cities:

- New York
- Boston
- London/Edinburgh
- Paris
- Frankfurt
- The Netherlands
- Italy
- Tokyo

The primary aim of the roadshow is to meet with existing shareholders as well as potential investors who have not participated in our recent IPO.
  In order for us to retain your firm in the selection process, and with a view to rotating brokers in the course of this year, we would appreciate it if you could provide us with the following information:

- Your recommendation in terms of target cities, target investors, and target timing (should you be aware of any other roadshow or conference taking place at this time of the year in the target city or should your teams be already involved in one, thus making it difficult for you to assist us efficiently).
- For each target institution: why we should meet with this institution; the type of funds they manage, by size and by nature (tech, general, French/European/global equities); their investment policy (hedge funds, long only, Value, GAARP, etc.); their exposure to our sector.
- For each fund manager and/or buy-side analyst: biography, title, area of coverage and responsibilities, level of understanding of our Company, main areas of interest, and concern regarding our Group.
- A draft itinerary for each target city/country, highlighting your competitive advantages in each market and providing references of roadshows your firm may have recently organized there. Note that the outcome of the selection process may lead us to allocating only one city to a broker as opposed to an entire country or region.
- Your commitment to sending us, within a week after the roadshow, a feedback detailed as follows:

- Date of meeting;
- Name of company and name of all investors having attended the meeting, including their contact details in a separate Excel spreadsheet;
- Their assessment of our.
* strengths/weaknesses, risks/opportunities;
* quality of management's presentation;
* our Investor Relations policy:
  - Any change in opinion on the stock, following the meeting, and if yes, in which direction;
  - Any opinion on the valuation of the company and on what could be a catalyst to the stock price.
* A detailed presentation of logistics organization around each event, and, in particular the following:
  - Name and tile of accompanying party on your side for each target city/region;
  - The list of logistic aspects you are committing to take care of or not.

We would appreciate receiving your response no later than 5 January. The selection process will be completed on 15 January, at the latest.

We remain at your disposal to answer any question you may have regarding this process.

We thank you in advance for your response.

Regards
Investor Relations

6.9 Earnings Announcement Timeline

DATE	ACTIVITY	Owner	Status	Comments
D-180	Select meeting format and location			
D-90	List broker selection criteria for the roadshow			
D-60				
D-45	Receive offers, select vendors, and broker(s)			
D-30	Quiet period begins			
	Plan webcast and document uploads			
	Update IR contact database			
	Send out invitations (meeting, conference call, investor luncheon, etc.)			
D-15	First draft earnings presentation and press release			
	Update analysts' consensus estimates			
D-13	Review of management's comments on draft press release and presentation			
D-11	Second draft earnings presentation and press release			
D-10	Logistics update: first list of attendants to the meeting			
	First roadshow outline and schedule			
	First draft script and Q&A document			
D-8	Review of all key documents with management			
	Draft press release and presentation submitted to legal department, auditors, corporate communications, and press officers for review			

6.10 Corporate Fact Sheet

XYZ Company		Key Shareholders/Key Executives				
Stock Market Data						
Number of shares in issue		1.	%			
Market capitalization		2.	%			
Sector/industry		3.	%			
Main index		4.	%			
Ticker symbol		5.	Employees			
Listing		6.	Treasury shares			
Last dividend		Chief Executive Officer:				
		Chief Financial Officer				
Company Profile		**Stock Price History**				
website : http://www.xyzxyz.com						
				2010	2011	2012
			High			
			Low			
			% Yield			
			x PER			
Key financials						
In Millions of USD	2008	2009	2010	2011	2012	
Revenues						
Gross profit						
Operating income						
Net income						
EPS						
Net debt						
Total shareholder's equity						
Cash flow from operations						
Capital expenditure						
Revenue by activity		**Analyst coverage**				
Financial calendar		**Contacts**				
Media contacts						
Investor Relations contacts						

6.11 Examples of ESG Performance Metrics

Environmental	
Greenhouse gas emissions Waste recycling ratio Energy consumption and efficiency Renewable energy use Water use	
Social	
Net employment creation Personnel turnover Salary gap Health &Safety compliance Human rights Stakeholder relations Female /Male Ratio	Donations in Cash Training qualifications and hours Absenteeism rate Percentage of workforce unionized Ratio of lowest wage to minimum wage Ratio of average wage to minimum wage Ratio of jobs offered to jobs accepted
Governance	
Board of directors experience % of independent board members Total board compensation Corporate governance reports Anti-takeover measures Litigation risks Business ethics	

6.12 Basic Site Map Template for an Investor Relations Website

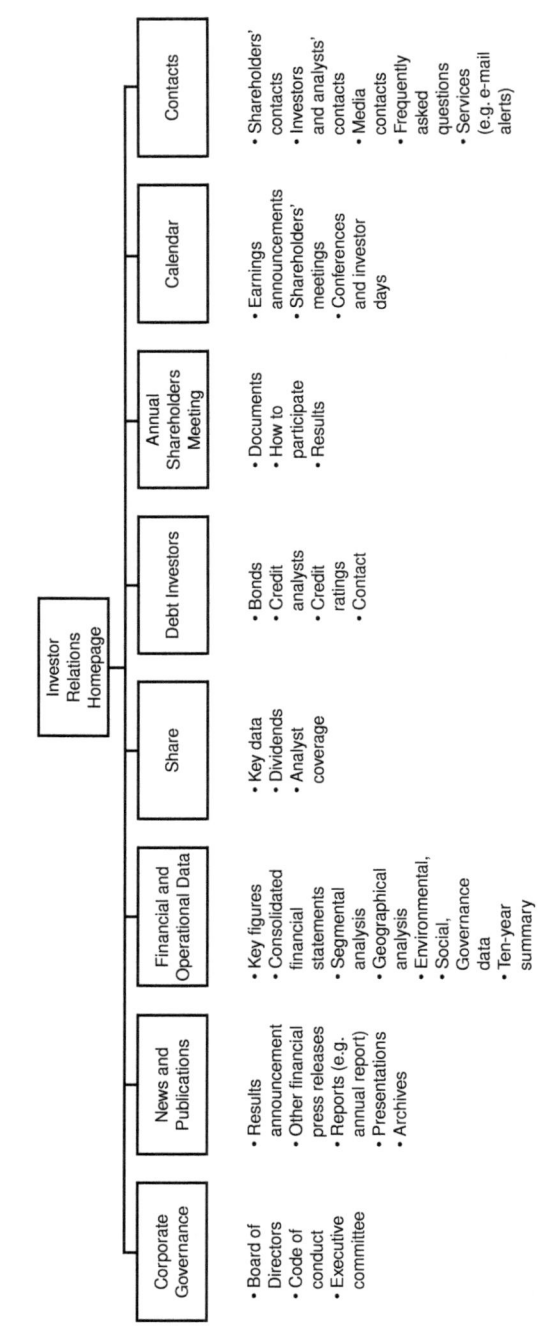

Index

This index is not intended to be a complete listing of all Investor Relations-related topics discussed in this book. It is an aid in finding classifications by selected common names or issues.

accounting standards, 34, 61, 69, 76, 80–81, 119–120, 150, 155, 180
   see also International FInancial Reporting Standards; US GAAP
activist shareholder, 99–103, 181–182
advisor, 54–55
aftermarket, 9, 11, 14–15, 23
analyst and investor days, 168–170
   see also capital market days
annual general meeting, 17, 30, 44–46, 60, 69–71, 73, 94
annual report, 7, 17, 28, 30, 42, 55, 60–61, 71–72, 106, 108, 111, 113, 139–140, 143, 150, 152–153, 154–157, 161, 180, 194
awards, 118, 194

bad news, 25, 59, 91, 115
balance sheet, 3, 69, 72, 88, 144–145, 155
black-out periods, 115
board of directors, 19, 28, 31–33, 38, 56, 103, 112, 128–129, 135, 197
boiler plate, 144
bond, 37, 71, 76, 92, 150
   see also debt Investor Relations
book value, 58
brand, 4, 75, 89, 115, 140–141, 152, 154, 181, 188, 202
broker, 9, 35–36, 71, 112, 163, 165–166, 168, 209, 211
budget, 24, 29, 44, 55, 62, 95, 111, 143, 153, 164, 188, 205
business model, 5, 19, 74, 79, 86, 103, 120–123, 125, 127–128, 130, 171, 198, 207
buyback, 73, 76, 133
buy-side, 14, 34, 50, 96, 100, 162, 168, 209
bylaws, 70, 93–94, 150, 183

capital expenditure, 76, 120
capital increase, 52, 64, 71, 76, 95–97, 157, 181, 192

capital market days, 168
   see also analyst and investor days
capital markets, 2, 15, 20, 25, 29, 63, 78, 198
career, 25, 32, 41, 46–49
cash flow, 58, 79, 99, 120, 125–126, 144, 155
checklist, 167, 171
chief executive officer (CEO), 9, 30
chief financial officer (CFO), 31, 103
chief operating officer (COO), 11, 103
code of conduct, 8, 74, 136
code of ethics, 33, 136
communications strategy, 14, 82–83, 89, 140
compensation, 3, 4, 54, 70, 86, 116, 120, 131, 133, 136, 192, 199, 213
competition, 2, 20, 23, 32–33, 38, 76, 79, 99, 112, 123, 138, 168, 179, 191, 193
competitive environment, 42, 79, 118, 198
compliance, 17, 24, 28, 33, 74, 80, 123–124, 188, 202, 213
conference calls, 9, 43–44, 46, 57, 68, 84–85, 109, 112, 135, 144–145, 147, 165, 170–174, 191, 211
conferences, 9, 39, 50, 65, 107, 112, 150, 168, 173, 179, 188, 191, 202
confidence, 2, 23, 47, 123, 172–173, 183
confidential, 2, 66, 125, 134
confidentiality, 40, 68
conflict, 52–53, 176
consensus, 16, 18, 58, 64, 83, 126, 131–132, 139, 189, 192, 211
consistency, 2, 13, 21, 23, 26, 28, 32–33, 87–89, 115, 125, 140, 145, 160, 183
consultant, 48, 53, 194
contact list, 56
convergence, 88, 141
corporate access, 35, 55, 163

corporate communications, 9, 28, 31, 36, 41–42, 46, 48–49, 60, 75, 88, 104, 140, 151, 153, 198, 211
corporate culture, 29, 34, 133, 135, 154, 169
corporate governance, 19, 33, 38, 73, 86, 118, 120, 136–137, 175–176, 189
cost of capital, 6, 59, 78, 81, 86, 133
counselor, 48
coverage, 35, 50, 52, 71, 75, 86, 129, 150, 152, 160, 163, 182, 202, 209, 212
credit analyst, 76, 150
credit rating, 37, 45, 150
credibility, 4, 8, 29–30, 41, 76, 90, 116, 119, 132, 134, 160, 183, 193
crisis communications, 88, 92, 128
cross-border listing, 78, 86
culture, 51, 175
currency, 4, 5, 45, 86, 100, 128, 148–149, 166
  see also foreign exchange
custodians, 37, 94
customer, 26, 28, 34, 37, 48, 58, 87, 97, 105, 118, 138, 180–181, 190

data sheet, 17
database, 16, 55–56, 94–95, 98, 167, 211
debriefing, 16, 170
debt Investor Relations, 20–21, 37, 45
delisting, 71, 77–79
depositary bank, 92
disclosure, 2, 9, 11–12, 17, 33, 43, 50, 52, 66–67, 69, 72–73, 75, 77–79, 82, 84–85, 87–89, 93, 107, 112–113, 115, 117, 122–124, 126, 130, 142, 147, 153, 170, 177–178, 198, 201
disclosure policy, 12, 33, 115, 178
disposal, 67, 128, 210
dividend, 45, 71, 76, 99, 112, 128, 133, 150, 155, 178, 181, 212
divisional, 11, 13, 38, 89, 172
domestic, 1, 6, 28, 43, 46, 65, 68, 74, 76, 78, 81, 96–97, 156
dry run, 10, 12

earnings announcement, 107, 150
earnings call, 55, 83, 172
  see also conference calls
earnings consensus, 15, 17, 39, 58, 131, 162
earnings estimates, 16, 82, 104, 114, 130, 162, 189, 192

earnings growth, 12, 100
earnings per share, 3, 58, 131, 133
earnings presentation, 46, 56, 95, 170, 179, 204, 211
earnings release, 9, 41, 42, 57, 59, 74, 83, 106, 109, 112, 114, 127, 131, 141, 143, 158, 170, 173, 199
earnings surprise, 132
electronic voting, 44
embargo, 68
employee, 4, 9–10, 28, 30–31, 33, 118, 138, 140–141, 178, 202
employee communications, 10, 202
Environmental, Social, Governance (ESG), 136–140
equity, 2, 11–12, 14, 18–20, 37, 40, 45, 56–57, 64, 74, 76, 78–79, 86, 99, 116, 120, 141, 147, 163, 190, 212
equity story, 11, 12, 14, 78–79
estimates, 32, 58, 83, 85, 118, 128, 151, 162, 211
ethical, 43
evaluation form, 205
event-driven, 101
exchange rates, 5, 61, 69, 116, 124
executive committee, 30–31, 84
executive team, 24, 173
exogenous factors, 74, 118
expectations, 1, 14, 19, 21, 24, 30–31, 45, 47, 52, 76, 101, 104, 106, 128, 132, 143, 172, 175, 183, 194, 202
extra-financial, 139

fact sheet, 83, 166, 179
fair value, 25, 50
feedback, 5, 39, 53–55, 91, 142, 148, 153, 163, 166–167, 170, 174, 202, 206, 209
financial advertising, 72, 108, 157
financial analyst, 1, 5, 9–10, 13–14, 16–17, 31, 33, 35–38, 41–42, 50, 52, 68, 72, 76, 81–82, 88, 112, 118, 165, 201
financial calendar, 17, 87, 111–113
financial communication, 9, 19, 24, 26, 34, 36, 38, 42, 51, 61, 63, 75, 87, 104–105, 108, 113, 132, 135, 144, 153, 155–156, 168, 194, 207
financial community, 40, 53, 59, 75, 88, 149, 168, 192, 202
financial image, 10, 18, 23, 45, 59, 193, 196
financial institution, 16, 37
financial intermediaries, 9

Index

financial markets, 1, 2, 10, 23–24, 26, 28–29, 32–33, 34, 36, 43, 61, 64, 68, 74, 76, 78, 82, 117, 119, 157–158, 163, 182–183, 198
financial press, 9, 28, 36, 43, 105, 113
financial statements, 4, 8, 33, 45, 65, 69–70, 80–82, 84–85, 107–111, 115, 133, 135, 144–145, 154–155, 172, 175
financial structure, 86
financing, 3, 6, 19–20, 37, 76, 134, 182, 191
financing costs, 3, 6, 191
fixed-income, 20, 37, 45
see also bond; debt Investor Relations
follow-up, 161–162
forecasts, 5, 28, 32, 34, 58, 70, 123–124, 126
foreign country, 4, 142
foreign exchange, 78, 86, 100
see also currency
foreign investor, 6, 72, 96, 191
foreign language, 87, 143, 173
foreign market, 30, 40, 43, 76–78, 86, 149
foreign press, 36
foreign shareholder, 74, 94, 175
forward-looking statement, 64, 123, 126–127
free float, 12, 18, 29, 32, 59, 74, 93, 97, 175, 190
frequently asked questions, 12, 17, 73, 145, 178
fund management, 35
fund manager, 14, 15, 31, 43, 56, 75, 96, 99, 102–103, 105–106, 137–138, 165, 209
fundamentals, 98, 121, 206
funds under management, 96, 100

geographic, 6, 15–16, 18, 57–58, 97, 119–120, 122, 125, 144, 163, 189, 191
global, 1, 29, 50, 58, 78–81, 85, 97, 122, 138, 146, 176, 201–202, 209
globalization, 78, 88
glossary, 10, 117, 142, 148
go public, 78
see also Initial Public Offering (IPO)
good news, 115
government, 1, 36, 65, 128, 179
graphics, 40, 60, 149
growth, 2, 3, 12, 18–19, 42, 58, 75, 85, 92, 100, 103, 117, 119–120, 122, 133, 138, 171
growth drivers, 42

guidance, 9, 12, 52, 64, 70, 81–82, 101, 106, 123–125, 127–132, 135, 171, 192, 202

half-yearly, 96, 107
hedge fund, 36, 93, 99, 101–102, 162–163, 165, 209
holding period, 101, 190
holdings, 4, 6, 64, 93, 95–96, 99, 102, 136, 181
hostile, 5, 93, 97, 99, 135–136, 164, 181
human resources, 28, 32, 119, 135, 140
hybrid, 2, 3, 177

identity, 10, 26, 89, 92, 94, 202
image, 3–4, 6, 9, 12, 25, 40, 45, 54, 61, 63, 67, 71, 75, 77–78, 82, 87, 105, 137, 140–141, 150–151, 153–154, 169, 175, 179, 192, 193
income statement, 69, 144–145, 155
individual shareholder, 1, 38, 93, 149, 174, 180, 193
industry, 9, 19, 35, 42, 52, 80–81, 86, 102, 112, 118, 123, 130, 138, 142–143, 148–149, 151, 154, 177, 182, 202, 206, 212
information kit, 9
information systems, 7, 8, 24, 44, 61–62, 96, 125, 128, 183
in-house, 11, 20, 26, 40, 46, 48, 50–51, 62, 176, 205
Initial Public Offering (IPO), 2–18
see also go public
innovation, 89, 115, 138, 147, 176, 179
inquiry, 33, 126
inside information, 53, 66
insider, 33, 63, 66, 112, 114, 127, 134, 141, 175, 178
institutional investor, 1, 5, 13–14, 16, 18–19, 34, 36, 38, 42, 45, 50, 60, 72, 74, 93, 95, 97, 99–100, 108, 150, 156, 160, 162, 165, 175–176, 190–191, 193
intangibles, 188
see also extra-financial
integrated communications, 4, 89
integrated report, 137–140
integrity, 106, 124, 193
intelligence, 26, 36
interactivity, 150, 179
interim, 17, 107, 110
internal communications, 10, 33–34, 82, 119, 151

international, 1, 4, 5, 13, 20, 28, 30, 34, 40, 43, 52, 58, 61, 67, 79, 81, 86, 94–95, 113, 118, 120, 141, 157, 168, 201–202
International FInancial Reporting Standards (I.F.R.S.), 84
internet, 78
interview, 83, 85, 193
investigation, 29, 59, 93, 95
investment, 1, 4–6, 9–15, 17–18, 24–26, 30–31, 34, 36–38, 43, 45, 46, 50–53, 55–57, 60, 62, 66, 68, 74, 76, 81, 84, 88, 95–98, 100–103, 113, 115, 117, 121, 123, 128, 130, 134, 137, 141, 147–149, 151, 155, 158, 160–161, 163–168, 179, 188–192, 196–197, 199, 201, 204, 209
investment bank, 9, 11–13, 34, 46, 50–52, 55–57, 60, 66, 68, 97–98, 117, 121, 158, 163–164, 166–167, 191
investment case, 9–11, 15, 76, 134, 179
investment community, 4, 5, 12, 14, 17, 26, 30–31, 36, 38, 43, 45, 53, 62, 84, 88, 102–103, 113, 137, 148, 151, 160–161, 163, 168, 179, 201
investment grade, 37
investment style, 98, 101
investor day, 46, 55, 112, 138, 169, 206
 see also analyst and investor days, capital market days
investor relations officer, 202
investor relations program, 9
issuer, 10, 12, 26, 37, 40, 51, 57–58, 64–68, 70, 72–73, 77, 92, 94–97, 99, 108, 126, 133, 155, 158, 164, 168, 173, 193

jargon, 105
journalists, 149, 162
 see also media relations; press

key performance indicator, 33, 85, 120–121, 129

language, 12, 14, 34, 40, 73, 86–87, 114, 117–118, 122, 141–143, 147, 155, 158–159, 166, 175, 179, 208
legal department, 73, 84, 105, 107, 115, 136, 211
legal requirements, 70, 108, 174
legislation, 70, 124, 139
listing, 1–4, 7, 18, 57, 60, 74, 76–78, 86–88, 107, 139, 191, 201

lobbying, 34, 80
lock-up, 18
logistics, 13, 39, 43, 45–46, 51, 55, 163, 165, 167, 169–170, 175, 205, 210
logo, 13, 67
long term, 1, 6, 29, 38, 59, 62, 101, 102, 106, 126–127, 138–139, 143, 196
loyalty, 4, 89, 99, 180

macroeconomic, 2, 75, 79, 97, 118, 125, 128, 130, 177
mailing, 9, 61, 95, 112, 142, 155–156, 180, 205
mailing costs, 112, 155
mailing list, 9, 142, 156, 205
management team, 3, 9, 47, 64, 125, 171, 173, 183
management time, 99, 101–102
market authorities, 13, 28–29, 33, 63, 66, 72–74, 107, 113–114, 117, 122, 126, 182
market capitalization, 5, 29, 35, 74–75, 101
market expectations, 29, 61–62, 92
market intelligence, 9, 28, 32, 44, 48, 52, 97
market share, 3, 89, 119, 154, 163
marketing, 9, 10, 12, 15, 20, 26, 31, 38, 41, 49, 56, 58, 65, 86, 95, 97, 99, 147, 153–154, 156, 164, 190
material information, 17, 105
measurable, 4, 24, 47, 55, 196
measurement, 26, 54, 188–189, 196
media, 2, 4, 11–14, 20, 25, 31, 36, 41, 42–43, 48, 50, 68, 70–71, 75, 82–83, 88–89, 107, 112, 151–153, 156–159, 162, 182, 194, 202, 205
media relations, 11, 20, 31, 36, 41, 82
 see also press
media trainer, 12
medium-sized companies, 4, 31, 36, 45, 51, 63, 75, 157
mergers and acquisitions, 64, 133
message, 5, 20, 21, 34, 41, 47, 52, 59, 76, 83–84, 88, 119, 121, 132, 141, 143–145, 147, 168–169, 172
microeconomic, 2
model, 6, 82, 99, 116, 120, 121
mutual fund, 36, 95

nationalization, 65, 182
net income, 131, 145

Index

news agencies, 36, 67
news flow, 5, 76, 105, 126, 175
newspapers, 4, 36
non-resident, 94, 176

objective, 5, 28, 38, 50–51, 59, 69, 87, 121–123, 154, 192, 199
obligation, 17, 71, 93, 127
offering, 3, 13, 15, 25, 92, 115, 202, 207
one-to-one, 38, 160–161, 165, 168, 191
one-to-one meetings, 161, 165, 191
open day, 168
operating expenses, 77
operating income, 58, 77, 131
outlook, 59, 70, 72, 74, 76, 83, 85, 107, 123–124, 126–127, 129–130, 144, 146, 150, 155, 160, 162, 171, 193, 204, 207
outsource, 20

payout ratio, 99, 120
peer group, 9, 129, 152
peers, 48, 54, 112, 142, 172
pension fund, 36, 100, 177
perception, 5, 15, 18, 28, 38–39, 51, 58, 62, 146, 192–193, 196
perception study, 15, 38, 192
portfolio, 4, 20, 36, 41, 52, 56, 62, 96, 102, 115, 121, 137, 141, 160, 162, 164–165, 168, 190
portfolio manager, 20, 36, 41, 52, 56, 102, 115, 121, 137, 160, 162, 164–165, 168
positioning, 11, 20, 52, 65, 118, 139–140, 154, 165, 202
post-IPO, 6
presentations, 36, 37, 42, 53, 82, 121, 137, 146–147, 150, 163, 168, 170, 202, 204–205
press, 9, 10, 13, 16, 28, 31, 33, 35–36, 37, 42–44, 50, 52, 56, 65–68, 70, 73, 83, 89, 104–107, 109, 113–114, 127, 131–132, 134–136, 140, 144–153, 158, 161, 165–166, 170–175, 188, 205, 211
see also journalists; media relations
press conference, 10, 65, 68, 158
press release, 9, 13, 16, 36, 42–44, 52, 56, 65–68, 70, 73, 83, 89, 105–107, 109, 113–114, 127, 131–132, 134–136, 144–149, 151–153, 158, 161, 165, 170–175, 188, 205, 211
price target, 16, 58, 59, 162

price-sensitive information, 8, 17, 30, 33, 64–66, 68, 84, 127–128, 142, 147, 161–162, 172–173, 178
private companies, 19
private equity, 19, 20
privatization, 10
privileged information, 29, 63–66, 114, 162
profit warning, 129, 131–132, 181
profitability, 99, 125, 135–136, 201
prospectus, 18, 123, 133
proxy, 60, 71, 94, 138, 176–177, 208
public company, 4, 7, 10, 12, 34, 178
public relations, 56, 77

Q&A, 12, 14, 17, 59, 74, 135, 145–146, 159, 161–162, 169, 172–174, 205, 211
Q&A session, 12, 17, 146, 159, 161–162, 169, 172–174
questionnaire, 167, 193
quiet period, 112–114

rating agencies, 31, 42, 45, 75, 137
ratio, 62, 121, 141, 213
recommendation, 13, 58, 68, 130, 162, 167, 192, 209
reconciliation, 83, 121, 155
registrar, 71, 92
regulatory change, 74, 80, 147
regulatory requirement, 13, 60, 77
remuneration, 4, 35, 48, 121, 133, 181, 199
reporting systems, 23, 61, 120
reputation, 2, 4, 26, 48, 53, 74–77, 100, 106, 115–119, 129, 131, 137–138, 140, 154, 157, 182, 192
research, 9, 11, 14, 18, 35, 39, 57–58, 61, 84, 102, 115, 120, 127, 130, 151, 162–164, 174, 194, 198, 202
research and development, 115, 120, 164
resignation, 64
resolution, 65, 95
retail bank, 96–97
retail ownership, 53
retail shareholder, 29, 37, 40, 44–45, 51, 60, 99, 142, 151, 158, 174–175, 181, 192
see also individual investors
retention, 58, 92, 138, 180–181, 190
return on capital employed (ROCE), 133
return on equity (ROE), 133
revenues, 17, 29, 35, 59, 67, 118, 138

reverse roadshow, 167
roadshow, 55, 147, 163, 165, 167–168, 209, 211

sales force, 36
save-the-day, 112
savings, 40, 61, 112, 138, 140, 148, 156, 158, 180, 194
schedule, 13, 47, 59, 107, 109, 114, 120, 162, 165, 169, 211
script, 147, 159, 172, 211
SEC, 122
   see also U.S. Securities and Exchange Commission
secondary offering, 29, 92, 163
sell-side, 15, 34–36, 43, 46, 50, 52, 56, 58, 85, 106, 112, 130–131, 135, 151, 160, 162, 168, 189, 193, 202
senior management, 47, 82, 91, 93, 103, 111, 121, 179, 189, 195, 202
service provider, 20, 44, 50–51, 54–55, 67, 111, 151, 201
share capital, 6, 12, 15, 72, 74, 93
share ownership, 4, 28, 31, 45, 92, 96–97, 141, 150
share price, 4–6, 12, 16–18, 25, 36, 44, 56–57, 63, 65, 67, 78, 87–88, 103, 125–126, 128, 135, 141, 178, 182, 188–189, 196
shareholder base, 4, 6, 15–18, 28, 30, 34, 39, 44, 56–57, 60, 64, 70–71, 78, 86, 92–93, 96–97, 121, 155, 157, 165, 173, 180, 189–190, 192, 195, 201
shareholder club, 178, 181
shareholder democracy, 70, 174
shareholder identification, 51, 55, 92–93, 95
shareholder letter, 45, 144, 157
shareholder loyalty, 92, 181
shareholder value creation, 132–133, 191
short selling, 101
short-term, 1, 23, 34, 98–99, 102, 121, 126, 131
site visit, 3, 179, 206
slideshow, 142
social media, 151–153, 180
socially responsible investment, 32, 35, 75, 120
socially responsible investors, 137, 179
sovereign fund, 36
spokesperson, 30, 32, 42, 202
spreadsheet, 40, 44, 85, 149, 156, 210
state-owned, 1, 10, 20, 100

statutory audit, 107, 123, 124, 133, 155
stock broker, 35, 158
stock exchange, 63, 78–80, 85–86, 96, 105, 118, 202
stock market, 20, 77, 80, 86, 94, 131, 139, 178
stock options, 141
stock price, 34, 38, 57–58, 84, 98, 105, 132, 141, 149, 155, 182, 196, 210
stock split, 64, 73
stock symbol, 149
strategy, 3, 4, 7, 10–11, 15, 18, 19, 20, 24–26, 31–32, 38–39, 42–43, 45, 47–49, 51, 56, 59, 62, 65, 71, 75–76, 84, 86–87, 89, 90, 92, 95, 97–99, 102–103, 106, 108, 111–112, 114–115, 118, 120–122, 124–125, 130–131, 133, 135, 137–139, 142, 145–146, 149–150, 154, 158, 163, 165–166, 171–172, 175, 181, 183, 188–198, 201–202, 207
supplier, 22, 26, 28, 34, 37
surveillance, 28, 55, 60
survey, 85, 170, 192, 201, 205

target, 5, 10, 14–15, 34, 36, 38, 51, 56, 59–60, 75, 82, 86, 97, 100–101, 106, 117, 127–128, 133, 140, 143, 166–168, 182, 190, 209–210
target price, 15
targeting, 49, 51, 96–98, 102–103, 142, 164–165, 191, 209
threshold, 93
time difference, 57
time horizon, 9, 34, 125–127, 129, 131
time zone, 68, 87, 171, 173
timeline, 11, 85, 142, 171, 205, 209
total shareholder return, 133
trade show, 9, 65, 107, 154
trading hours, 67
trading volumes, 17, 50, 57, 74, 149
training, 13, 19, 81, 153, 164–165, 205
transaction, 1–3, 13, 52, 65–66, 72, 115, 119, 134–135, 148, 158, 163–164
translation, 125, 142, 143, 179
   see also foreign language
treasury, 21, 32, 37, 45, 62, 73, 150
trust, 37, 129, 133, 161, 180, 183, 193

underwriter, 97
US GAAP, 155

Index

U.S. Securities and Exchange Commission (SEC), 105

valuation, 1–3, 5, 10–12, 19, 25–26, 32, 36, 48, 50, 54, 58, 78–79, 85–86, 95, 99–100, 102, 115, 121–122, 125, 127, 129–131, 134, 137, 139, 141, 146, 188–189, 191, 198, 210
valuation model, 10, 36, 85, 115, 121, 125
valuation multiple, 3, 11, 95, 99, 191
value creation, 6, 122, 132, 134, 138, 201
venture capital, 1, 4, 18, 92
video, 13, 83, 148, 151, 153, 177, 179
visibility, 4, 13, 20, 29, 36, 50, 53, 87, 121, 147, 156
vision, 19, 24, 28, 98, 115, 119, 169, 198
visuals, 135, 145–146, 159, 172
volatility, 93, 99, 102, 105, 128–129, 131, 166, 189
vote, 70, 95, 150, 174–177
voting right, 71, 73, 93

webcast, 170, 205, 211
website, 9, 44–45, 67, 87, 106, 135, 147–149, 151–152, 157–158, 172, 177, 205, 212
wire services, 36

XBRL, 80

Lightning Source UK Ltd.
Milton Keynes UK
UKHW022032050221
378325UK00010B/1716